No Way to Build

No Way
to Build
a Ballpark
and Other

Irreverent

Essays

on

Architecture

by Allan Temko

Winner of the Pulitzer Prize for Criticism

Chronicle Books ■ San Francisco

To the memory of Scott Newhall (1914–1992) — these screeds were his fault: *qui facit per alium facit per se.*

The author thanks Jay Schaefer and Karen Silver of Chronicle Books, and the staff of the San Francisco Chronicle library, especially Kathleen Rhodes, Johnny Miller, and Sally Kibbee, for helping to put this book together. And of course the redoubtable Dolly Rhee, as always, helped mightily.

The articles in this book have appeared as follows: "San Francisco's Changing Cityscape," "Working in the Suburbs," and "San Francisco's Newest Tower" in Architectural Forum; "Reshaping Super-City: The Problem of Los Angeles" in Cry, California, "A Fountain Deposited by a Dog with Square Intestines," in San Francisco Magazine; "Architecture in Transit: BART" and "A Still-Remarkable Gift of Architecture to Oakland" in the AIA Journal; and "No Way to Build a Ballpark" in Harper's Magazine. All others have appeared in The San Francisco Chronicle.

Printed in the United States of America

Library of Congress Cataloging-in-Publication Data
Temko, Allan
    No way to build a ballpark : and other irreverent essays on architecture / by Allan Temko
    p. cm.
    Includes index.
    ISBN 0-8118-0352-X
    1. Architecture, Modern — 20th century — California.
  2. Architecture — California. I. Title
NA730.C2T46 1993
720'.9794'0904 — dc20   92-28858
                       CIP

Editing: Sharon Silva
Book and cover design: Katy Homans and Sayre Coombs
Cover photograph: Candlestick Park, San Francisco, California.
Copyright © 1991 San Francisco Giants. Used by permission of the San Francisco Giants.
Page 2: Downtown from Diamond Heights, San Francisco, California, 1991. By Liz Hafalia.
Courtesy The San Francisco Chronicle.

Distributed in Canada by Raincoast Books,
112 East Third Avenue, Vancouver, B.C. V5T 1C8

10 9 8 7 6 5 4 3 2 1

Chronicle Books
275 Fifth Street
San Francisco, CA 94103

Table of Contents

INTRODUCTION Activist Criticism 7

I. THE EVOLVING CITY
San Francisco's Changing Cityscape 17
Reshaping Super-City: The Problem of Los Angeles 22
San Jose's Grand Plan for its River 30
Working in the Suburbs 34
The Dilemma of Berkeley's Shore 40

II. URBAN CENTERS
A Giant Drawn Concrete Bow 45
Misgivings 49
A Chance for Greatness 52
A "City of Tomorrow" Today 56
A Fountain Deposited by a Dog with Square Intestines 59
San Jose Center Sets Standard in Public Architecture 63
Architecture in Small Towns Yields Big Results 66

III. WORK PLACES
San Francisco's Newest Tower 73
The Rich New Temple in the Financial District 78
Bold State Offices to Save Energy 82
Levi's Choice — Be Good or Be Great 86
GM's Fremont Plant — The Beauty of Function 90
An Architectural Joy in Silicon Valley 93
IBM's New Palace of Technology 96
A 27-Story Collection of Architectural Errors 99
Eighteen Decent Floors of Art Deco Revival — Then Pow! 104

IV. ARCHITECTURE OF TRANSIT
Let's Build a Splendid Bridge! 109
Colossal Boondoggle: S.F.'s Airport Mess 112
Architecture in Transit: BART 115
The Expensive Errors in the Ferry Business 120
A Poetic Conquest of Space 124
A Work of Engineering Art on the Bay 129
Southern Pacific Depot in Jeopardy 132

V. SCHOOLS, JAILS AND CHURCHES
    The Right Architecture for an Acropolis   137
    A Winning Pavilion at Santa Clara   139
    Finding Form Once Again on the Farm   143
    A Campus that Went Astray   146
    Inventive, Generous Design for San Francisco Sheriff's Lockup   150
    Cathedral Plan — A Good Start   153
    The Restoration of a True San Francisco Monument   156

VI. RETAIL SHOPPING
    Wright's Jewel in Maiden Lane Defaced   161
    After the City of Paris   164
    Shopping Centers — New Visions in the Suburbs   169
    The Nut Tree — An Oasis of Good Taste   172
    The Port's Architectural Fiasco — Pier 39   175
    Theatrics Packing 'Em In   179
    Rincon Center — Overblown, but It's Fun   183

VII. HOTELS, HOSPITALS AND HOUSING
    It's Designed for the Good Times   189
    The Marriott Debate: A Hotel Architects Detest and People Are
       Crazy About   193
    Resplendent Palace Hotel Reopens   198
    Two Hospitals Too Big for Their Blocks   202
    The Social Art of Architecture for the Poor and Sick   206
    Italian Look for Delancey Street   210

VIII. STADIUMS AND MUSEUMS
    No Way to Build a Ballpark   215
    A's Coliseum an Architectural Marvel   221
    A Still-Remarkable Gift of Architecture to Oakland   224
    Davies Hall — Prose, Rather than Poetry   235
    SF MOMA: An Extraordinary Work for San Francisco   239
    Blowing It on Wilshire Boulevard   242
    What to Do with the Presidio   247

IX. BOOKS AND EXHIBITIONS
    Architectural Theater of the Absurd: The Work of Frank Gehry   253
    Wright's Monumental Contributions: Frank Lloyd Wright:
       In the Realm of Ideas   257
    The Mystery of Julia Morgan   260
    The West's First Modern Architecture   264

INDEX   268

Introduction: Activist Criticism

Thirty years ago, about the time I became architecture critic of The San Francisco Chronicle in 1962, Americans were just learning that they would have to fight for a decent environment. Suddenly the country was being ruined before our eyes, smashed, raped, poisoned, stunk up, and, not least, disfigured by inhumane and even hideous buildings. "Corn. Kitsch. Schlock. Honky-tonk. Dreck. Schmaltz. Merde." These charitable appraisals of Disneyish confections on San Francisco's Pier 39, below Telegraph Hill, could have been applied in the early 1960s to junk sprouting all over the San Francisco Bay Area, to say nothing of the rest of the United States. I was writing for the world at large — in The Chronicle and in national magazines — but Northern California was the place to take a stand. It had much more to lose than Detroit or the Bronx.

Locally, in one of the loveliest spots on earth, Candlestick Park showed how not to build a ballpark. The double-decked Embarcadero freeway was a prototype, aped in Seattle, of how to ravage an urban waterfront. The Vaillancourt Fountain looked as if it had been deposited by a giant concrete dog with square intestines. The new San Francisco Federal Building was a literally toxic monument to bad government. Massive downtown highrises, strewn along the maldesigned BART line, inaugurated the "Manhattanization" of San Francisco, flattening hills, blocking views, depriving downtown streets of sun. Uncontrolled filling of the bay threatened to reduce the vast landlocked harbor to a mud puddle rimmed by "slurbs" — neither suburbs nor cities but a continuous nonurban slime, oozing over farms and orchards.

Not only fast-buck speculators and highway engineers, but also architects and planners — supposedly non-yahoos, who should have known better — joined in the devastation. Lewis Mumford likened Americans to passengers in a motorcar without steering wheel or brakes, hurtling towards chaos.

A new environmental politics was needed, and with it a new journalism, not Mumford's rarefied jeremiads in The New Yorker, but war-in-the-trenches attacks on ugliness, an assault spearheaded by America's most uninhibited daily newspaper. The San Francisco Chronicle, under the editorship of Scott Newhall, was a disrespectful, oddly raffish, wickedly entertaining, and, at its best, beautifully written paper that retained some of the wildness of the Old West.

In those days there were still spittoons and sawdust on the floor in a city room that could have been a stage set for *The Front Page.* I had put in a brief stint there in the late 1940s, when I was uncertain about my career and torn between journalism and teaching at the University of California at Berkeley, but now The Chronicle dealt me a royal flush, in spades, and I bet my life on it.

Newhall was for me an editor of rare perfection. Aristocratic in background and taste, he was profoundly democratic in social outlook. The peccadilloes and vagaries of humankind, and occasionally of the animal kingdom (such as the shamelessly naked horses he proposed to diaper), were to this genial Californian an unending source of merriment. He took glee in puncturing pomposity and assailing incompetence, especially at City Hall, and he had unerring insight into Jesuitical, Talmudic, or — what he knew best — WASP chicanery in the public and private realms.

Newhall was also unafraid of baroque prosody, and that won my heart. Once, to avoid repeating the sobriquet *vandals* in denouncing some architectural butchery, I was momentarily stumped for a synonym; Newhall volunteered *Visigoths.* Later, for the inadequate passenger concourses at the San Francisco Airport, through which he hopped irately on his wooden leg, he suggested *cattle chutes.*

Ten years older than his apple-cheeked architecture critic, Newhall was a mystagogue of mischief. Our behavior, scandalous by today's standards, reminded me of Penrod and Sam smoking sassafras "tobaccy" behind a Booth Tarkington barn.

Unbeknownst to the publisher, he found a lawyer, our now-noted friend Matthew Weinberg, to fight one of our causes célèbres. Together we got the south Berkeley community to sue BART because, on the pretext of excessive expense, the transit bureaucracy was trying to renege on placing the Ashby station underground, as had been specified in a bond issue. Among other evils, this would have erected a barrier between black and white neighborhoods, but our case (with me rooting not so anonymously from the sidelines) was won handily when another friend of The Chronicle, the great structural engineer Professor T. Y. Lin of the University of California, testified that BART's hacks had overestimated the extra cost by $1 million or so. "Take away a zero," he told the judge, who promptly ruled in favor of better design.

Naturally The Chronicle reported such *faits divers,* and occasionally I contributed unsigned editorials (taking care to sign them carefully between the lines) that praised the infallible discernment of the architecture critic.

Another series of articles — unique in newspaper annals because they brought the design of a major bridge under scrutiny — led to a new concept for the $70 million Hayward-San Mateo Bridge across the southern part of the San Francisco Bay. Thanks to the Chron, it is now one of the most slender and elegant spans in the world. The state engineers had concocted what I called a "Rip Van Winkle" bridge, whose timid bolted framework could have been technically achieved in the 19th century. The double-decked truss appeared reactionary even to the engineering profession. It particularly outraged structural artists such as Professor Lin and Myron Goldsmith, the brilliant architect-engineer of Skidmore, Owings & Merrill, who designed the Oakland Coliseum. With their help, I was able to clarify technical, aesthetic, and even economic problems in a series of four lengthy articles, plus an editorial.

The bridge bureaucracy began to capitulate. After some dickering behind the scenes in San Francisco and Sacramento, Governor Edmund G. "Pat" Brown, Sr., convened the bridge commission. Dressed to the nines in a Brooks Brothers suit, I rose to testify before the commission, like David Copperfield before a row of Uriah Heeps. At one point the head engineer promised to hire a certain architect as design consultant; I broke in to mention his demise several years earlier. When a commissioner chastised this violation of *Robert's Rules of Order,* a legendary Chronicle reporter in the press row, J. Campbell Bruce, leaped to defend me.

"What does Allan know about rules?" he yelled. "He's an artist. A poet. He lives in a garret. He's the real representative of the people of California, not you." Pat Brown quelled the donnybrook, and the commission went on to kill the earlier design. Instead, we got a daring ribbon of steel two miles long, with a main span of 750 feet that is only 15 feet deep at midpoint — and Pat Brown, in the midst of his successful reelection campaign to defeat Richard Nixon, was praised in a front-page Chronicle editorial.

There were occasions, of course, when the editors and I disagreed, but my work appeared prominently nonetheless — I used a full page of the newspaper to denounce the design for Embarcadero Center, which most of the editors genuinely liked. Without undue obeisance to its developer David Rockefeller ("a handsome swain," I had opined, with whom San Francisco "needn't go all the way on a first date"), Scott himself informed readers of the editorial page that The Chronicle's "stylish" architecture critic wrote "with his own quill pen," and not for the paper as an institution.

When the paper backed me, we almost always won. When it didn't, I often lost. But it was always a joy, the kind of above-the-fold-of-the-page fun that sold newspapers. In the 1960s, The Chronicle — the resurgent "Voice of the West" owned by descendants of the pioneer scandalmonger M. H. De Young — was locked in a circulation battle with Hearst's San

Francisco Examiner, "the Monarch of the Dailies." We were beating the bejesus out of them, not only because our writing and editing were incomparably more inspired, but also because the Ex had yet to learn that environmental squabbles were hot news. The Hearstlings tended to side with the Chamber of Commerce, highway technocrats, ward heelers, and other enemies of the public weal.

A case in point was the proposed despoliation of Golden Gate Park, the city's supreme work of environmental art, by a six-laner that would have cut through the Panhandle and, after taking out some 300 mature trees, veered northward to the Golden Gate Bridge. Even though landscape architect Lawrence Halprin, as consultant to the state engineers, gave his imprimatur to the desecration, it was plainly a crime that had to be stopped.

The Examiner was in favor of the new plan. But The Chronicle riposted with fang and claw. One of my better lines — "when a highway engineer sees a public park, it is like a sex maniac eyeing a virgin" — was forged in the heat of the struggle. A curious civic organization, dubbed something like "defenders of the park," or "foes of the freeway," arose under the one watchful eye of Warren Hinckle, a then little-known but precocious Chronicle feature writer who went into action, wearing his eye patch, like a hero of the I.R.A.

Thereupon we cooked up a spontaneous protest at the polo field in the park. The turnout was terrific. When I arrived with my family, at the same moment as our ally Supervisor George Moscone and his clan, crowds were pouring down the greensward, drawn by Turk Murphy's Dixieland band.

Precisely how many people attended remains unknown because the Chron and the Ex each counted the house according to editorial policy. Both took aerial photos, the Ex from so high an altitude that the crowd appeared insignificant in the expanse of the park, the Chron so low that thousands were packed in a dense view, presumably with thousands more beyond the photo. I think our banner headline put the crowd at 50,000, the Ex at 5,000. Perhaps 20,000 showed up altogether.

There were at that time two freeways threatening the city. A second brute was intended to extend the Embarcadero freeway northward around Telegraph Hill, through Fisherman's Wharf (which would be no great loss), but then going offshore to mar Aquatic Park and Fort Mason, before wiping out Marina Green and pulverizing a stretch of the Presidio en route to the Golden Gate Bridge.

The Chronicle seemed likely to win only one of these controversies, mainly because the automobile and construction industries, their unions, and certain financial interests had peculiar powers of persuasion with a malleable group of supervisors. But several of the wavering pols were invited to Newhall's office, and we defeated both freeways by one-vote margins.

Every fight has its own rationale, but I never doubted that each, in its own way, was a striving for excellence, or at least for something better than mediocrity. The new St. Mary's Cathedral is not a great contemporary church, on the order, say, of Le Corbusier's Ronchamp or Frank Lloyd Wright's Unity Temple. But the design by Pietro Belluschi and the famous Italian engineer Pier Luigi Nervi has some great things in it, such as the towering hyperbolic paraboloid vaults, 180 feet high, which are structural marvels.

What matters is that the finished cathedral is incomparably superior to what the city — not just the Roman Catholic community, but all of San Francisco — would have gotten if The Chronicle hadn't objected to the original choice of architects. That was about as far as the newspaper could go, short of hiring architects on its own.

But that was farther than any newspaper had gone before. It is worth recalling that we were literally pioneers. Nowadays some 30 or 40 architecture critics write regularly for American newspapers, and perhaps a couple of dozen elsewhere in the world, but when I joined up in the 1960s only Ada Louise Huxtable of The New York Times and Wolf von Eckhardt of The Washington Post were on duty. Both are excellent, but their East Coast newspapers were much more decorous, even squeamish, than the rambunctious Chronicle.

Easterners tended to regard us *de haut en bas,* but the Post especially, and the Times also because of the magnitude and complexity of New York, never came close to equaling our record in practical results: better architecture, historic preservation, transportation, waterfront and coastal protection, creation of parks, and bolder urban and regional planning. In recent years, it's true, The Chronicle has squabbled with San Francisco's city planners when they started to dictate architectural design, and festooned downtown with pseudohistoric buildings topped by silly Post-Modernist "hats." Otherwise we supported their goals of lower and thinner buildings, retail activity at street level instead of barren abstract plazas, and contributions by developers to affordable housing, public transit, childcare facilities, art, and open space.

Historically, this was a paradox. The Chronicle as a Republican institution usually has been more conservative than its overall tone, except in matters such as environment, civil rights, and sexual proclivities. Yet I have always been free to take the high road, even if it meant offending advertisers, for instance Neiman-Marcus, for whom Philip Johnson did a vapid building — "gift-wrapped," I called it — on Union Square after tearing down the old City of Paris.

That, too, was good newspapering, although it occasionally led to intramural tiffs. "Although my confrere Herb Caen cooingly refers to Stanley Marcus as a 'merchant prince,' " I wrote, "back in my own Tolstoyan surroundings in Berkeley, mowing the grain at Yasnaya Polyana, we call him a wealthy tradesman." Caen of course took a whack back at me (I'd say that we are even with each other over the years), but it has all been part of life at The Chronicle.

So my romance with the Chron has endured a few rocky moments and even temporary separations, including a divorce I thought final when Scott Newhall stepped down as executive editor in 1971. I departed slightly before him, to the relief of the publisher, to return to the halcyon groves of academe across the bay. Then, quite unexpectedly, I found myself again with Scott when he had an inspiration to turn San Francisco Magazine into a West Coast version of The New Yorker.

For a short time we were once more a pair of Peck's bad boys, while I wrote some of the more insouciant pieces reprinted in this collection, but then he went bonkers and ran for mayor against Joe Alioto, Dianne Feinstein, and the ineffable Harold Dobbs. The race was distinguished by crushingly expensive full-page ads in The Chronicle depicting Newhall as the central personage in Custer's Last Stand. He came in last of the four. And there went our magazine.

Although that was my one real brush with politics (Newhall had shanghaied me into campaigning for him), I had also worked for President John F. Kennedy on the plan for Pennsylvania Avenue and other chores, and had put together a Governor's Design Awards program for Pat Brown of California. My writing brought me in close touch with a succession of San Francisco mayors, starting with the vague Jack Shelley. When I exhorted him to higher things, such as well-designed low-cost housing, he invited me to an inner sanctum — the room where Dan White would later kill George Moscone — which Shelley had fitted up with a fully stocked bar, complete with his certificate of membership in the bartenders' union. "How's your dandruff, Allan?" he asked. "I'm using Head & Shoulders."

Alioto liked me less, and in his farewell TV interview as mayor singled me out as a foe of progress and American enterprise. He was piqued by my irreverence toward his proudest erection, the Transamerica pyramid, which I mildly described, among other things, as the biggest architectural dunce cap in the world.

Yet this demurrer had been voiced in public forums and chance publications, not in The Chronicle, since we were still separated. A brief reconciliation in 1974 did not work out, but three years later it was bliss eternal when I was asked to return by William German, a good friend who was managing editor under the young publisher Richard Thieriot.

Composed and reflective rather than impulsive, but with a fund of dry humor, Bill German is a very different person from Newhall. Certainly he is a "more serious" editor who has packed a lot of hard news into The Chronicle, at the expense of merriment, but with a desire for substance and, I suppose, national respectability.

The Chronicle was probably fated to change along those lines anyway, since it had vanquished the Examiner and was now a larger and richer paper with the morning field all to itself. That made little difference to me, but I missed the no-holds-barred competition from the Ex. A certain bureaucratic constraint, a loss of daring, was perceptible in the city room, together with a quietus due to the disappearance of eccentric but wildly gifted writers and, oddly enough, to the absence of typewriters. The electronic technologies, handsome in themselves, did not improve the quality of prose, and conceivably harmed it.

But I resumed exactly where I left off, happy and free. There were literally innumerable battles to be fought, and some of the best are included in this book. Our readers, always the best informed in the country so far as environment is concerned, and organized far more powerfully than could have been anticipated 30 years ago, have now made controversies into political issues that decide elections. All around us we see the achievements of courage and foresight. The Embarcadero freeway has finally come down, and the great waterfront is once more exhilarating in its openness and vitality. The Presidio is part of the Golden Gate National Recreation Area. Whether we will be equal to the coming challenges, as a people, remains to be seen, but we will have a good run at them.

In retrospect, it seems that we have been better at stopping bad things, like the freeways, than at creating good things. We have very few buildings as good as the Oakland Museum, and too many dogs like the Marriott Hotel, a hallucinatory "jukebox," which came out pretty much as originally designed despite my protests. So did Pier 39. Levi's, on the other hand, not only responded favorably to criticism, but also gave a $7 million park to the city. That occurred at least partly because The Chronicle, taking a line from the company's ads, said "Levi's shouldn't be just good — they should be great!"

The potential for greatness has been the idea all along. Every building cannot be "a palace of democratic excellence," as I called the Oakland Museum, but a popular desire for better architecture and urban design is unmistakable in the United States. My own writings, over the past 30 years, have been part of that ground swell in environmental consciousness; they display the full range and power of the fight for finer things. They also reveal the education of a critic, who started out believing that architecture could change the world, instead of the other way around.

Now we all know better. Buildings inevitably express nonarchitectural forces: politics, economics, and, not least — if the architecture is to be socially just — civil rights. Our new principles have been forged in a crucible of incessant social and technological change. But some things never change. Architecture, at its highest, is still fine art.

In these articles, I hope there are lessons for all urban regions, even if they have not been graced, as San Francisco has been, with a *joie de vivre* and half-Mediterranean *dolce far niente*. So these essays on architecture are also an autobiography, or a love story, since I first saw the city in 1944, white and immaculate on its hills, with the great suspension bridges spanning the bay, and brimming with innumerable delights and irresistible temptations for a 20-year-old ensign en route to the Pacific.

If San Francisco has grown less lovely, so has the world, but nothing can deprive the city and its incomparable setting of the love and loyalty we must feel, as citizens of a *civitas* that has become as legendary as Athens or Florence, Siena or Rome. Or for that matter — as these fighting and often angry, but always affirmative articles should show — the pride that people everywhere should feel in making cities worth their urban salt.

No Way to Build a Ballpark

I. The Evolving City

The cable car, dipping over Nob Hill, rushes downward as the panorama of city, bay, bridge and sky unfolds in every direction. San Francisco stands brilliant on its hills, burnished by sunlight, compact, intense, proudly cosmopolitan — the most pleasant of American cities. Towers rise at all levels of the terrain, massed together downtown, standing isolated on the slopes and hilltops. Those at the crests lift nearly as high as the great skyscrapers of New York, commanding a port whose grandeur is rivaled only perhaps by the beautiful bay of Rio de Janeiro. For almost 50 miles to north and south, where it is lost in golden haze, the harbor unites the regional metropolis of the 3.5 million people who live on its shores in a territory almost as large as New Jersey. And because this is the Far West, with its tremendous open space and wonderful light, the whole scene can go crimson at sunset.

To find so powerful a modern metropolis in such a setting, almost Latin in mood but plainly American in vigor and enterprise, is a stroke of luck in this age of urban crisis. If renewal can succeed anywhere, it should here, in a city which is not only young and blessed with natural beauty, but was also, like a fortunate person, born to wealth. An almost incredible treasure was carried down from the mines during the first years of the city's existence, and wealth has been accumulating in the great banks and commercial houses of downtown ever since. Today the per-capita income of more than $2,600 a year is among the highest in the country.

This prosperity is reflected in the city's *savoir vivre:* its easy but elegant manners, its appreciation of food and wine, its support of the arts, its deep-rooted, but scarcely slavish, sense of history. Apollo, protector of cities, has been exceptionally kind to San Francisco, a city that is dear to the sun.

Yet when the Philadelphia urbanist Aaron Levine was invited last year to criticize San Francisco's lagging renewal program, he could speak of "euphoria," and warn that, when cities go, they go fast. The note of urgency was justified, for, although it had been clear to the city's able planners immediately after the last war that San Francisco was "badly run-down at the heels," more people were living in the slums today than in 1945, and blight was spreading.

Twin Peaks looking toward downtown, San Francisco, California, 1990.
By Liz Hafalia. Courtesy The San Francisco Chronicle.

Nevertheless, the redevelopment program seemed hopelessly stalled. Three major projects, the great Golden Gateway scheme to replace the obsolete produce market, and the smaller but ambitious projects for the Western Addition and Diamond Heights, all model enterprises which dated back to 1956, 1951 and 1949, respectively, were tied up by red tape, litigation and — most important — apathy, incompetence and even venality at high levels in the municipal government. A scandal erupted at City Hall, resulting in the resignation of the mayor's principal aid, who owned stock in a syndicate dealing in slum properties; federal officials impatiently started an investigation of the city's "slowness"; the general outlook appeared so dark that *Forum* only last September described the city's renewal prospects as "poor."

Today the situation has changed so dramatically, and the city is proceeding so impressively in other sectors of the urban struggle, that San Francisco's experience can stand as an object lesson for the rest of the nation. Land acquisition has been virtually completed in the Western Addition, and is already complete on Diamond Heights, and proposals from developers are being considered. For Golden Gateway, in an effort to ensure high architectural quality based on a philosophy of humanism that goes "beyond the expected returns to the investors," the city is conducting one of the great urban design competitions of modern times.

If any single man is responsible for this remarkable turn of events, it is M. Justin Herman, former western administrator of the U.S. Housing and Home Finance Agency, who, after prodding, cajoling and threatening the city for eight years in an effort to spur it to action, was finally asked to assume direction of the Redevelopment Agency, and do the job himself. That few men could do as brilliantly, he has demonstrated in only eight months.

Yet Herman's success in salvaging the sinking renewal program is only a symptom of a profound change for the better in San Francisco's urban health. Not only the city's gifted architects and planners, as well as enlightened officials and businessmen, but the populace as a whole, shocked into recognition that the very future of San Francisco is at stake, have abandoned complacency. Never before have San Franciscans, who are not quick to find fault with their city, been so concerned by the fate of their surroundings.

They have reason. The tasks confronting San Francisco, as it strives to preserve and enrich its historical *cachet*, clear its slums and defend itself against the automobile, are staggering. More than $100 million of new construction has been recently completed, and no less than

$500 million more is to be spent in the next few years. But even if all the work contemplated is actually carried out, more will remain to be done. In spite of its jaunty, bay-windowed charm and occasional real elegance, the city which was hastily rebuilt after the disaster of 1906 has aged with tragic swiftness. Abject tawdriness typifies streets as important as Market and Kearny; and spacious Van Ness Avenue, a potentially magnificent boulevard, passes between the Beaux-Arts monuments of the Civic Center to become a nightmarish automobile row.

The auto menaces the city everywhere, as was painfully revealed by the demolition of the Montgomery Block of 1953, the most precious memento of the pioneer community. Long a home to artists, it could easily have been brought into the group of splendidly renovated early structures of Jackson Square, but it was leveled to make room for a parking lot. Throughout downtown, block-busting garages have sprouted up to accommodate as many as possible of the 630,000 cars which enter the city on a typical business day, and the parking authority has come to regard the subsurface of every public square as a possible underground storage space. Yet, no matter how adroitly these squares are transformed, they are never quite so sympathetic again. Something indefinably valuable is lost when the natural contour of the city, with its depth of rock and earth, is replaced by a suave terrace of concrete. Union Square and St. Mary's Square have already been thus undermined, and the turn of Portsmouth Plaza, where Old Glory was raised over the city, will come next unless a citizens' law suit, claiming violation of the city charter, succeeds in blocking its conversion.

Perhaps even more fateful for the city has been the plan of the state-highway engineers to run a network of freeways over the hills, dismembering San Francisco as Los Angeles has been dismembered. Thanks to public indignation, which here for once has been effective, the program was checked and is now being reconsidered. Yet it was not checked before the system had forked into downtown, directing one prong at the Civic Center and jamming another double-deck expressway down the Embarcadero, ruthlessly cutting in front of the old Ferry building at the foot of Market Street, and robbing the waterfront of sunlight and the famous bay views.

"Progress usually means giving up something worth-while for something less attractive," The Chronicle ruefully quoted architect Edward Durrell Stone, and recommended that the freeway be torn down. Yet at the same time, casting a critical eye over the city, the newspaper also saw cause for hope: a prodigious display of civic responsibility by the Crown Zellerbach Corp. Eighty years before, the company had started as a stationery store in a basement; it now wished to pay a debt of gratitude to the city which had helped it become a wood-products empire with holdings from Canada to Mexico.

The gesture was handsome. Soaring 20 stories as a transparent enclosure of green glass, the company's new headquarters created a magnificent gift of urban space, carved from what had been a declining waste on lower Market Street. Only one-third of the triangular, parklike site — certainly a local record for urban land use — is occupied by the tower, which lifts two stories free of the ground on 18 formidable columns that ascend the full height of the structure as its only vertical supports. Elevators and other utilities are housed in the massive service shaft which flanks the southern facade.

Whatever the shortcomings of this concept (the unprotected glass facades, to name one obvious weakness, suffer severely from the sun), this far-western cousin of Inland Steel and of Lever House nevertheless deserves comparison with the serious architecture of its time — a claim which hitherto could not be made for any tall building in San Francisco, including the elephantine, white Equitable of 1955. Together with the nearby John Hancock Building — so profoundly different although it too was designed by Skidmore, Owings & Merrill and completed about the same time — Crown has inaugurated a new phase in the city's development which the Chamber of Commerce has dubbed "The Big Build."

By the standards of any city, the build is big, even though none of the major structures would attract much notice if deposited in the Manhattan skyline. Probably the most ponderous will be the $50 million Federal Building, a 20-story block that will dominate the north side of the Civic Center. Perhaps the most ill-advised is the 22-story shaft by Mario Gaidano which owner Ben Swig proposes to plunk on a corner of the notable old Fairmont Hotel; it will irreparably mar the scale and mood of the massive granite pile. In some ways the most interesting should be the ingenious, but clumsy, combination hotel-motel, built around a garage, which William Tabler has devised for Conrad Hilton.

With luck, as many as 50 major structures will go up during the coming decade, including those in Golden Gateway. What makes the whole, roaring boom fascinating is that, although laissez-faire prevails in most cases and economic motives predominate, an imaginative planner could not have picked more logical sites for most of the buildings that are being erected. They are admirably spaced from the waterfront to the Civic Center in spots that are ripe for renewal. The Hilton Hotel, plaza and adjoining office building, for example, will occupy a full block in the sleazy Tenderloin, where land was cheap, but will be within easy walking distance of both the smart shops and theaters around Union Square and the Civic Center where conventions are held. The magnitude of the $35 million undertaking promises to improve the entire vicinity; and chic restaurants are already installing themselves nearby.

The city is on the move. Throughout downtown demolition and construction are under way. If much is architecturally disappointing, or worse, there are compensations in the very fact of newness, and amenities such as trees and planting. Welton Becket's Bethlehem Steel Building, just below John Hancock on California Street, is clearly outclassed by its splendid neighbor. Bethlehem's dark gray tile exteriors, brightened with white and stainless steel, manage to look garish rather than dignified, at least in contrast to the strength and sobriety of Hancock's granite. But the building has its greenery, and a charming roof garden by Royston, Hanamoto & Mayes, complete with waterfall. And again, there is the outlook on the city.

Everywhere, as San Francisco moves on its hills, swept over crest after crest by the resolute grid of streets, its character changes. So does the language, color and dress of the people — and the weather, when portions of the city are covered by fog blowing through the Gate, and the rest remains in the sun. The city is subtle. The architect can only try to capture its nuances, as Frank Lloyd Wright did in the V. C. Morris Store in Maiden Lane, in the days before the ugly little street was over-publicized, overpraised and overdecorated.

On the other hand, the architect can try to capture the totality of the city's romance. Now beginning to rise on the slope of Nob Hill is a tower which may do just that. Anshen & Allen's American President Lines Building will be a glittering shaft of white and gold, capped by a bright hovering roof that should shine for miles in the sunlight, across the bay.

On the shores of the vast harbor, which until a few years ago were dotted with isolated towns and villages, there now extends a continuous urban strip, gradually broadening as subdivisions mount the hills. Population is growing at the rate of nearly 15,000 a month so that in a generation it will have doubled, and stand at 7 million. Socially, economically and geographically the region is an entity; and, although it remains a political mosaic of 83 municipalities and nine counties, area-wide cooperation has already been achieved in smog-control and water-pollution agencies, as well as in the rapid-transit district which next year will ask the voters to approve an outlay of more than $500 million for the first phase of a system which alone can liberate the region from the tyranny of the automobile.

At the center of this great metropolitan complex, giving it heart and cultural meaning, is San Francisco — "The City," as Manhattan is also called by Greater New York. Yet there the comparison must end. For if

Manhattan has been rendered increasingly uninhabitable by insane congestion and Brobdingnagian scale, "The City" of San Francisco remains an uncommonly delightful place to live for its relatively stable population of 800,000. As they build, and gain the wisdom to plan, these San Franciscans are preparing for a period of greatness.

April 1960, *Architectural Forum*

■ RESHAPING SUPER-CITY:
THE PROBLEM OF LOS ANGELES

Shrouded by toxic smog in which the nervous neon winks, the Super-City of Southern California is even more darkly obscured by hostile mythology. Much of the mythology is self-generated, like the special brand of phantasmagorical urban junk that festoons many parts of Los Angeles. Yet Southern Californians are not especially dissatisfied with their environment; and it would seem that hatred of their new urban culture, most notably on the part of genteel Easterners and San Franciscans, is more inspired by fear of the future than by justifiable abhorrence of the present.

Nevertheless the future of Southern California is potentially magnificent; and by many standards, not necessarily those of the Los Angeles Chamber of Commerce, it is already one of the most civilized places on earth, where Aldous Huxley — who had such sane misgivings about the future — did not disdain to live and where Igor Stravinsky and Charles Eames live today. In virtually all of the creative arts, particularly movies, TV, electronic music, and other nonofficial art forms that have sprung out of our own technological age, Los Angeles more than holds its own with San Francisco, just as Cal Tech holds its own with Stanford, and UCLA, in many departments, has drawn even or outstripped Berkeley. This is not to draw invidious comparisons between Southern California and the Bay Area, but merely to indicate the formidable creative strength of the southern part of the state.

Even to speak of the "problem" of Southern California, therefore, is to beg serious environmental questions. In spite of its undeniable virtues, however, Southern California represents a deeply disturbing phase in urban history. Never before has so far-flung a pattern of random, low-density settlement erupted so swiftly, ruthlessly and senselessly, chopping away hills, spreading over the fertile plain like an oozing Camembert. We may be delighted by the Super-City's cultural strongholds, from

Robert M. Hutchins' Center for the Study of Democratic Institutions at Santa Barbara to the Scripps Institute of Oceanography and the Salk Center at La Jolla, but between them extends a scene of environmental devastation that is made doubly tragic because of the splendor of the site.

Few civilizations have had the opportunity to build in a setting of such sweeping natural grandeur, blessed with a climate which until recently was one of the most benign on earth. Precisely because of its beauty, this land demanded the most exquisite sensibility on the part of developers, for it wounds easily. Where a delicately balanced ecology prevailed, there has been fearful disruption of natural processes, such as water runoff. Quite literally, hills have burst into flame, or collapsed in slides of mud, like horrors in Dante's *Inferno*. Soil and water, like the air, have been poisoned.

More serious still, individual man has found his basic need for urbane social intercourse thwarted by excessive diffusion of cultural resources. Over hundreds of square miles, there are few places to walk, few occasions for the civilized surprise, the beautiful chance meetings, the freshly discovered, unique thing, which are almost birthrights for citizens of richly venerable cities such as London and Rome. The only discernible urban structure, on the scale that the Super-City requires, is the freeway network. To make this a truly great city, rather than simply a mammoth one, all sorts of new structures must be interwoven logically in a strengthened urban tissue. And because the Super-City itself is unprecedented, these must be unprecedented and revolutionary structures. Old solutions do not exist for this utterly new and exhilarating problem.

In fairness to Southern California it should be made clear that many of its vexing difficulties can now be recognized as universal problems of advanced technological civilization. They can be found in all rapidly expanding urban regions, often in more aggravated form than in Southern California, which has not experienced the massive power failures and water shortages that have plagued the Megalopolis of the Atlantic Seaboard.

Indeed, rival urban regions everywhere would like to share some of Southern California's so-called problems, such as its disproportionate dependence on the lucrative aerospace industry. As a Department of Labor study revealed last year, 18 new jobs, almost all of them in "growth" industries, are created in California for every new one in New York; and Southern California, with nearly 60 percent of the state's industrial capacity, is where most of the jobs may be found.

And so the newcomers continue to arrive: the Yankee from Maine such as the taxi driver from Bangor who drove me cheerfully on the freeways last month, as well as the black Alabaman who, together with about half of the residents of Watts, cannot afford to own a car. Yet he too, for many complex reasons, comes to Southern California, the first urban region in the world to become almost completely dependent on the private automobile.

Considered as a population magnet alone, this is clearly one of the most attractive places on earth. If there were no smog, as the late Catherine Bauer Wurster observed, there would be even more people.

In the vast urbanized area that extends continuously along the coast from Santa Barbara to Mexico, spreading inland to engulf Riverside and San Bernardino, and sweeping beyond, into the increasingly befouled desert, about 10 million people already occupy several thousand square miles of developed land. Even if immigration were to be reduced by massive shifts in the national economy and changing settlement patterns, natural increase alone will swell Southern California's population enormously in the next generation. Very likely 20 million — and possibly 3 or 4 millions more — will dwell in the Super-City by the turn of the century, with no end of growth yet in sight.

Not only people, but machines are proliferating, and they must also be taken into account if any realistic attempt is made to create a biotechnic civic order where all now appears to be disorder. To establish such a new order of man, which will meet not only his physiological and psychological needs, but also satisfy the increasingly complex technical requirements of industrialized society is the real problem of Southern California, as it doubles in population. In other words, the random pattern of expansion must be replaced by rational *city-building processes*, which will enable both public and private investment to yield tremendous dividends in amenity and efficiency.

If this sounds simple, or simplistic, the harrowing examples of the East Coast power and water crises show that it is going to be infernally difficult to change the process of urban expansion and give it a more coherent direction. The traditionalist planning of the Bay Area Rapid Transit system, predicated on the notion that San Francisco would retain its historical supremacy as a core metropolis, when a regional city had already sprung up around the periphery of the great bay, demonstrates the folly of applying conventional wisdom to new challenges. At still another scale of development, the weak conceptual design of large projects such as the "megacampuses" of the University of California at La Jolla, Irvine and Santa Cruz, together with the disastrous expansion programs at UCLA and Berkeley, shows how crude a state of the art prevails in both the planning and architectural professions.

Yet such projects were planned and executed as public works, and were protected from the pressure of market forces. If this is the best we can do in the public sector, the outlook in private development is even more discouraging. To speak glibly of creating "The Great Society," as is so fashionable nowadays, is to deny or minimize the staggering difficulties which were implicit in the very phrase, "The New Frontier." There is something oddly perverse in a nation defining its goals without specifying the means it needs to achieve them.

It would be much more meaningful today, in a period of swift and incessant scientific and technological innovation, to formulate policies which will enable us to deal with an unprecedented scale of dynamic development; and then to create appropriate political, social and economic instruments with which to execute those policies.

To do this, however, we must first take the great step of recognizing the whole bewildering phenomenon of the expanding environment as a single thing: an amalgam of interacting physical and social systems of which our present knowledge is woefully incomplete, and over which we probably can never exercise full control. Yet surely a modicum of rationally informed control would produce substantial immediate returns. The jammed freeways are part of a physical system, for instance, which leads, say from Watts to Beverly Hills, both of which are physical expressions of social and economic systems. The polluted air hovering over both communities is affected not only by the exhausts of millions of internal combustion engines, but the outpourings of thousands of industrial plants on which the wealth of the whole society is based. None of these plants, however, has been sited according to a comprehensive regional plan of development, even though rudimentary zoning and air pollution regulations do have some effect on their locations. No more oil refineries, for example, are to be built within the jurisdiction of the Los Angeles Air Pollution Control District, and it was partly because of its increasingly rigorous supervision of industrial processes that Kaiser Steel's big mill was located at Fontana, just across the Los Angeles County border.

Nor are any of the much advertised, new "planned communities" (which Edward Eichler's research has shown are radically different from British and Scandinavian government-built "New Towns" and therefore best regarded simply as very large real estate promotions) part of a coordinated program of regional growth. A few overriding factors — the strength of the market, plus the availability of water and the freeway — usually determine the feasibility of these big projects.

Here is surely one area in which the problem of authentic planning of Southern California could be attacked boldly. For private profit is directly dependent on massive public improvements. It is no accident, for instance, that one of the three southern termini of the $1.75 billion State

Water System (minimum cost, including interest: more than $3 billion — some critics say possibly as much as $10 billion) will be at the edge of the 44,000-acre Newhall Ranch, site of the "new town" of Valencia. No accident, either, that a freeway will serve Valencia, almost on order from the Newhall interests.

The point here is not that there was abject collusion between the developers of Valencia and the state bureaucracies which plan the water and freeway systems. Rather, there was entirely proper cooperation and exchange of views. But there was no truly comprehensive planning in spite of the magnitude of public capital expenditures which obviously would have a decisive effect on settlement patterns in Southern California. No state agency existed which could have coordinated the planning of individual systems, including the subsystems of Valencia itself, within an orderly regional framework. In the same way there is no agency, nor even a single advisory official on the governor's staff, to anticipate the effect on urban growth of new programs such as the saline water conversion effort which is now being ambitiously pushed by the federal government. Although it makes excellent sense to combine the conversion plants with nuclear power stations, virtually no thought has been given to future locations of these facilities. [Note: soon after I became a foe of nuclear plants.] Should they all be situated, as the big Long Beach station will be, on islands just a few hundred yards from prime recreational areas? And where will the salt be stored? What will it be used for? In the same way, as was forcefully argued in the last issue of *Cry California* by Richard Reinhardt, there was no coordinating agency to consider the *total* environmental impact of the linear accelerator at Stanford which necessitated the additional power line that was so crudely laid across the terrain of Woodside.

Only if we do coordinate large public and private undertakings on this scale can an authentic regional order arise amidst the inchoate settlement patterns of Southern California. The existence of huge private landholdings, of which the Irvine Ranch is the hugest, is potentially a tremendous advantage. But thus far Irvine departs only in minor features from smaller-scale developments; and very probably, apart from the formalistic layout of its university, will end up very similar to the big Janss-Conejo development, which also was ostensibly "planned" but in fact is scarcely distinguishable from the subdivision surrounding it.

But surely these large projects can be built in such a way that they solve more problems than they create. Surely they can be integrated with an overall regional infrastructure of unparalleled comeliness and efficiency. Surely a much higher level of civic design can be achieved in the projects themselves, incorporating fresh advances in technology such as microtransportation systems that will dispense with Detroit-style vehicles. Surely some equitable relationship can be established between public interest and private profit *on this scale*, where developers have the financial staying power to see the projects through to the end.

Yet first we should try to define our ends more carefully and sensitively than any society has yet attempted. The detached, single-family home, for example, is often decried, but it obviously remains the first preference of families with young children. Traditional urbanists, who find so much to admire in Pompeii, a city closely organized around private pools and courtyards, which nevertheless enjoyed magnificent vistas of Mount Vesuvius and its foothills, fail to see that an analogy exists in Southern California with its tens of thousands of private patios and swimming pools (which are spotted from airplanes by tax assessors).

What is wrong with such developments is primarily their architecture, but in principle the single-family residence does not seem incorrect. Substantial increases in density would doubtless improve the overall settlement pattern. Nothing would be gained, though, by transforming Pasadena into the Bronx, just as nothing has been gained by the construction of thousands of barrackslike "garden apartments" in Southern California in recent years. In fact, more multiple dwellings are now being built than single-family homes, with a sharp increase in density patterns — precisely what most urbanists have advocated. The mess has become denser, but it is still a mess: the freeways are jammed; hillsides which stood for millennia suddenly slide after heavy rains; the town of Thousand Palms, a few miles eastward of heavy development at Palm Springs, finds itself buried by blowing sand.

What had been sought by the Southern Californians was not so different from the amenities of the Pompeians, but what had changed between classical antiquity and modern times was the scale of development made possible by industrial technology. Let me emphasize that this technology goes far beyond the automobile in determining settlement patterns. The swimming pools represent a formidable technological achievement, as do the refrigerators and freezers which have utterly transformed food merchandising and consumption, the telephones which revolutionized communications, the TV sets which have barely begun to effect profound cultural changes.

Because the full complexity of technological innovation was never grasped by the bulk of society, and because the new scale of development was never acknowledged, the settlement process remained piecemeal, with calamitous results for natural ecology and the quality of community life. Not even the plutocratic enclave of San Marino, the avowed enemy of governmental action and comprehensive planning, could escape this fate. The San Gabriel Mountains, which once provided San Marino with an incomparable backdrop, are veiled in smog which the patricians must breathe together with the proletariat of Watts.

From the air these two communities, tragically — perhaps mortally — at odds with one another, can be seen as part of a single thing: the bewildering expanse of urban plasm which covers the entire coastal basin. Where scores of individual communities once stood plainly delineated, separated by miles of fragrant orange groves, there is only one community. By day, from a jet, it may appear to lack any regional structure whatever, except for the freeways which lace it like veins. At evening, however, when a glorious spectacle of colored lights makes it one of the most stirring works of nonobjective art ever to germinate from unconscious social forces, the interacting dynamics of the Super-City are unmistakable.

Unlike the Megalopolis of the Atlantic Seaboard, which has coalesced around the congested and degraded, but still massive, cores of older cities, Southern California has only faintly assertive nuclei, when observed in so large a perspective. Yet this impression is deceptive. One of the greatest myths perpetrated by the enemies of Los Angeles, for instance, is that it has no urban core.

While it is true that a large number of aging buildings, few of them higher than two or three stories, were destroyed to make room for parking lots, this was certainly not harmful to the city in the long run. The market in this case simply cleared land more rapidly than government-sponsored redevelopment ever could have, and provided downtown with a substantial reserve of open land for imminent development. All of these parking lots will be built on before another generation has passed; and the new structures will be decisively superior in every way to the gimcrack little buildings that were destroyed. But will they be good enough? Will they be part of an admirably reorganized downtown, served by both regional and subregional transportation systems, freed from the tyranny of the automobile and yet accessible to it? This is the real question to which critics such as Victor Gruen, if they took the trouble to come from Beverly Hills to look at downtown, should have confined themselves. For Los Angeles' downtown never disappeared, never was eviscerated, as the traditional urban theorists apparently believe. Not one first-class building, so far as I know, was demolished; and the one outstanding historical monument, the Bradbury Building, is still very much in business, fully rented like most of the other major structures, and apparently here to stay for a long time.

In fact, although it has grave failings architecturally, and remains as old-fangled in most respects as the ancient European cities which the traditionalists admire, downtown Los Angeles is a remarkably pleasant place, in which it is still possible to dine well, attend concerts, browse in bookstores, and shop at Brooks Brothers or Robinson's. Moreover, some three million square feet of office and commercial space — something like the entire downtown capacity of Oakland — is now under construction or planned in the core, with five or six times as much to come in the next decade or two.

If the central business district were to be plunked down in San Francisco, its imposing city blocks, department stores and public buildings would appear very formidable indeed. Yet in Southern California, because of the new scale of settlement, it appears weak; and thus it provides a valuable insight into the nature of the Super-City's evolving form.

For the central business district, augmented by the apartments, hotels, stores, restaurants, plazas and subsurface road system of the $500 million Bunker Hill project, which has finally gotten under way with the construction of a 40-story tower, is only one of the great regional components from which the new civic order must be fashioned. Shooting westward from this concentration, something like the tube of a thermometer fourteen miles long, the towers of Wilshire Boulevard present an altogether new kind of urban profile, broadening to join Alcoa's Century City in West Los Angeles, and, a few miles farther along, the academic city, studded with highrise towers, that has arisen around UCLA. At its best, this sumptuous urban passage through Beverly Hills, Brentwood, Bel Air, Westwood and Pacific Palisades is surely one of the most gracious environments yet created in America. At the end of Wilshire, Santa Monica is still another element of this far-flung urban configuration.

If each of these developments were linked with other massive additions to the Super-City, such as the highrise complex of office buildings, banks and hotels that now surround the international airport, and further connected on a larger scale, with the nuclei of San Diego, Santa Barbara and San Bernadino; and if at the same time gray areas such as Watts were renewed, and integrated, on the same scale, an urban civilization of unprecedented force and graciousness would appear. A period of cleansing and reorganization could follow the period of resistless expansion which has proceeded decade after decade, as population doubled and redoubled. Oil fields, such as Signal Hill, could be reclaimed as precious land reserves, and thanks to improved drilling techniques, opened to settlement as soon as the wells were made unobtrusive.

There is room enough in the Super-City not for 20 but for 30 or 40 millions of people if only we have the wisdom to conserve the resources which remain unspoiled, and to renew the resources which have been wantonly damaged. We must decide where we should build, and where the wisest course would be to leave land undeveloped, according to the full scope of future needs. Not the pathetic 8,000 acres or so now planned, but the full panoply of the Santa Monica Mountains would constitute a true regional park on the civilized scale of the future. Literally hundreds of other recreational spaces, some large, some intimate, but all meaningful in terms of human needs, would have to be reclaimed from the degraded coastal plain, as if from a pestilential fen. All this would require political and social maturity such as Americans have yet to prove they possess, as well as efficient management — of combined water and recreational resources, for instance — such as we have never achieved in spite of pretensions of "Yankee know-how." For obviously there is much, at this still primitive stage of human development, that we do not know, that we cannot do. The only way to learn is to accept the reality of the new scale of urban civilization, to rejoice in its challenge, and above all to realize that we possess the wealth and the strength to make it the good thing it can easily and swiftly become.

Spring 1966, *Cry, California*

■ SAN JOSE'S GRAND PLAN FOR ITS RIVER

The miserable ditch called the Guadalupe River, on the edge of downtown San Jose, finally has a chance to be a great urban gateway.

Over the next couple of decades, a consortium of city, regional and federal agencies — with substantial help from the private sector — plans to clean up the Guadalupe, and to broaden some stretches into lakes and lagoons as the stream threads its way through a three-mile park.

The ambitious plan not only includes playing fields, tennis courts, beaches and other recreational facilities, but also sites for museums, a sculpture garden and a new repertory theater that are part of San Jose's long-range strategy to make its wretched downtown an inviting place.

If San Jose, which has sabotaged its own environmental opportunities for years, can pull this off, its saving of the half-dead river will be one of the more spectacular comebacks since the resurrection of Lazarus.

Yet it should work, if only because so many public agencies and community groups have a stake in the plan's success.

The plan has been put together over the past two years by the San Francisco planning and landscape firm of EDAW Inc., in close cooperation with the Army Corps of Engineers, the Santa Clara Valley water district, the city and county park and recreation departments, and especially the San Jose Redevelopment Agency, which led the entire project.

It will take $150 million in public and private funds, a sum which might have seemed impossible a short time ago, but seems feasible now.

San Jose will provide the most money, perhaps $80 million or more, through an ingenious financial ploy that has turned most of the city into a single vast redevelopment area.

Under the plan, lucrative outlying developments in Silicon Valley are subsidizing the inner-city redevelopment projects. About $40 million in cash and city-owned land is already available as San Jose's share of the $80 million Technology Center of Silicon Valley, which will be the showplace of the Guadalupe River park.

Situated on the west bank, near West San Carlos and Prevost streets, the Technology Center is intended to be the world's finest high-tech and modern science museum, an attraction comparable to the Monterey Aquarium, which drew 2.3 million visitors last year.

However, the Technology Center and its accompanying scientific "discovery center" for young children are only the most splendid features of this bold and sensitive concept for the Guadalupe, which far outdistances several previous ill-fated beautification schemes.

Those schemes, over the past 25 years, failed because none came close to solving the interrelated problem of urban design, community needs and, most crucial, flood control.

The Guadalupe can be very destructive after rainy winters. Therefore, the most fascinating component of the new park design will be a $50 million flood-control system, which Congress is expected to approve within the next five years.

Although the system has been technically devised by the Corps of Engineers, who have a long record of environmental butchery, the design by EDAW has integrated it so deftly with the landscaping or hidden it in huge underground culverts, that the engineering will be hardly noticeable.

The river, flowing northward from Virginia Street to the edge of the San Jose Municipal Airport, will pass through six distinctly different zones in the park. Each zone would derive its character from the flood-control devices and varied activities along the shore.

The transitions between zones should be gracious. Flowing water will provide a sense of continuity, and so will riverside walkways — sometimes narrow and thickly planted, sometimes broadening in terraces and promenades, and running freely again in paths through open lawns. All this should renew San Jose's historic relation to the Guadalupe. The 18th-century pueblo was founded on its banks, but the tawdry modern town has turned its back to the river, contaminated its water and degraded the charming Victorian cottages along the shore into a Chicano slum.

The plan calls for the eradication of the slum, but the task will not be simple. San Jose is currently facing a lawsuit from the few remaining Hispanic families, some of whom have lived beside the river for 40 years.

They were being booted out under eminent domain until the Legal Aid Society went to court in their behalf and demanded permanent affordable housing, claiming the right of an ethnic community to stay together under the 1968 Federal Housing Act.

The plan can also encounter difficulties with private developers adjacent to the park. They will be responsible for the landscaping of their adjacent segments of public shoreline. Their contributions could amount to $10 million or $20 million.

So far, their record has been bleak. Lincoln Properties has built a disgraceful pair of midrise office buildings, just north of the Technology Center site, designed by the Texas architect, Harwood K. Smith. (The same developers and architect, by the way, are putting up a howler of a highrise on Market Street in San Francisco at the site of the old Hoffman Grill.)

The San Jose Redevelopment Agency, directed by Frank Taylor, a professional architect, is supposed to be enforcing strict aesthetic controls. But somehow the invertebrate city planning department — a quite separate agency — got into the act; and between the two bureaucracies, yahoo developers have continued to pepper the city with speculative junk.

On the other hand, the Corps of Engineers — once a great sinner — has apparently gotten true religion.

The corps, whose proposed $50 million federal contribution is indispensable, started out with typical heavy-handed flood-control schemes. Fortunately, project manager Arijs Rakstins, was finally persuaded by EDAW and redevelopment director Taylor to pitch in creatively, and to begin the control system about three-fourths of a mile upstream at Virginia Street, instead of the corps' original starting point at West Santa Clara Street.

That has made possible the most inventive part of the plan, where the Guadalupe, having passed under the goliath interchange of Interstate 280 and Route 87, broadens into a lake in front of the Technology Center.

The river here will not be the Guadalupe, but a stream fed with well water — pure enough for children to sail boats on — and kept at a constant water level throughout the year. The clear stream will continue all the way down to West San Fernando Street, where this artificial lake will be contained by a dam.

The real Guadalupe, meanwhile, will be shunted beneath the west bank in a pair of gigantic box-culverts, and will re-emerge in the old riverbed beyond the massive overpass of Route 87 near West San Carlos Street.

A second, broader lake will be formed a short distance downstream at the confluence of the Guadalupe and Los Gatos Creek. It will be essentially a holding basin for spring runoff. Instead of the water vanishing in summer, it will also be held at a decent level the year-round, stretching as far as another barrier at Old West Julian Street.

Thereafter, the banks — as far as the airport — will be shaped as natural containment forms, earth structures rather than dikes, although done as "sculptural" stepbacks of concrete. The riverbed will be planted with hardy vegetation, which will survive even when the water runs low in hot July and August.

Innumerable details remain to be worked out in this grand design. There is not much that can be done with ponderous elevated freeways, and their access ramps, which entangle acres of the future park in concrete spaghetti, but the proposed street and pedestrian bridges present stirring opportunities.

The street and pedestrian bridges should not be left to hokey city engineers, but should be built as a consistently elegant series of related spans.

Lighting, paving, benches and other park furniture should be unified from beginning to end. The greenswards should not become a dumping ground for cornball sculpture, such as the Berkeley waterfront, but should be reserved for works by great artists, but not too many of them.

Will half-barbarous San Jose have the civic will to carry it off? The time is here, and there could be no better place to prove the city's capabilities in the technological age.

December 27, 1985

In the halcyon days before World War II, when the population explosion had scarcely begun in the Bay Region, and the peninsula below San Francisco was dotted with towns and villages which were still separated by farms, orchards and great estates, there were few places where suburban life could be seen to finer advantage than in the unhurried university town of Palo Alto, just 30 miles south of the metropolis. Founded in the '80s as a tiny faculty village for the university that Senator and Mrs. Stanford established in memory of a beloved only son, Palo Alto had developed into a classic, well-to-do suburb of homes, schools, churches, parks and tree-lined streets. Each morning the Southern Pacific took executives and professional men to the city. Except for the shops on University Avenue, and the restaurants on El Camino Real (which still served adequately as a north-and-south highway), there was little business activity, and no manufacturing whatever. Considerable acreage remained under cultivation. The marshy bay front, which the farsighted municipal government acquired cheaply and early, was populated mainly by birds. And extending westward — as the key to Palo Alto's future — was the incomparable 8,800-acre Stanford campus, affectionately known as "The Farm," lifting from the agricultural plain in oak-studded hills.

Today, although the town appears in many respects unchanged, and even improved, the old, tranquil suburban pattern has been transformed irrevocably. The suburb has become a city, a subcenter of the vast regional metropolis which now rings the bay; and things will never be the same down on the farm, which has quite suddenly become one of the foremost centers of scientific research in the world.

The census best reveals the magnitude of the change. Where fewer than 17,000 people lived in 1940, and only 25,000 10 years later, there are nearly 55,000, and the population continues to climb. More people now enter Palo Alto to work and shop each day than commute to San Francisco or to the sprawling new, submetropolis of San Jose at the south end of the bay. Each day some 70,000 cars enter and leave Palo Alto, and some 50,000 others merely pass through on four heavily traveled north-and-south arteries, including the tremendous freeway which runs beside the bay.

What had been open fields even three and four years ago are now subdivisions, whole square miles of them, including the celebrated developments of Joseph Eichler, who soon after the war saw a young market in California for contemporary design, and has erected some

2,000 mass-produced modern houses (by Anshen & Allen and Jones & Emmons) in Palo Alto alone. There are hundreds of duplex units, and the first high rise apartments have commenced to change the profile of the town. The business community, too, has undergone a profound change. University Avenue, the old commercial street, is rapidly becoming a professional and financial center (16 brokerage houses are in operation where there were only 4 in 1955); and the leading local merchants, together with the branches of San Francisco stores such as I. Magnin, have shifted to a huge shopping center — largest on the peninsula — which, although this would have seemed incredible a decade ago, is located on the Stanford campus, and attracts customers from a score of neighboring communities.

In the most significant development of all, the smokeless electronics plants of the space age — Varian Associates, Hewlett-Packard, Lockheed, General Electric — have also been welcomed on the campus, close to the university's laboratories where many of their products have been perfected; and last November, after the most bitter election campaign in the city's history, a narrow majority voted to allow Ampex Corp. to build a 350,000-square-foot, 4,000-employee factory in the hills.

For Palo Alto there can be no turning back (although some past and present errors of judgment may be rectified). Together the city and the university, not invariably in full harmony with each other, are moving toward a new kind of environment. In their efforts to achieve a "balanced," largely self-sustaining community — efforts which are being duplicated less dramatically in other strong American suburbs such as Pasadena and Princeton — can be seen one of the most crucial struggles of the present urban revolution.

Indeed, if Palo Alto successfully integrates industry and commerce with its exemplary residential and cultural resources, and at the same time controls the automobile and wisely conserves its remaining open land, then the city in another generation — when population should reach 100,000 — may well bear a healthy resemblance to the visionary Garden City conceived by Ebenezer Howard at the close of the last century. Unlike most communities which had tried to be "garden cities," Palo Alto is large enough, and fundamentally strong enough, to make the concept succeed.

A series of impressive recent civic accomplishments have given unmistakable evidence of that strength. First of all, in 1950, when the old village system of government obviously could not meet the city's needs, the administration was reorganized on a managerial basis. In Jerome Keithley, a young, hard-driving administrator who refused what might have been a bigger job as manager of San Diego in order to remain in Palo Alto, the city has found one of the finest public servants in the state. Keithley and his team of youthful assistants, including planner Louis Fourcroy, are staunchly backed by a city council which, as might be expected in Palo Alto, is especially distinguished by its cultivation, intelligence and concern for the public interest. Quite simply, the council — which is conservative in national outlook but likely to be extremely liberal on the local scene — wants nothing but the best for the community.

During the '50s, it got something close to its wish. In 1953 a new city hall, designed by Palo Alto architect Leslie Nichols, was opened in a spacious parklike Civic Center. The informal building of redwood and brick, quite residential in character, was joined a few years later by a handsome public library by Edward D. Stone, who at the time had gone to Palo Alto to design Stanford's rather grandiose medical center which, whatever its architectural shortcomings, has provided the university with a magnificent research and teaching establishment, and the town with a community hospital of the first national rank. Stone also designed a smaller branch library for the city, at the same time that landscape architects Royston, Hanamoto & Mayes were creating in 18-acre Mitchell park a most delightful recreation area.

These improvements, as well as the municipal golf course, small-plane airport, and yacht harbor which were created by the bay, plus a group of architecturally undistinguished but solidly constructed new schools (most of them accompanied by adjoining parks), and an extensive road improvement and street-tree planting program, all cost a great deal of money. Yet, during this same period the tax rate, which in 1950 had risen to an all-time high of $1.29 per $100 of assessment, dropped spectacularly to only 80 cents.

How did the city perform this Indian rope trick of finance? Good management is one answer, and private construction, of course, also provided additional tax revenue. But the main explanation is somewhat more complex. As the city felt its urban power growing, it became aware that its stores — especially those in the big Stanford Shopping Center and in the charming tree-shaded Town and Country center on El Camino Real — served not only Palo Altans but a quarter of a million people from surrounding communities, a figure which should double in the next 20 years. In 1957 a local sales tax was imposed, which last year yielded Palo Alto $1.2 million.

Even more income poured in from a source which may be surprising: the city's booming utility business. Long ago Palo Alto (which for this reason has been called the "world's most conservative socialistic community") decided that it could retail gas, electricity and water, together with sewage disposal and garbage collection, much more efficiently than could private utility companies. Even though it charges approximately the same rates as private utilities elsewhere in California, Palo Alto's profit on this operation runs close to 25 percent. Last year revenues totaled $3 million. The chief power lines, of course, run straight to the Stanford campus and its landscaped industrial park, because the electronics plants — Lockheed, for instance, where the Polaris missile was developed — consume tremendous energy.

How the great campus, which surely is one of the finest tracts of open space remaining within a densely populated metropolitan region, came to be made available for industrial and commercial development is one of the fascinating land-use stories of modern time.

Although Senator Stanford in 1885 endowed the university with what was then the enormous sum of $21 million, which at the time was more than the combined endowments of Harvard, Yale and Columbia, the shrewd old railroad magnate saw that the institution's real wealth was its land, and he specified that the 8,800 acres might be leased, but never sold. There was something more than acumen in this limitation of the founding deed. The senator was deeply devoted to his Peninsula estate, with its ancient oaks and redwoods, its wheat fields, its stables and corrals, and the wooded uplands where cattle grazed.

The university's earliest buildings carefully respected the mood of the terrain. The faculty lived in redwood bungalows, and the monumental academic structures of buff-colored stone — a splendid complex of neo-Romanesque buildings by Richardson's successors Shepley, Rutan & Coolidge — were linked together around the spacious quadrangle by deep, shadowy arcades. None of the later buildings has approached their robust generosity of form, or their refinement of detail; but in spite of the overall mediocrity of the more modern standard buildings, the campus remained a remarkably pleasant place.

Yet, by 1946 the university's endowment had risen only to $32 million and had been far surpassed by the leading eastern schools. Stanford suddenly found itself land-poor in an inflationary economy. Income from farm leases dwindled below outgo for taxes (only the educational plant is tax-exempt). Moreover, as land grew scarce on the Peninsula, the Stanford properties were eyed for public use. Palo Alto took 51 acres for a high school. The Veterans Administration condemned 87 more for a psychiatric hospital.

The university, seriously in need of funds, turned to hard-headed alumnus Alf Brandin, a former football star and insurance executive, who became Stanford's business manager. Guided by a plan prepared by Skidmore, Owings & Merrill (SOM) in 1953, Brandin launched the land-development program. On the northern flank of the campus, acreage was assigned to the shopping center, just off El Camino Real, and farther back, a group of medical and professional buildings near Stone's new medical center, and a luxury residential district, where thus far only some very showy garden apartments by John Carl Warnecke & Associates have been built. Indeed, except for two crisply elegant, but extremely modest, office buildings by Knorr-Elliott, this entire area must be considered an architectural disappointment.

On the other side of the academic complex, 450 acres were assigned to industry, with leases — as in the commercial development — to run for 99 years. Much has been made by Brandin and other university officials concerning the aesthetic quality of these smokeless plants. Yet, although it is true that the 40 percent ground coverage and mandatory landscaping represent higher standards than in conventional developments, very few of the structures can be described as handsome; some are extremely coarse. Furthermore, even 40 percent ground coverage — a figure which may have seemed satisfactory on paper — proved to be too generous concession on the part of the university. The sites are much too crowded.

Gradually, at the close of the '50s, the factories inched up the slopes toward the hills. Then, last year, Stanford and the Ampex Corp. caused a furor when Brandin announced the university's intention to open 250 more acres for manufacturing, of which Ampex — as a starter — would take 80. What disturbed the citizens such as Palo Alto architect Morgan Stedman, who led the fight against the proposal, was that Stanford seemed bent on exploiting its lands according to the available market. Neither the university nor Palo Alto (which annexes the Stanford properties as they are developed for nonacademic use), charged Stedman, had an up-to-date plan which dealt comprehensively with the future of the city.

The charge was true. Palo Alto's only plan was an interim report prepared by Harold Wise & Associates in 1955, and never formally adopted by the city council. Skidmore, Owings & Merrill's university master plan of 1953 was also badly dated; and, in fact, Stanford had not consulted SOM on planning matters since 1956. The university, furthermore, had no supervising architect. Virtually the only supervision to be exercised over Ampex was by Brandin and Stanford's staff planner Harry Sanders. Enough indignation was stirred up to force a referendum, and both sides carried the issue to the voters, who decided (four to three) to allow the university to open a new 250-acre industrial tract.

If the vote was a defeat for advocates of planning, they nevertheless gained certain points. The Ampex plant will cover only 20 percent rather than 40 percent of its rolling site; there will be a minimum of grading although the terrain undoubtedly will be badly scarred. More important, there seems to be little chance that Stanford will be allowed to invade the hills farther until Palo Alto itself has a master plan, which will be drawn up as soon as possible by one of three nationally known firms which are being considered for the job.

Far on the other side of the city, the municipally owned tidal flats, another victory has been scored for a planned environment. Here, with the support of City Manager Keithley, the Utah Construction and Mining Corp. proposed a $36 million partnership with the city in order to reclaim 600 acres along the bay for industrial building sites, as well as for a golf course, a series of landlocked lagoons and a commercial-professional area. The offer was tempting and before the Ampex controversy grew intense, it seemed likely to be accepted by the city council. On November 14, however, just after the election, the council decided to kill the project and went on record against all large undertakings until Palo Alto had the benefit of the best professional planning counsel.

"We've been on a development binge," ruefully remarked Councilman Carl Stephens. "It's time to sober up a bit."

The city seems ready to take the advice. Palo Alto's momentum has been so swift, and its ambition so strong, that this would appear to be an appropriate moment to pause, so that the magnitude of the task ahead can be measured. By a wonderful stroke of luck, thanks largely to Dr. Russell V. Lee (chief of the famous Palo Alto clinic) who owned an immense tract of land in the hills to the south, the city has acquired a superb, 1200-acre upland park, and beside it had annexed no less than 11 additional square miles of hill territory. This virgin land is roughly equal to the present area of Palo Alto, so that the city has now become a double city, linked by a long annexation corridor that snakes through intervening communities. Years, perhaps decades, may pass before the hills are fully developed — indeed, if they are ever developed entirely. Possibly it will occur to the city and the university that the hills, so precious now, will be incalculably more precious in another half century, that they constitute not only a regional, but in a strict sense a national, treasure. And, if the people of Palo Alto and Stanford are not able to save them, perhaps the governments of California and the United States can.

In the meantime, lesser chores await the planners. A new freeway, running through the hills, is planned by a state division of highways and exceptional care must be taken that the route does not cut savagely across country. El Camino Real, presently bordered for block after block by tawdry drive-ins, gas stations, motels and cheap shops which make it resemble a Los Angeles strip, must be cleansed and landscaped. University Avenue should be closed to traffic, and turned into a pedestrian mall. More towers must go up — not only apartments, but office buildings — so that, from their terraced roofs, the view to the east may be toward a continuously green shore of the bay; and to the west, where the hills roll upward in green folds above forested canyons, there will be the bright sight of the Pacific beyond the crests.

January 1961, *Architectural Forum*

■ THE DILEMMA OF BERKELEY'S SHORE

Nowhere is the tragic gap between this region's full potential splendor and its present needless squalor more apparent than in Berkeley, where the Campanile of the University of California — a classical emblem of civilization — may be sighted, distantly but distinctly, from the garbage dump on the East Bay mud flats.

Between these paradoxical extremes Berkeley is not truly a fine university town, but a nondescript and, in places, cheap and vicious, ordinary western city that happens to have one of the world's foremost universities in it.

Until recently the small-town chamber of commerce mentality has belligerently withstood, on one side, the bitter patrician criticism of unenlightened professional people in the hills, and on the other, the smoldering indignation of the Negroes in their horizontal ghetto close to the bay.

Lately however, a promising new mood has been perceptible in Berkeley, not least in the deliberations of the now liberal-minded City Council, which at last seems resolved to find sound and if possible, permanent solutions to the community's problems, especially the problem of the degraded waterfront, one of the most unsightly stretches of the entire bay shore.

Indeed, tonight, the council will hear a number of proposals in this connection from groups such as the Save the Bay Association and the East Bay Chapter of the American Institute of Architects, both of which are opposed in principle to any more large-scale filling of the bay, and which also advocate, again in broad principle, that as much of the shoreline as possible be allocated to recreational and cultural pursuits.

At the same time the council will hear from Edgardo Contini, senior partner in the well-known Los Angeles architectural and planning firm of Victor Gruen Associates, who have prepared for the Santa Fe Railroad — the principal private landowner in this part of the bay — a sweeping program of reclamation and development along the entire waterfront from Oakland to Point Richmond.

Over the past half century some 30 "plans" — most of which have been merely coarse filling proposals — have been prepared for this crescent-shaped area, but the Gruen concept is by far the most persuasive of them all, and doubtless must command the serious consideration of all concerned.

A proposal of this magnitude concerns not only the directly affected communities — Oakland, Emeryville, Berkeley, Albany and Richmond, which are now so foolishly at odds on this question — but the whole regional city of the bay, including its historic core of San Francisco.

At present we have no effective multicity governmental apparatus to direct the metropolitan entity, much less a plan for its physical development, and therefore even if the Santa Fe and its planners wished to integrate their scheme with a total program for the bay, they would not, for no such program exists.

This alone is good reason for postponing any undertaking on this scale and, moreover, for the state Legislature to declare a moratorium on large filling operations until a regional plan is formulated.

Possibly a decade — about the time needed for the realizations of the rapid transit system — would be required before a feasible plan could be developed and approved.

But what is ten years — and one must constantly remind compulsively impatient Americans of this — what is ten years in the long-term development of an environment which we should be bound, morally and economically, to leave to our descendants in better condition than we found it?

The cardinal virtue of the Gruen scheme, in truth, is that even though it deals with only a fraction of the bay, it shows the undeniable advantages of comprehensive planning of this kind of the grand scale.

For this is clearly a multicity concept which overrides irrational municipal divisions, and attacks the problem of the East Bay as a totality. Under this scheme no less than five cities would enjoy a visually and functionally unified frontage on the vast harbor. People and buildings would be brought into intimate relationships with the water, on a much more profound basis than in piecemeal single-family allotments such as on Belvedere Lagoon. Like Venice, this might be a genuine water city of exceptional richness and grace.

But would the water city be organically united with the older cities on the other side of the freeway barrier?

For what the planners have in fact proposed is a sixth city beside the other five — a linear city of 100,000 people strung along a transportation line and fluidly bending outward to open space — with an independent urban *raison d'être* of its own.

Even if this city were designed for sparsely settled prairies, therefore, and open water was replaced by public meadows in the concept, this would still be a stimulating contribution to contemporary urban design.

It happens, however, that the city is proposed for a densely settled, intricately organized, metropolitan region, and it would certainly cause severe disruptions not readily apparent in the adroitly drawn diagrams.

What is good for the Santa Fe might well, in the end, be good for the region as a whole, but the region should know, and be prepared to pay the price.

For the seemingly generous reservation of more than half of the legally developable acreage as open water — that is, half of the 14,300 acres within the bulkhead line established by the U.S. Army Engineers — proves to not be generous at all. The Santa Fe is simply recommending that the people be given their own water.

For of the total area only 4,700 acres — much less than half — is privately owned, and 9,600 are already in the public domain. Of the private holdings, 3,400 acres are the Santa Fe's, and these or their equivalent — for some swapping of inshore and offshore real estate is suggested — the railroad proposes to develop entirely.

By assembling all of the various holdings in a single project, the Santa Fe has in fact made their own full stake less evident, even though the planners indicate — in a candid admission — that about half of the submerged properties are for practical purposes unbuildable anyway because of the condition of the bay bottom.

The only large recreational area proposed is "Berkeley Island" jutting far into the bay, which will be consecrated to a golf course (to be swept by wild winds), because its mud fill will settle considerably.

So much for the allocation of open water. The related question of land use, also seemingly humane because it is largely given to residential development, rather than tax-producing heavy industry — which pays heavily for appropriate sites — also shows a less-than-selfless attitude on the part of the Santa Fe.

The truth, as the planners concede, is that so much industrial land is now being anarchically developed in the Bay Region — without any thought being given to the total requirements of the area — that it is infernally difficult to market industrial sites in this relatively expensive corner of the bay.

For this reason, a residential community, with some facilities for research and development, was decided upon. Yet it is commonly known that residential development of this kind, particularly on filled land, is the most expensive in terms of municipal services.

Who is to pay for these prettily conceived schools? Who is to provide the police and fire protection for their comely neighbors? Who is to maintain their sewage lines and streets?

In considering these questions tonight, the Berkeley City Council — which has had considerable difficulty maintaining, not to speak of improving, its school system — might also ask, what will the huge proposed commercial development, across the freeway at the foot of University Avenue, do to the aged business district centered on Shattuck Avenue?

There the shopkeepers have already been hard hit by the big regional shopping center in nearby El Cerrito.

A still bigger competitor, only a few blocks away on the waterfront, might put them out of business permanently.

And why develop the foot of University Avenue for commercial purposes when, over its entire length, this now tawdry — but potentially splendid — thoroughfare needs comprehensive improvement?

The rapid transit station at the intersection of Sacramento and University avenues would provide an admirable nucleus for an expanded business district.

The subject of transit introduces several others which show the Gruen concept to be extremely vulnerable when examined in the light of total environmental needs. Will we truly need still another giant freeway along the East Bay, as the state engineers insist, or can their habitual butchery of the environment be avoided here, too, through imaginative design?

So much is at stake here — nothing less than the whole future of one side of the bay, whose climate, for instance, might be affected by the filling of 7,000 additional acres — that the most searching studies are obviously necessary if real solutions are to be found.

And even if Berkeley and its neighbors decide that the whole vast scheme is desirable, it will take more than attractive pictures in a brochure to make it an architecturally handsome community.

November 19, 1963

Embarcadero centers #4 to #1, from left to right, San Francisco, California, 1982.
By Mike Maloney. Courtesy The San Francisco Chronicle.

II. Urban Centers

■ A GIANT DRAWN CONCRETE BOW

San Francisco has another structural wonder of the world, ranking with the great suspension bridges of the 1930s spanning the Golden Gate and the bay, in the George R. Moscone Convention Center.

The arching exhibition hall — 880 feet long, nearly 300 feet wide and 43 feet high — is the largest underground room ever built. In many ways it's also the finest. For Moscone Center, finished in 1981 at a cost of $126 million, is not only a technological feat but a work of architectural art.

Because the huge facility has been placed mostly below the surface of the surroundings streets, and landscaped as a park above, Moscone Center also marks a serious attempt to humanize large-scale urban design. The master plan for the Yerba Buena Gardens project calls for a number of structures atop the eight-acre roof — including a domed, big-screen movie house, recreation pavilions and meeting rooms — embellished by a fountain and pool.

Whether or not the grandiose plan is ever realized, it can't be fully successful: Planners discovered that a high water table under the convention hall would make total undergrounding impossibly expensive. This is why the great concrete box pops out of the ground. The steep sides, planted with greenery but still forbidding, jut as high as 20 feet above the bordering sidewalks.

This half-undergrounding also cost at least an extra $25 million, and perhaps as much as $40 million; city officials have never revealed precisely how much.

The cost overrun, enough to finance the repairs Golden Gate Park needs for the next century, hasn't overly bothered this most insouciant of American cities, which spent twice what domed stadiums cost Minneapolis and Seattle for a space too low for professional basketball games.

But Moscone Center will easily accommodate the Democratic National Convention, even though it was never planned for the purpose — proof of its tremendous adaptability. And besides, it's not only big but beautiful.

Granted, the overall design is flawed in places, particularly in the cumbersome trusses of the glassed-in entrance pavilion at street level, but the project as a whole is a stirring achievement by architects Hellmuth,

Obata & Kassabaum and the masterly engineer, Professor T.Y. Lin of the University of California at Berkeley.

What makes Moscone Center unique is the great subterranean space, far larger than its nearest rivals: the modern concrete shell of the crypt at Lourdes and the ribbed concrete ceiling of Italian engineer Ricardo Morandi's underground automobile showplace in Turin.

Moscone Center's 16 heroic arches, however, can be better understood in terms of bridge construction than in terms of more conventional earth-covered roofs. There are longer concrete arches, all in bridges, including the 1,000-foot span of the Gladesville Bridge in Sydney, Australia, which is the longest of all. But none of those arches has to support rooftop loads of soil and structures up to three stories high, whose weight will average some 300 pounds per square foot, and at certain points perhaps twice as much. What's more, there are no interior columns to support these loads, which press down on an unobstructed, clear-span volume of approximately 9.5 million cubic feet.

To negotiate this kind of space, the architects, led by Gyo Obata and engineer Lin, were largely inspired by the bridges of Robert Maillart, the Swiss structural genius who from the early 1900s onward devised arches of bewitching elegance, stiffened — or "braced" — by deck slabs integrated with their curving shapes. In an analogous way, Moscone Center's arches are braced by great transversal roof girders that pass through their crowns.

But Lin, the "father of prestressed concrete" in this country, was able to be technically bolder than Maillart because of structural advances made since World War II, such as "post-tensioning" with steel cables. The post-tensioning system used here enabled Lin to flex the 275-foot arches like gigantic concrete bows, aiming an unseen arrow of force upward at the top of their rise.

These technicalities underlie the aesthetics of Moscone Center like the metrics of a poem. There are 16 arches in all, arranged in pairs set 60 feet apart down the length of the 800-foot space, and their lean profiles set up a grand processional rhythm as they spring in succession, with astonishing lightness, 40 feet to their crests, across the 290-foot width of the hall.

The architectural decision to use 16 arches in pairs, rather than 8 colossal single arches, is the secret of the overall impression of grace. Each arch is only 5 feet thick, or about 1/60th of its overall length, making a depth-span ratio that is mathematically remarkable in a structure of this size.

Like many other types of great structures — airplane hangars, for instance, or covered arenas, such as the 400-foot cable-slung Oakland Coliseum, Moscone Center was more spectacular before it was enclosed.

When the space was still open at the Third and Fourth street ends, but the ceiling of T-shaped, prestressed concrete beams — each 80 feet long — was already in place above the arches and bracing girders, sunlight poured into the vast interior with an almost mystical beauty, as in the nave of an ancient shrine or basilica.

Yet this is an uncompromisingly modern structure, revealing the emotional power of rationalist International Style architecture in a period of trendy Post-Modernism.

Paradoxically, the only major design weakness has been a failure of the structural nerve in the ponderous 120-foot trusses spanning the entrance pavilion on the surface. These tubular concoctions — relatives of the pipe-trusses in Obata's Space Museum in Washington, D.C. — are strangely heavy in comparison with the fearlessly conceived arches, which are more than twice as long and which perform a far more difficult task underground.

But if the trusses killed the chance of the glass-enclosed pavilion to be a masterpiece in its own right, it nevertheless opens views to the downtown skyline beyond the tundra of the intervening redevelopment area, which planners promise us will one day be gardenlike.

From the entrance — which is big enough for 20,000 visitors to pass through in an hour — there are also stirring glimpses downward to the great hall as the space drops 30 feet to the lower level. Handsome escalators and granite staircases shoot downward in spectacular diagonals from landscaped terraces and balconies. In spite of terrible murals, the result of an ill-conceived $500,000 city art program, the drama of these multilevel spaces is Piranesian.

It has all been enhanced by very decent graphics, furnishings, carpets, fine granite pavings, stainless steel hardware and large sheets of glass. The colors are particularly sensitive: reticent in backgrounds of soft browns, beiges and grays; livelier in the Op-Art decoration of the elevator shafts; and nothing short of magnificent in the strong white of the great arched hall, where the Democratic National Convention will be.

Credit for the ingenious setting for the convention goes to the firm of Gensler & Associates, but as Arthur Gensler freely admits, the design was virtually dictated by the demands of the TV networks, whose three-story studios — prefab buildings within a building — dominate the scene.

To anyone who has seen the astonishing electronics paraphernalia — miles of colored wires and cables strewn through the hall and outside to mobile communications units — the implications for the political future are harrowing.

What had been a relatively innocent ritual has been turned into a media spectacular. Hokey decorations have been replaced by the slick, high-tech staging of a political Superbowl in which the TV medium is the true commercial message. Indeed, most of the installations — seating, lighting, apparatus, amplifying systems — have been rented from companies that supply sports events and rock concerts.

Visually, however, there is no sign of frenzy, or even confusion (although the scene doubtless will get hectic when the convention moves into high gear). The staging is too adroit for that. Virtually everyone — except the print media, positioned parallel to the far ends of the dais — will get a clear view of the proceedings. Most of the audience will be especially close to the central rostrum (although the scaffolding for massed TV cameras will be centermost and closer). Only in the stands at the far ends of the hall will the experience be something like watching a football game from the end zone.

There are bound to be minor problems, such as finding the refreshment bars. But the overall impression should be handsome. The mood will be modern. Traditional World Series–style red-white-and-blue bunting has been minimized. A decent Scandinavian blue — "architect's blue" — will predominate.

The lighting may punish the politicians on the platform, but considering the heat put out by a grid of 900 high-powered incandescent lamps that have been brought in to augment the permanent mercury vapor lights, the audience should be kept reasonably comfortable by specially installed air-conditioning ducts and giant rented chillers.

Spectators may cheerfully contemplate the grand lines of the architecture as the convention drones on. The vast floor, perfect for displaying yachts, computers, medical equipment, recreation vehicles and farm machinery at trade fairs, has been leased out in chunks of rentable space, like any sales display.

But the arches soaring up from behind the VIP boxes, over the massed cameras and microphones, and curving downward behind the long dais on the other side of the hall, nearly 100 yards away, provide a powerful backdrop for the whole political show. There's something civilized in that.

July 15, 1984

Now that the reconstruction of the Civic Center Plaza has been largely completed, and the poverty of the design is painfully apparent, a number of disappointed citizens — including the mayor and other high officials who forget that they themselves are ultimately responsible for such fiascoes — have voiced misgivings about the new look of this great urban space.

For where there had been a stately, old plaza which was completely at home in the neoclassical Civic Center, there is now a hodgepodge of Modernist cliches. Once again — but this time on the very threshold of City Hall — San Francisco has wantonly destroyed one of its historical embellishments in order to build an underground garage, as well as an equally subterranean, cheerless exhibition hall.

And once again, so far as the beauty of the cityscape is concerned, San Francisco lost more than it gained by a purported "improvement." This is learning the urban facts of life the hard way.

As the skimpy landscaping testifies, the new plaza is really a roof garden. Only three feet of earth covers the underground facilities (that is, where any earth is provided at all). Yet a minimum of five feet — which would have cost an extra $1 million — is required to sustain deep-rooted trees.

Consequently, sycamores and olives — which will never grow to appreciable size — were planted, rather than, say, noble elms which would have matched the scale of the massive public buildings on every side. Therefore, although the designers have asked that we be patient for another five to ten years (in spite of the fact that the plaza has been torn up for most of the last five), so that the trees can come into their own, there is grave reason to doubt that this design will ever prove to be an appropriate centerpiece for one of the finest groups of public buildings in the country.

For much more is wrong with this scheme than merely the tiny, woebegone trees and the scanty lawns. The weak lines of white flagpoles, the crudely spurting fountain, the protruding elevator shaft and vents of the underground facilities, and especially the overall coldness of mood, show modern architecture at its most melancholy, carelessly willing to destroy the past but unable to equal its accomplishments.

Where there had been richness, harmony, symmetrical order and monumental scale in the old plaza, there is now inadequate scale, confusion of line, fussy detail, modified symmetry, and — more serious still — an air of provincial cheapness.

And as can be expected in this age of civic parsimony, short-sightedness and piecemeal planning, the plaza is cheap in several senses of the word.

"Nothing," Shakespeare wrote in *King Lear*, "will come of nothing." This was sadly the case here. The budget was paltry. Only $650,000 was appropriated for a project which required at least three times as much for successful realization (although the sum was more than double the $250,000 the supervisors originally hoped would suffice).

Thus the undertaking was doomed from the start. Whatever may be wrong with the older buildings of the Civic Center (and their main fault is that they are copybook architecture), they are not cheap — in contrast to the new state buildings on the northern side, which succeed in looking flimsy and garish at the same time.

On the contrary, these ornate, neo-Baroque monuments — particularly Arthur Brown's resplendent City Hall which cost some $4 million before World War I — for their time were models of American municipal pride, generosity and foresight, conceived with European grandeur.

There are few places in the country, except in the universities, where so strongly unified a group of large public buildings can be found. The City Hall, the Civic Auditorium, the old State and Federal buildings, the Public Library, the Opera House and the War Memorial all share the same cornice line, the same system of classical proportions, the same elaborate scheme of historical decoration, the same expensive (and therefore long-lasting) materials such as granite and bronze.

The original plaza was part of this lordly composition, just as Thomas Church's sensitively scaled Court of Honor between the Opera and the War Memorial, with its eloquent brickwork and hedges of yew, remains part of it today. The Court of Honor, reminiscent of a portion of the famous Place Stanislaus at Nancy in France, sports no Modernist gewgaws, but it is in harmony with the powerful monuments which flank it.

This lesson escaped the designers of the new plaza, who surprisingly enough were not political hacks, but the prominent architectural firms of Wurster, Bernardi & Emmons and Skidmore, Owings & Merrill, working together with Douglas Baylis, one of the better landscape architects of the Bay Area.

Probably this was a case of too many cooks spoiling a dish, into which various city officials also stuck their thumbs. Instead of a serene flow of neoclassical space, the designers produced a badly cut-up pattern. They dispensed with a strong cross axis between the State Building and the Civic Auditorium — indeed smack in front of the facade of the

State Building is the ugly bank of elevators leading to the garage below, to which they scarcely wished to call attention.

Instead, they concentrated on the long axis between City Hall and Market Street, thus somewhat distorting the calm of the space, and transformed it into "an avenue of flags." Presumably this was to serve as a reminder that San Francisco was the first meeting place of the United Nations. But apart from the questionable ideology of this premise (are we so rustic that we must resort to such showmanship?), the visual effect of the white flagpoles, not unlike those in veterans' cemeteries, is extremely unhappy.

By paradox, however, in this setting they appear not so much mournful as excessively festive and light, and better suited for a World's Fair or a carnival than for an august Civic Center. These thin, strident uprights, clamoring for attention, cannot compete with the formidable colonnade of the City Hall, which crushes them visually, so that they seem merely messy.

Between the flagpoles, in front of City Hall, is a fountain that draws inordinate attention to itself, but nevertheless reveals an almost total lack of appreciation of the possibilities of water in a monumental setting. The banal arrangement of the triple bank of jets suggests a giant bathtub gone wild, but the fountain acts neither as a descending cascade (which it actually is), nor as a placid reflecting pool, for which its form would be appropriate. The flow of water is too heavy. It was turned on full force at the request of the politicians, and therefore also makes a good deal of noise, which should please them. As a piece of architecture, however, the fountain doesn't have much meaning.

The fountain's low walls are of granite, and there are more strips of granite set at intervals — not very carefully studied intervals — in the surrounding paving. But this sparse use of a fine material (some of it salvaged from the old plaza) merely calls attention to the adjoining concrete aggregate which, except for the panels filled with black Sonora stone, could be seen in thousands of suburban backyards.

As for the heavy-looking benches which sit like lumps on the plaza, they do not qualify even as backyard architecture. Not only are the seats of wood painted a nondescript WPA color, but the ugly lights underneath them look almost as bad by day as by night.

At night, all the tawdriness, all the confusion of this plaza, dotted with low-lying lamps, blazing with light amidst the crashing torrent of the pool, appear still more exaggerated. But as yet we have been spared floodlighting of the slope of lawn opposite the Civic Center, where the city's nurserymen will soon install floral tableaux of the sort which embellish railway stations. Here, in flowers, may soon be written: "Welcome Rotarians!" or "Happy Father's Day!" Thus we repay our fathers who, when they wished, built better than we.

May 29, 1961

■ A CHANCE FOR GREATNESS

The time has come for San Francisco to be entirely serious about Embarcadero Center.

In sheer size and complexity, as well as in possible splendor, the $150 million complex is the most ambitious construction project in the history of the city.

Dominated by three tremendous office buildings and an 800-room hotel, enlivened by shops, restaurants, a wine museum, theaters and other cultural facilities, and tied together by a potentially magnificent series of elevated plazas and esplanades which will be embellished by fountains, sculpture and other works of art by famous masters, Embarcadero Center will cover the entire 8.5 acres of the southern half of the Golden Gateway Redevelopment Area.

In a single formidable building campaign that will take at least a decade, it will complete the Golden Gateway project, and what is more important, extend the financial district to the now sadly degraded waterfront.

To give a fuller perspective of its magnitude, and of its possible ramifications through the whole of the central city, the proposed 2,851,000 square feet of office space exceeds the total lost in the fire of 1906, when downtown San Francisco was almost totally destroyed.

It also amounts to a good third of the first-class office space created here since World War II, which has caused sober reflection by owners of less imposing buildings who recall that much of central Manhattan was left tenantless by the construction of Rockefeller Center in the 1930s.

On the other hand — and this consideration should be overriding in a city which wishes to remain the financial and administrative center of the West — even this much new office space is less than one-seventh of the 20 million square feet under construction or contemplated in downtown Los Angeles.

The hotel, too, will be the largest — and perhaps in some ways the most interesting — ever built in a city which has prided itself on great hotels since the old Palace opened its opulent doors in 1875. The new theaters also can come only as a relief to a citizenry which has long been afflicted by the flea-bitten Geary and Curran.

Never, indeed, has so large a chunk of San Francisco been developed as an architectural entity since the Civic Center was created in a unified classical style in the first decades of the century.

The potential rewards of such an approach are immense, and redevelopment director M. Justin Herman deserves much credit for refusing to develop the area piecemeal, as he was under much pressure to do. Instead he held out until he could find developers with the financial strength and lasting power to see the project through correctly to the end.

For a project on this scale — which is necessarily a new scale for San Francisco — should not only be a superb improvement for the city, but one of the greatest urban designs in the world.

At present, to state an unhappy truth bluntly, Embarcadero Center is merely big, and very far from greatness.

The preliminary plans reveal many oversimplifications and, most notably in the case of the colossal central slab which will be two blocks long and 25 stories high, appalling crudities which can, and must, be rectified before the huge undertaking is allowed to go ahead.

Yet unless the city acts more wisely and deliberately than it has to date, and thus far it has acted with almost indecent haste, there will be nothing to stop the developers from closely following their present unrefined designs which, on the basis of their public statements, they clearly intend to do.

This would be a tragic and needless loss for the city because Embarcadero Center, in spite of its obvious shortcomings, does contain a glimpse of greatness.

The seeds of splendor must be carefully nurtured by public diligence, however, if they are to grow and flourish in the harsh economic world of large-scale construction, where many promising projects are coarsened, rather than improved, and end up more than not expiring in an architectural gas chamber.

Here I am thinking not only of BART, but of several ill-fated works of the San Francisco Redevelopment Agency, particularly the Golden Gateway residential group just north of Embarcadero Center, and badly botched Diamond Heights.

To achieve veritable greatness in Embarcadero Center, instead of mere bigness, is therefore the supreme issue before the city.

But the issue has been unfortunately obscured by the goggling provincialism hereabouts aroused by the wealth and prestige of the Rockefeller family, who have evoked as rapturous a local response as did the visit of the Prince of Wales a generation ago. Hence the pioneer sourdough soubriquet, Rockefeller Center West, applied to a project which in every respect, except for size, should surpass New York's now historic Rockefeller Center of the 1930s.

This is not to say that the Rockefellers do not deserve the highest praise for the exemplary architectural standards of projects in which they have been personally deeply involved, such as David Rockefeller's Chase-Manhattan Bank, or Laurence's Mauna Kea Hotel in Hawaii. Their "stewardship" of enormous wealth in such cases has been outstanding.

Furthermore, their money — unlike much of the paper which flies about in urban real estate deals — is real money, for which San Francisco can rightly draw a sigh of relief after its experience at Red Rock Hill in Diamond Heights.

And even if David Rockefeller were not the principal partner in what, as I shall show, is actually a very mixed consortium of investors in Embarcadero Center, the project would be inevitably compared with Rockefeller Center in New York, which after three decades remains the finest — if not the most generous (for only 17 percent of the site was left open) — example of integrated urban design in the United States.

Rockefeller Center, it should be remembered, was studied and restudied by a large and resourceful group of architects over a period of ten years while its original program was greatly refined and enriched.

The locations, dimensions, purposes and overall appearance of the buildings were several times completely changed, always for the better.

Similar procedures now, which need not require nearly so long a period of architectural gestation, would yield immense dividends for San Francisco.

So swiftly and adroitly has Justin Herman propelled Embarcadero Center through the usually tortuous processes of municipal government, however, that both the Redevelopment Agency and the Planning Commission have approved the preliminary plans without the slightest qualification.

More precisely, there has been scarcely a murmur of criticism from any public official with the significant exception of the able new planning director, Allan B. Jacobs, who in an astringently phrased, but very damaging statement, revealed grave difficulties in the present plans.

Nevertheless the Planning Commission, in a unanimous vote which may have ominous implications for Jacobs' future effectiveness in a city which conducted a nationwide search to find him, refused to grant his specific request that a fresh study be made of the elephantine central slab, as well as the entire concept.

Thus, as matters stand officially, the Board of Supervisors alone can now guard the city's interests, when they begin hearings on Monday, by subjecting to the most measured scrutiny the overall concept of Embarcadero Center, the architecture of its individually very large buildings, and the complete credentials of the entire Rockefeller team of developers, for whom redevelopment director Herman has shown almost immodest devotion.

Although it is difficult to liken doughty Justin Herman to a blushing maiden, he might well be reminded that a girl need not go all the way on a first date, and had better yield her treasures slowly, even if the swain is as eligible as a Rockefeller.

Still another point to be considered without any querulous intent, is that Rockefeller's associates in Embarcadero Center have never executed a project that approaches the masterpiece that the city of San Francisco demands now.

They have done some big things, but as is now apparent in Trammel Crow's large but hopelessly mediocre Dallas Trade complex, bigness is no guarantee of greatness. His share in Embarcadero Center is more substantial than is readily apparent, moreover, because he happens to be a major shareholder in the George A. Fuller Construction Co., whose president, Cloyce K. Box, also represents a one-third interest in the non-Rockefeller half of Embarcadero Center.

The final third is held by John Portman, an Atlanta architect who is little known here, but a man to reckon with in his own city, where he has single-handedly rebuilt much of the downtown area.

From humble beginnings he has become, within the space of 15 years, one of the financially most successful architects in the country because he is not only the designer but the promoter of very large projects, which he owns wholly or in part. In other words he is a developer who happens also to be a professional architect.

I do not mention this invidiously, but it is an important, sensitive question. One of the most dangerous things an architect can do, is to place himself in a position where he stands to profit personally by modifying a design.

Ideally the role of an architect should be analogous to that of a physician, who prescribes what is right (to the best of his skill), even if his client may have other notions. For this reason doctors, when they themselves are ill, call in other physicians to treat them.

I am bound to add that I have considerable personal regard for

Portman, who is surely no less gifted than most of the local worthies who have attacked him. Only because he is to be both "managing partner" and designer of Embarcadero Center does it seem reasonable to suggest that the city convince the developers that an architect of the greatest international distinction, unencumbered by any investment in the project, might be added to the Embarcadero Center design staff. Rockefeller Center, I must repeat, was not entrusted to a single architect, but to a large group of leading designers.

The Redevelopment Agency, it is true, has called in its own specialists: a design advisory board headed by Dean Emeritus Pietro Belluschi of MIT. At their request Portman has made several important changes already, including total redesign of the hotel, after submitting an original design that has never even been released to the public.

Yet this "watchdog committee" does not seem to have been sufficiently forbidding; and it was disappointing to hear Dean Belluschi remark, suavely but lamely, that they gave Embarcadero Center "wholehearted approval," even though there are many problems yet to be solved.

The problems in fact remain staggering, and the supervisors should not only question Dean Belluschi and other members of his board individually, but also planner Jacobs, to determine what the problems really are.

May 6, 1967

■ A "CITY OF TOMORROW" TODAY

Whatever one thinks of the massive office slabs of Embarcadero Center, and it's no secret that I consider them a colossal blunder in civic design, cutting off sunlight and views across a wide swath of downtown, there's no denying that the great multilevel shopping esplanades at their base are one of architect-developer John Portman's most successful ideas.

Financially, socially, and to some extent architecturally, in spite of needless crudities of design, this ingenious complex of shops and restaurants, singles bars and open terraces, sunken courts and curving staircases, fine art and kitsch, is a veritable triumph.

Here is what used to be called the "City of Tomorrow" today.

Extending three full blocks from Battery to Drumm streets, between Clay and Sacramento, spanning the intervening cross street on bridges, and soon to jump across Drumm when the fourth and final tower of the mammoth development is built next to the Hyatt Regency, Embarcadero Center has already reached a state of "critical mass" — to borrow a physicist's term. After a rather dreary beginning, when the first building stood alone in 1971, it is now exploding with a rich mix of social energy. This is not an abstract Cartesian cityscape by Le Corbusier, in which individuals move across ruled pavements like ants on graph paper. It is a true pedestrian's environment, to which thousands of office workers descend at noon, and again at 5 p.m., from the office buildings towering overhead.

More thousands assemble from elsewhere in the financial district, ascending on stairs or escalators, or from the Hyatt Regency and other hotels. Still more come south from the apartments and town houses of Golden Gateway, crossing to Embarcadero Center on overpasses from the formal plaza of the powerful X-framed Alcoa Building across the way.

To appreciate what Portman has done right at Embarcadero Center, indeed, it is necessary only to see what is wrong with Alcoa. In purely architectural terms, as an abstract form in space, Skidmore, Owings & Merrill's Alcoa is far superior — in every way more lucid and noble — than Portman's jumbled, unashamedly commercial, but happily crowded terraces across the way.

In comparison, Alcoa seems almost lifeless, mounted on an enormous dead garage which has every appearance of a tomb for automobiles.

On the north, where the base confronts the blank walls of an identical garage podium of the Golden Gateway residential buildings, pedestrian activity is almost nil. The freeway off-ramp, forking into Washington Street, turns it into a monoxide alley.

Even though the south side of Alcoa and the freeway on-ramp create a similar situation on Clay Street, it is saved from a fiasco by the spirited retail business at the base of Portman's building. This is one of the most vivid illustrations in the country of Jane Jacobs' theory that a large number of shops and eateries at sidewalk level is indispensable to the health of the city.

Portman's buildings may be vulgar (which originally was only another way of describing the popular speech and manners of ordinary people), but — like the spectacular design of the Hyatt Regency — they are fun; and all this amounts to a vindication of Portman's ambitious social and economic theory of architecture.

For his purpose is nothing less than to reconcile serious design with U.S. speculative building, which by and large is the greediest construction in the world.

To Portman, however, there is no contradiction in his aim. Not for nothing, someone remarked, is his middle name Calvin; and his architecture — if its hedonistic festivity could be overlooked — might be described as the Protestant ethic translated into highly profitable structure and space.

Each square foot of these buildings is meant to make money for Portman the architect in his other role as entrepreneur. Not only in San Francisco, where his principal partner is David Rockefeller, but in vast projects such as Renaissance Center in Detroit, where he has teamed up with Henry Ford II, and in his own city of Atlanta, whose downtown core he has almost singlehandedly rebuilt in an extraordinary complex of hotels, office buildings, furniture and apparel marts.

The sheer volume of this dual practice nearly precludes architecture as a fine art, even though Portman — quoting Frank Lloyd Wright, Louis Kahn, Eero Saarinen and other famous architects, as well as philosophers such as Emerson — obviously wishes his building to be judged at a high level of the contemporary movement.

Yet for all their gusto, they show unmistakable marks of haste, even improvisation. From basic structure to details such as paving and planters, much of the San Francisco design was borrowed wholesale from the earlier work at Atlanta, and simply adapted to a long narrow site. Consequently his escalators are strangely jammed together, so that one wonders if there is enough headroom between levels, probably because some draughtsman in Atlanta never figured it out. Nothing in Portman's local work is so finely drawn as the magnificent escalator lobby of Alcoa, which Skidmore treated as a meticulous piece of minimalist sculpture.

Portman's entrances are maximalist. He puts out "people scoops" — canopies of bronze-colored plexiglass — to yank passersby into his commercial space, crowding them on his stairs and escalators, where they notice that — far from conceiving a clear, open structural base for his building — he has merely neglected to fill in the spaces between the columns on the first three floors of his skyscrapers.

In this structural forest, stores and restaurants are installed almost at random, as they are around the courts and on the upper terraces. But this is his strength. All the impromptu variety and unpredictability of historic cityscapes — which took decades to coalesce — have been instantly provided; and what is more, the concept leaves room for individual architects to pit their own designs — in shops and bars and restaurants — against the overpowering towers which otherwise might simply crush them.

There are few better places, indeed, to observe the new high level of retail merchandising design that now prevails in San Francisco.

Of all the stores, the delightful two-story premises of Design Research by William Turnbull show best how a skilled architect — far more fastidious in detail than Portman has time to be — can overcome the heavy frame of the skyscraper to create an ambience that is residential in scale. With wonderful humor Turnbull has opened spaces between floors, as well as a cheerful skylight, hung out banners (something Portman does, too), and even made neon decorative devices.

The carefully selected furniture and kitchen equipment, clothing and yard goods at Design Research of course enhance the effect. But the real test of Portman's environment is the range of business it can handle. Even McDonald's, which serves 4,000 people at lunch each day, has a very decent presence, but most of the eateries and food stores — with their plants and wooden tables — are much better: Mrs. Robinson's, La Fuente, the Natural Grocery and — if you want to get with it — Scott's (almost impossible to enter after work) and Crisis Hopkins, which has a jazz band out on the terrace on fair Friday nights.

All this adds up to urban vitality, everywhere enriched — or at least complicated — by works of art that are more or less serious, and sometimes, as in Willi Gutmann's big stainless steel group, better than that. Portman simply slings his art around, so that often one wonders if it is not in the wrong place, whether Guttman's and Louise Nevelson's (very weak) sculpture were not put in the sunken courts by accident, rather than on the high terraces where they would have stood out to better effect.

But the crowds do not mind, do not seem to notice. They enjoy the art, the pubs, the shops — even a few which are terribly corny, like Shapero's phony "old-fashioned" drug store. Most of all they seem to enjoy being with one another, or just watching other people; and that is Portman's social gift.

December 12, 1977

■ A FOUNTAIN DEPOSITED BY A DOG WITH
SQUARE INTESTINES

halprinize *hal- pri-niz vt;* halprinate (*at*) *var.* [Early Anglo Saxon]:
   1. to build or design in a superficial manner and in cliché form, e.g.
   such as to reconstruct the Taj Mahal in poured marbleized concrete
   plaster. 2. to plan and construct the Trevi Fountain in *papier-mâché*
   or gutta-percha. (*Webster's International Dictionary*, San Francisco
   edition, 1972.)

In case you have been hoping that those leprous 12-ton chunks of concrete heaped together in Ferry Park are symptoms that the Embarcadero freeway is decomposing because of a bad case of skin cancer, it's a pity to report that, far from falling apart, the freeway is alive and well in hapless San Francisco, and the pseudomonumental oddity huddled in its monstrous shadow is supposed to be a work of art. Like, wow! man, like it's a fountain: "One of the great works of civic art that has been created in this country," as it has been described with characteristic modesty by one of its chief perpetrators, landscape architect Lawrence Halprin. Like, you can tell he's an artistic-type "eco-architect" because he wears jewelry and a beard; and, you know, he'd "never lay a trip on anyone" because people must do their thing.

He has, however, enabled the even more hirsute Canadian sculptor, Armand Vaillancourt, to do his own very strange thing on the waterfront, at a cost of more than half a million dollars, laying several tons of almost incredibly ugly, brutal, pretentiously simple-minded, and literally insipid concrete blocks on the city — unless, as a flippant citizen suggested, these technological excrescences were in fact deposited by a giant concrete dog with square intestines.

Another citizen, apparently as coldly sober as he was hotly enraged, drove a pickup truck across the surrounding plaza, into the pool, and smashed against the fountain, knocking off sizable chunks of eroding concrete in a unique and altogether eloquent style of civic protest.

Vaillancourt, to be sure, has been largely an artist-in-absentia, appearing in San Francisco at rare intervals (and failing to show up even for the trial run of the fountain last month), although he is collecting a baronial fee of $40,000 for his episodic labors. According to persistent report, the scrofulous surfaces of the concrete (which were cast in Styrofoam molds) are substantially the work of the insouciant workmen at a Petaluma cement plant, doing *their* thing, at a few bucks per hour.

Be this as it may, Halprin is disposed — now that the fountain is on view in its full crudity — to give maximum credit for the coarse forms themselves to Vaillancourt, reserving for himself, again with typical self-effacement, those qualities of the jumbled masses which are likely to evoke some public approval, including the heroic size of the fountain, its placement in the park, the opportunity to walk through it and over its top, and the exhilarating view of downtown which it provides.

The fountain is much more of a collaboration than that, and Halprin stands responsible not only for selling the design to the city, but also for having meddled with it considerably since then. Certainly its overall composition — which is little more than a dissonant crescendo delivered in a disconnected series of heavy blows — has been largely orchestrated by the locale maestro while the evanescent Vaillancourt to all intents and purposes has been caught in a bear trap in the hyperborean wilds beyond the border. Thus the fountain is really a joint work; and, although it may be unsporting to recall a wager made in an outburst of passion, San Francisco would do well — particularly if Halprin contemplates more *chefs-d'oeuvre* on this order, at public expense, within the city limits — to recall his perfervid declaration during one of those numerous hearings in which city officials muffed the chance to cancel the misbegotten design, when he promised that, if the fountain did not turn out to be as "great" as he anticipated, "I am going to slit my throat."

Whether or not the formal dedication of the fountain will be the occasion of this act of hara-kiri, the public is entitled to a strict accounting of the fiasco, not only from Halprin, but also from Justin Herman, the gauleiter of the Redevelopment Agency, who has been mighty chary with facts and figures concerning the full cost of the fountain, perhaps because the total is still clicking up, like a taxi meter that has been left running on a public expense account. Even so, the basic reason for extravagance is already clear: the perversity of the design itself, thwarting the natural flow of water because of its illogical angular shapes, required all sorts of special engineering — as well as a hidden internal structure of steel — to make it stand up at all. These silly forms may have seemed structurally feasible to "eco-architect" Halprin on paper, but in three-dimensional reality — which is what architecture is actually about — the fountain has been needlessly difficult to construct. "Ugliness is waste," said Bernard Shaw, and in the case of the phantasmagorically frightful fountain the Shavian theorem holds true.

Vaillancourt's original concept, before it was halprinized, was foolish enough — calling for widely diffused concrete toadstools weakly exuding fluids — but at least it did not oppose the nature of water in this deliberately uncouth way. Water resists angular shapes, and demands curving and fluid forms. It is no accident that pipes are round, or that tanks are spherical and cylindrical. (Indeed, when some badly mistaken architects cutely built a faceted water tank in the East Bay a few years ago, it promptly collapsed when pressure built up in the angles.)

Now, it is easy enough, when using concrete in the same way as natural rock, and allowing water to flow over its surfaces, to shape the material as arbitrarily as you wish, for the water, in turn, will wear it into natural patterns. Halprin himself, with considerable success, has used concrete this way in his fountains in Portland, Ore., which, if not profoundly designed, are nevertheless pleasant things.

But the whole problem changes when concrete is used as a freestanding structure in space; and it brings into question the arbitrary requirement — set by Halprin in the competition which Vaillancourt won, but which was conspicuous for the unexalted quality of the several submissions — that the fountain must be built of concrete. His reason was obvious, for The Freeway looms immediately behind the site, and he thought that concrete was necessarily a strong-man material with which he could oppose the mindless power of the highway engineers. But at least the engineers knew what they were about *structurally*, no matter how illiterate they may have been socially and aesthetically. The Halprin-Vaillancourt team did not, as they had to call in their own engineer, William Gilbert, plus specialists from the University of California, who spun the computer wildly in an effort to guarantee the stability of the illogical structure, which defies almost every known law of dynamics and equilibrium. When asked about the vagaries of the structure, engineer Gilbert remarked: "Nobody's *guaranteeing* anything"; and he has in fact not given signed approval to several modifications of the design which were made, in the last stages of the project, to cut skyrocketing costs.

The result, masked by concrete surfaces that in large part are nothing more than stucco, has been a concealed fountain in steel. Not just steel reinforcement, as in the post-tensioned components of the fountain that are under least stress, but actual boxes of one-inch plate steel — and special Corten steel at that — which might be suitable for bridge construction. These cumbersome forms were then tacked together with difficult welds; and although engineer Gilbert is confident that they will ride out a sizable earthquake, I'm not so sure. For already one heavily bent set of steel boxes has sagged downward to rest upon another group of the same, even though they were supposed to be separated by several inches.

So far as the aesthetic impact of the ensemble is concerned, however, it makes not the slightest difference. Everything has been done so ineptly and haphazardly, with such crass vulgarity, that a mistake of this kind simply doesn't register in the overall impression of a trick badly done. To Halprin and Vaillancourt this may be *joie de vivre*, but it is really sad. For all of Halprin's grandiloquence about social honesty, the fountain is structurally a dishonest lie, and the joke, in the end, is on himself. These drooping members — they can hardly be called erections — are in fact evidence of technical impotence, the very opposite of the great manly creations of Bernini, say, in the Piazza Navona, or the thunderous spectacle of the marvelously refined and complex Trevi Fountain. None of the great fountains of the world is brutal, just as none of them is literally square.

Perhaps the lesson to be learned from all this is that weakness, when *parading* as strength, can only end in brutality and empty posturing.

April 1971, *San Francisco Magazine*

■ SAN JOSE CENTER SETS STANDARD IN PUBLIC ARCHITECTURE

While San Francisco has futzed with Moscone Center, turning a half-buried blunder into a fiasco, San Jose has completed a smaller but brilliantly conceived convention center that is the best public architecture the Bay Area has seen in a generation.

In a single magnificent stroke, San Jose's $103 million convention facility not only has healed a ravaged edge of downtown, but also has literally brought the cityscape inside the building by running a great, skylit pedestrian way through the 1,000-foot length of the structure.

This noble indoor street, set behind a remarkable sculptural facade, is an essentially new idea in convention center design.

Except for a shorter and less spectacular interior street in Baltimore, there is nothing quite like San Jose's in any of the adventuresome convention centers that are springing up in Seattle, San Diego, Los Angeles and even unexpected places like Columbus, Ohio.

Unlike the dull, windowless "boxes" that formerly typified convention facilities (and occasioned the extravagant undergrounding of Moscone Center), the new centers make warm overtures to their cities.

But none invites the city directly within, as San Jose's does in an ingenious two-level arrangement in which the convention needs are met by an upper concourse that is deftly closed off to the general public.

The visually open and airy upper concourse serves as a long foyer and lounge, as well as a circulation "spine," for three large exhibition spaces, a banquet hall, small meeting rooms, offices and backup areas.

But it is the public esplanade below, soon to be enlivened by shops, kiosks and food bars, that makes the difference between a better-than-average convention center and a work of social art.

Filled with natural light that pours down through vaulted clerestories that curve and recurve their crowns 49 feet above the handsome geometric pavings, this tremendous processional colonnade — three football fields long and the equivalent of five stories high — is a fine place to stroll between San Jose's rapidly reviving business district on the east and the new cultural facilities that will border the Guadalupe River on the west.

It is a connector, rather than a barrier, between the two halves of the downtown, which are finally coalescing into a "critical mass" after years of planning and rebuilding that still has a way to go.

The effort required the whole city to be turned into a redevelopment area, so that lucrative outlying projects for high-tech industries could bankroll the convention center and other improvements in the core, which had been eviscerated by "urban renewal" schemes of the 1960s.

The transformed downtown won't come fully into its own for a few years, although it is already showing vitality in an open-air shopping paseo (a happy variation of an open-air mall), a much-needed Fairmont Hotel and office buildings that are peppy additions to a formerly moribund downtown scene but vary architecturally from mediocre to terrible.

Several charming plazas and parks have been created, and there has been a perceptible increase in foot traffic near the light-rail trolley line that threads the urban core to its present terminus — a nicely designed stop, by the way — just in front of the convention center on San Carlos Street between Almaden Boulevard and Market Street.

Eventually, the rail line will continue across the river to an $80 million museum, the Technology Center of Silicon Valley, whose first element, a Discovery Museum for small children, is under construction. From there the transit system will go on to IBM and the other big electronic factories and labs in the southern reaches of the Santa Clara Valley.

At the center of this fast, unfocused pattern of settlement is a convention center that makes excellent environmental sense.

Yet the building is not just a practical piece of urban planning. It is Modern architecture of a very high level, free from Post-Mod trivialities and pseudohistoric kitsch but classic in its adherence to timeless principles of scale and proportion, structural candor, humanely organized space and the play of sunlight and shadow over strong surfaces.

The building's principal architect is the distinguished Italian American Romaldo Giurgola (his most famous recent work is Australia's house of Parliament in Canberra). San Jose's redevelopment director, Frank M. Taylor, also made important contributions, and so did his urban design consultant, Thomas Aidala.

Together they have set a new standard of architectural excellence for San Jose.

Seen across the cityscape, the convention center is a model of urban order. Its three great curving roofs, covered in gleaming aluminum that will soften with time, correspond to the different dimensions of the three main exhibition spaces — 200, 230 and 270 feet across — although the interior does not strictly reflect the outer forms.

The successively expanding volumes, like three rising notes in a scale, swell gently above the 1,000-foot front of the building and they set up a majestic counterpoint with the great horizontal facade.

The complex composition should be symmetrical, but it has been nudged off-center by a bit of history — the crude public library, painted an unfortunate yellow, that has been kept for the sake of economy. The library hardly bears comparison with the dignity and strength of the convention center's gray concrete facade, but it has forced the architects to offset its presence with a ceremonial portal adorned with an astonishing ceramic mural — 50 feet high and 120 feet across — by the Danish artist Lin Utzon.

She has created a wonderfully free but profoundly coherent porcelain "tapestry" — of royal Copenhagen white, cobalt blue, deep orange and a paler blue — that is a rare example of convincing architectural art.

It may seem almost overpowering in its present context, but this is not the permanent condition of the site. At either end of the block, a midrise hotel is planned — including one on the west to be designed by the Giurgola office and another on the east which, with the side of the library, will compose a three-sided court at the main entry.

Then the sloping entrance plaza and fountain will not be so exposed as today. It will become a densely charged architectural space, paved in light gray Vermont granite and darker Vermont bluestone. Beside the sunken pool, the ornamental bluestone spheres — three feet in diameter — will be still more potent emblems of classical order.

Through this plaza, past the rushing water where inner city kids splash and play, thousands of conventioneers and local citizens will crowd into the luminous interior spaces once the South Bay has grown up to the wonder of this architecture. Others will enter directly, through the hotels and through charming side entrances.

The facades at either end are appropriately less imposing, finished not in concrete but in pink, gray and bluish stucco, Mediterranean colors that have started to bleach out subtly under the strong sun of the Santa Clara Valley. But the powerful half-curves and counter-curves of the vaulted arcades jut beyond the ends of the building, playing an intricate structural game above deep shadowy recesses.

Inside, the detailing is equally distinguished, and once again Lin Utzon (daughter of Jorn Utzon, architect of the famous Sydney Opera House) had a major role in designing the elegant "shark's tooth" patterns of the light gray and dark gray terrazzo pavements.

Much else is worth noticing, including the half-round and square-shaped hybrid columns that do very different things with space between the advancing colonnades. The glass balustrades, capped with oak railings, are particularly fine. So are the mighty sconces and other custom-built light fixtures.

Only when the big exhibition spaces are entered is there disappointment. The architects had ambitious hopes for these rooms, whose ceilings were supposed to be coffered and the walls finished in expensive fabrics, as they have been partly done in the banquet hall. But the money ran out, partly because so much was spent on the lordly public spaces.

About $3 million was chopped from the budget at the last minute, and ceilings and walls suffered most. The triad of exhibition spaces, whose partitions can be drawn back to create a single clear-span area of 165,000 square feet, revert to brutal industrial boxes, lighted by harsh metal-halide lamps.

Yet there is a deeper sense of architectural loss in these 30-foot-high spaces. The curved roofs on the outside of the building seemed to promise tremendous arching spaces within, but Giurgola and his associates could not figure out how to achieve them — in any case, not at a reasonable price.

Instead they settled for ordinary bowstring trusses of steel that are concealed above the banal flat ceilings, which don't require careful finishing for unseen mechanical systems or expensive acoustical protection (the building is directly under the flight path to the airport).

The architects, more than anyone else, are keenly aware of these compromises, for a moral question of structural truth is involved — say, the truth of the immense cable-hung ceiling of the Oakland Coliseum Arena. As if to make amends, they and the structural engineer, Leslie Robertson, have made a structural tour de force out of the diagonal bracing of the enormous two-level, 1,300-car garage beneath the exhibition halls, also 1,000 feet long.

Yet nothing can deprive this building of its basic integrity. Not since Oakland built its parklike museum in the 1960s have we had so original and sincere public building in this part of the world — a building that reaches out to the surrounding urban fabric as a gift of intelligence.
July 10, 1989

■ ARCHITECTURE IN SMALL TOWNS YIELDS
BIG RESULTS

Good architecture in small towns is hard to find nowadays and easy to love. To come across a fine new community center in Petaluma, and better still, a perfect little Pacific Gas and Electric Co. service facility in Geyserville, is therefore a joy and a revelation.

Both designs are by the Santa Rosa firm of Roland/Miller Associates, which recently won an America Institute of Architects award for each of them.

Headed by the 55-year-old partners Craig W. Roland and John K.

Miller, it is an interesting office of a dozen architects, plus a few other workers.

As regionalists, rather like good regional architects in Sweden, say, or Switzerland, they know the land and the people and understand local needs. Hence, their best works to date, at Petaluma and Geyserville, have been specifically tailored for two very different communities.

Although Miller was the partner in charge of both projects, the Petaluma and Geyserville buildings could scarcely be more unlike in size, purpose, form and mood.

What unites them is civic dignity and warmth, a striving for excellence that recalls the local pride of such communities 75 or 100 years ago, when the agricultural center of Petaluma and the hamlet of Geyserville were in some ways more civilized than today.

Of the two projects, the PG&E facility in Geyserville has an edge in design, but the much larger Petaluma community center presented a more complex and challenging problem.

The latter town, once compact and comely, is in the throes of exurban sprawl that it resisted but could not control as development quickly pushed its population to 50,000.

The community center is intended to give a civic focus — a sense of order and shared cultural life — to the inchoate east side of town, and it succeeds admirably.

There are really two Petalumas.

The original settlement of the 1850s on the west side of the river, first a wealthy farming center and later the "chicken capital of the world," has kept much of its old charm. Although the chickens and eggs have vanished, there are still wonderful grain elevators and mash plants near railroad sidings and river landings, superb Victorian ironfront buildings, and delightful 19th century and early 20th century housing that turns to splendor in the old feed merchants' mansions on D Street.

By contrast, Petaluma's east side — largely open fields until the 1960s and '70s — has become a morass of drive-in strips, shopping centers, gas stations, tilt-up warehouses and miles of insipid housing tracts.

Leaving U.S. 101 on East Washington Street, and turning north on McDowell, there is a feeling of widespread environmental crime.

Then suddenly — beyond a lagoon crowded with ducks, geese and all kinds of chattering birds — the community center appears in quiet monumental grandeur, at the center of lawns and playing fields.

It is instantly clear that this calm, unified building, topped by large and small pyramidal roofs, is one answer to Petaluma's problem of civic identity.

A tall, open-frame clock tower on the north announces its presence in a friendly way, although the metal structure has been somewhat forced (with a shopping center showiness unworthy of the rest of the architecture) to make it a "sculptural" feature. If the vertical form also seems off-center, it is because the 27,500-square-foot building is only the first element of a three-part recreation complex that will be completed by a performing arts center and an athletic field house in this new municipal park.

The two remaining structures will be built as money becomes available, at phased intervals of three or four years. Roland/Miller in much the same way have done another handsome community center complex at Rohnert Park — in redwood regional style, with broad overhanging roofs — during the past decade.

The Petaluma group should be still more impressive.

By the late 1990s, the clock tower will be a balanced part of the whole composition, which will be linked together by long, curving colonnades that start out in the loggia at the tower's base that now seem to lead nowhere at all.

In the meantime, Petaluma has a handsome bargain in the $3.3 million main building. Its exterior drama has been achieved by simple, economic means: consistent materials, monumental scale and noble proportions.

The long, masonry walls are made up of dark gray concrete blocks, roughly surfaced like cleft stone, set off by accents of still darker gray blocks that look almost black.

The restrained palette could have seemed somber but, in fact, the muted grays, like very dark Oxford flannel, are not forbidding. They impart a gentle urbanity, precisely what east Petaluma has lacked. And because dark gray goes with everything, their neutral tone has allowed the architect tremendous freedom in the massing of minimalist geometric forms.

Handsome in themselves, the solid masonry blocks open up — at strong harmonic intervals — in great rectangular portals and deeply recessed windows, commanding broad views of the lake, that respond richly to sun and shadow.

These are not the masterly proportions of Kevin Roche's Oakland Museum, but John Miller has given Petaluma its most carefully considered architecture in decades.

It also presents some elating surprises. An inspired touch, relieving the long horizontal emphasis of the lakefront facade, is a small "clubhouse" pavilion, projecting toward the water.

Its metal pyramid roof and matching metal walls have not been finished in gray, but a teal green that is almost teal blue in certain light.

This sets up a counterpoint of form and color with the large gray pyramid covering a multipurpose hall and the teal green clock tower in the distance.

Unfortunately, the loggia below the tower has been stained a different green, a terrible green that was bound to look discordant on concrete masonry instead of metal. Someday it will be overgrown by vines.

Otherwise, the architecture is quite assured. The spare geometry continues in the interior, but far less austerely than outside. A succession of beautifully organized lofty spaces, with plenty of natural light from clerestories and tall windows, contain an exceptional assortment of recreation facilities and meeting rooms — all immaculately kept — that have set a new standard for cordial community life in Petaluma.

This straightforward building has unexpected subtleties, starting at the main entrance. Here, the basic rectangular layout has been split asymmetrically by a wedge-shaped entry hall — a happy triangular space — that skews the structure into two halves, so that the building without appearing to be bent follows the curving shore of the lake in an easy and natural way without compromising its geometry.

Still, there are flaws.

To the left of the entrance hall is a multiuse assembly hall and theater, with adjacent kitchens and service rooms, which can accommodate large banquets. This was potentially the most stirring space in the building, expressing the pure form of its pyramid roof, but the chance was botched by a ponderous overhead structure and bulky utility ducts.

Nonetheless, people rightly like it.

They have fun here at parties and performances that Petaluma could not enjoy before, and the other half of the building is very nearly all they could have hoped for.

There are lounges, another dining room and kitchen and rooms for citizens' political groups, service clubs, conferences and purely social gatherings. The shops for ceramics and other crafts are well equipped.

Best of all is the clubhouse, with its fireplace, comfortable furniture and big windows facing the lake, which has become very popular for wedding receptions and private parties.

Not least, a preschool classroom, incredibly neat and clean compared to most big-city child care facilities, with a protected terrace overlooking the lake, literally opens the way to Petaluma's future.

■ Less than an hour's drive up Highway 101, where Roland/Miller's unassuming IMCO office building — hung with blue awnings — can be sighted en route at the northern limits of Santa Rosa, the old resort and farming village of Geyserville (population 800) seems to have scarcely changed since the 1930s.

The chief virtue of the new PG&E service center is that it seems to have been there all the time.

The three gabled buildings and a covered outdoor work space, their clapboard and metal siding painted a warm yellow with white trim, are strung along the old Redwood Highway a few hundred feet north of the freeway exit.

"Lined up head to tail" is the architects' description, but there is nothing donkeyish or hokey about this accomplished architecture. It raises local vernacular architecture to fine art.

The corrugated metal roofs and siding are essentially the same as the rusting roofs on nearby industrial structures, workshops and outbuildings. The yellow color, almost a peach, is very close to the yellow or faded orange on the old garage and Mickey's fountain cafe — a museum piece virtually frozen in time since 1945 — a short distance up the road. Just as the older commercial buildings do not overwhelm the nearby modest bungalows, PG&E's buildings fit into the environment with utmost tact.

This is what "contextualism" is all about. Instead of aping historic architecture, which Post-Modern city planners think is the way to respect context, John Miller as a rational Modernist sought the fundamental principles of older structures in Geyserville. Individually, most of them do not even qualify as architecture, but collectively they create a humane and gracious environment that even PG&E, not always so gentle architecturally, realized should not be parodied or degraded.

The result is a model of economy and good sense. Geyserville is a place where people like to pay their utility bills in person, so the customer service building is closest to the heart of town.

Next comes the operations office, where the utility's maintenance of the Highway 101 corridor is managed by a small staff of supervisors and dispatchers. Then comes the outdoor repair area, with its own pitched roof, where mechanics can work on large machines undercover. Finally there is a storage-automotive building, a spare parts and repair facility for the blue PG&E vehicles parked in the corporation yard.

That's it. But the interior of the storage-automotive building is exquisitely framed in wood. The great windows are as carefully proportioned as the windows of the operations and customer service buildings. Every detail has been designed with love.

What is more, the buildings have been sensitively placed on a difficult site. The northern end of the Anderson Valley is a flood plain, often underwater along the railroad tracks. So the buildings were moved as far as possible up the slope, closely grouped on one side of the corporation yard instead of being scattered over the four-acre site.

The residents of Geyserville had worried about the design of the new buildings, and John Miller showed them the drawings in the lovely old Grange Hall a mile away. Approval was unanimous. Geyserville, which knows what it has been, could now see where it should be going.

July 5, 1990

III. Work Places

■ SAN FRANCISCO'S NEWEST TOWER

Black and solid in the sunlight, responding eloquently to sky and
weather, the John Hancock Building is a romantic creation for a romantic city, in which it could not be more at home. Indeed, this western
headquarters for a conservative Boston insurance company has taken its
place in San Francisco's vigorous financial district with such imaginative
tact, and such refreshing freedom from Modernist dogma, that it can
scarcely be appreciated except in the context of the cityscape. This is
perhaps the first measure of its excellence.

Whatever its other virtues — which include a happy recollection of
the uninhibited early skyscrapers of Louis Sullivan — Hancock is first of
all a brilliant urban concept. Although at only 14 stories it plays a powerful role in the skyline, Hancock has been designed primarily to be seen
by the pedestrian approaching through the busy downtown streets, past
the formidable banks, steamship lines, exchanges, insurance companies
and corporation headquarters which for blocks present massive and
continuous facades.

If few of these old buildings are truly distinguished, taken en masse
they nevertheless constitute an admirable urban scene. Beaux-Arts
monuments, laden with classical orders, rise on two-story colonnades or
arcades that provide them with imposing entrances and interiors; and,
like Renaissance palazzos, they are capped with strong cornices which
enable them to meet the sky with unmistakable finality.

To the credit of Hancock's architects (who, although this may seem
astounding to those familiar with the firm's other work, are the San
Francisco office of Skidmore, Owings & Merrill) it was decided to
accept the historical challenge of California Street as an opportunity
rather than a handicap. Clearly, a street with so firmly established a
character presented problems almost as vexing as those which have
defeated the contemporary movement on Park Avenue in New York,
where SOM and other Modernists have been content to remake
entirely a handsome existing environment by erecting a series of
glass boxes — granted, a few of them extremely elegant boxes. In a
city as sun swept and unconstrained as San Francisco, however, a
"New York building" would be even less satisfactory, as SOM's

transparent Crown Zellerbach tower on Market Street has already demonstrated.

The problem, obviously, had to be completely re-examined; and it is fascinating that the concept developed for Hancock actually harks back to the pioneer period of the Modern movement, which after three quarters of a century still remains the most winning moment of office building design in the United States. Like Sullivan's venerable Wainwright and Guaranty buildings, Hancock was given a clearly defined base, a middle and a top. And like John Wellborn Root's grandly sober Monadnock Building, the last triumph of the bearing wall, Hancock also celebrates the strength, calm and opacity of traditional masonry, but in conjunction with a modern industrial material — reinforced concrete — to do the structural framing.

If these affinities with the early modern in a sense make Hancock an old-fashioned building, the lessons of the pioneers have been faithfully translated into the new architectural vocabulary of the present. The result is an uncompromisingly experimental structure, suffering some of the *gaucheries* inevitable in such experiments, but with a prodigious originality that can be grasped as soon as its unique arcade of reinforced concrete — drawing the eye past older arcades in the foreground — comes into the pedestrian's view.

Quite suddenly, one after the other, the lithe arches are seen springing, logically changing shape as they rise to meet the weight of the granite-sheathed walls of the square tower above, and creating at each of the corners a deep, heraldic recess reminiscent of a neoclassical shield (yet actually dictated by structural needs). Nowhere in the United States has concrete been used more cheerfully than in these arches, so precise in outline and warm in texture, given a rose tint by the basalite aggregate which was bush-hammered and washed with acid to bring out its full tone.

At their crown the arches project outward some five feet above the terrace, which breaks their supporting columns in midrise, and provides the key to Hancock's very special role in the city. Not only does the terrace overhang the shop fronts below, sheltering pedestrians as nowhere else in San Francisco, but it also provides a platform of greenery from which the tower — set well back from the sides of the site — can ascend unimpeded by its neighbors. Thus Hancock has been ingeniously united with the surrounding city at street level, where continuity is welcome, but at the same time rises *solus*, as Sullivan said the tall building must.

The tower, furthermore, lifts with controlled opulence. Even in this city, where less than a dozen towers exceed 20 stories [this was in 1960!],

Hancock does not qualify, at 14, as a "skyscraper." But what it lacks in height it makes up in richness. The plaques of polished Minnesota granite, actually charcoal in color, turn jet when seen as an ensemble in San Francisco's rapidly changing light. The granite makes no secret that it is applied; and thus it is as "honest" and architectonically as valid a device as Mies' largely decorative use of nonstructural metal members to express his fireproofed (and therefore hidden) steel skeletons. The staggered, overlaid pattern of the granite gives a baroque effect of low relief.

The bronze around the windows of course makes the effect richer still, and is admirably in scale: the glass is not framed so much as trimmed. Moreover, the gray glass has been chosen with care. Its color, in large sheets, approximates that of the stone, and because of the chaste flush mountings the windows appear as a heavy film, rather than as pronounced openings in the wall, enhancing the impression of mass. Only at night do the windows blaze forth individually.

Like San Francisco, Hancock is complex, subtle, full of unexpected secrets, yet candid. Set in the midst of imitation Florentine palaces, it is truly palatial. With generosity and ingenuity its architects have shown what the best Renaissance designers, if they had been working in a technological age, might have done with industrial techniques and materials, hesitating neither to use stone (which after all is today quarried and polished by machines), nor even to attach the precast concrete panels of the parapet to a roof frame of steel. Structurally, the technique is as justifiable as the hiding of reinforcing bars within concrete; and visually — which is what counts in this building — the effect is handsome.

Hancock, then, is a palazzo of today, transmuting Renaissance ideology into a thoroughly modern idiom, and using classical forms only to obtain richness and diversity. If this is the ground on which the building should be considered, then one may ask fairly if it satisfies Alberti's dictum that the essence of beauty resides in "the harmony and concord of all the parts achieved in such a manner that nothing could be added or taken away or altered except for the worse."

This awesome verse from a bible of architecture is perhaps more dreaded by contemporary designers than by any of their predecessors, and Hancock's architects — as the splendid change of proportions between base, shaft, and summit show — took it to heart. A glance at the terrace, cutting through the arcade across the whole width of the structure, reveals, however, that they have not hesitated to spoil the base for the sake of the overall concept. Both the Renaissance and Gothic masters taught with incomparable authority that a curved line should be allowed to develop energy, so that, at the key of an arch or a vault, it is spent with maximum drama. If this were done at Hancock, the mezzanine floor would have been eliminated, and the entire base of the building would have stood open and lordly. At the very least the first two floors should have been recessed, and the arcade left unbroken.

Although Hancock is a palace, it is a monument of the modern mercantile community and not of a ducal regime, and attends to the economic as well as the aesthetic use of space. Hancock was designed with the client's requirements in mind. Although the company needed only one floor for its regional executive office, not an entire building, it did wish to display a corporate image commensurate with its wealth, age and dignity. How far its building is from being simply a crass moneymaker can be appreciated by contrasting it with the Equitable Building only three blocks away, erected by a comparable institution on a comparable corner site. Equitable is crammed on its lot, rising 25 stories — 11 higher than Hancock. It provides no greenery — not even sidewalk trees, such as Hancock's sycamores. It even fails to provide for underground parking, while Hancock accommodates 40 cars in its basement.

Hancock's only mark of identification is its traditional signature on a small oval medallion attached to the exquisitely wrought bronze balustrade of the terrace just above the main entrance: a far cry from the ludicrous advertising clock on the roof of the Equitable. Nevertheless, everyone knows which building is the Hancock. Not only in the building's monumental appearance, but in the elegance of its appointments, including the greenery, Hancock obtained a corporate image scarcely less impressive than the headquarters of the nearby Crown Zellerbach Corp., which is set in a luxurious private park.

As soon as one moves under the balcony, beneath the flags of the state and nation hung like Renaissance banners from almost horizontal staffs, one realizes this is a special arcade indeed. The underside of the balcony is finished in strips of teak. The shop windows and doorways are handsomely trimmed in bronze, and the overall appearance is controlled. There is a clear indication of welcome, a feeling of expectation, as one passes through the triple bay of the entrance. The lobby, however, is a disappointment.

The space which flows through the glazed doorways is abruptly checked — scarcely 10 feet inside the entrance — by a wall of the service core. This surface of cream-colored, unfilled travertine might have been less oppressive if it had been left unadorned — as are the rest of the lobby walls where the same classical material is left handsome and discreet in itself. But the entrance wall has been hung with bulky concrete bas-reliefs which are not only woefully out of scale — perhaps two or

three times larger than they should be — but also undistinguished.
[The reliefs were later removed.] Perhaps these pieces of precast sculpture were meant to symbolize the Hancock nationwide or worldwide
associations, for they include patriotic motifs as well as a fish and a
sextant. But in actuality they call attention to the small dimensions of
the lobby. Here was an appropriate place for a sitting group but there is
not so much as a bench.

As soon as the Hancock suite is reached, the building comes into its
own again. The garden with its jetting fountain is immediately seen
through the glass doors of the reception room and the glazed archway
beyond: a little urban oasis. The lofty, vaulted offices, sweeping around
the perimeter of the building, are even more than one expected from
outside.

Not for some time have spaces like these appeared in a major American office structure. Their close contact between indoors and out — in
the heart of the city but above the hurly-burly of the street — is a heartening sign. From every desk, including those of the stenographers farthest from the windows, there are views of the garden and the city
through the broad arching bays. There is also a sense of elation in having the ceiling so high overhead. Even small private offices only one bay
wide seem to have generous dimensions, because of the vaulted ceilings.
The detailing everywhere on this floor is particularly accomplished. The
colors are serene: beige, off-white, warm browns; the woodwork is teak.

French doors offer a strong invitation to the L-shaped garden (the
joint work of SOM and landscape architect Lawrence Halprin) which so
adroitly enhances the building at the rear of the site, and which is continued, in planters of box hedges, on the balconies overlooking the
street. The focal point of the terrace is the little patio first seen from the
reception room, with its splashing fountain which was carved at the
quarry from a single eight foot square of the same granite used in facing
the tower. Grass grows between the concrete paving blocks, which
branch off in single files from the patio through small areas of lawn
enlivened by birches and sycamores, laurel and wisteria, jasmine, peri-
winkle and a variety of other plants.

The upper stories are entirely column-free: the plan could not be
more "Miesian," simplified to a square — the compact central service
core placed within the larger square of the exterior walls. Both inner and
outer walls are bearing members, and the 32-foot space between them is
modular and flexible. The 5-foot, 1-inch module is curious: by adding
an inch to the original module they contemplated, the architects found
that additional space equal to that of a whole floor could be obtained;

and since 14 stories was near the physical limit of the concrete, they decided to go not higher but slightly wider. The cost of custom fabricating ceiling tiles and other standard fixtures was offset by the increased rental income.

On the upper floors one can appreciate the advantages and disadvantages of the window pattern. In comparison with an all-glass tower such as Crown Zellerbach, where acrophobia can result if one moves too close to the transparent wall, Hancock's intermittent pattern of solid and void is reassuring. Yet a tower should grow lighter and more open as it ascends, and this is something that Hancock, a classical building, does not do. Could the upper portions of the building have been give a treatment as revolutionary as that of the base? Perhaps. But the chance, if it exists in a building of this kind, was not seized upon. Perhaps it will be, in the building which next picks up the thread — one of the most essential threads in the many-colored fabric of modern architecture.

The significance of the Hancock building to modern architecture should not be underestimated. That its architects have turned from their Miesian doctrine is alone an architectural event of some importance, in view of the stature of the firm and its unswerving allegiance to Mies' design precepts for more than two decades. Hancock also marks the emergence of Edward Charles Bassett, SOM's 38-year-old chief designer in San Francisco, as an unusually gifted architect. Perhaps it is no accident that SOM has seen the light of romance, for the light is San Francisco's, catching the square, black, powerful structure which overlooks the bay.

April 1960, *Architectural Forum*

■ THE RICH NEW TEMPLE IN THE FINANCIAL DISTRICT

By all odds the most interesting new building in town — and our finest bank architecture since the superb Roman temple of the Bank of California was completed just across the street in 1908 — is the resplendent West Coast headquarters of the Bank of Tokyo at the corner of California and Sansome.

Inexplicably, the Bank of Tokyo has changed its local name to "California First Bank," a sobriquet which denies both its own history and the special Japanese-American qualities of the new building.

But otherwise the big international bank has gone all out architecturally, spending plenty of yen to give itself a strong and sumptuous identity on a prime site in the financial district, where the price of $371 per square foot for the land was the highest ever recorded in California.

There is no architecture anywhere quite like this immaculate essay in concrete and glass by Skidmore, Owings & Merrill.

Outwardly the beautifully composed small tower — at only 20 stories an admirable size for downtown — is deceptively simple, held aloft by widely spaced cylindrical uprights that soar from the great open banking room at its base to the richly indented roofline, where the found forms emerge as monumental sculpture in shadowy recesses, 330 feet above the cable cars clanging past on California Street.

But, as the very elegance of detailing reveals, Bank of Tokyo in fact is a complex work of civic art that takes a good deal of understanding.

At first glance it may be regarded solely as a unique office structure, but hardly freakish like William Pereira's Transamerica Pyramid, with its giant dunce cap. Nevertheless, it takes a gracious independent stance against the heavy cubes in the skyline, for instance the coarse Union Bank and Mutual Benefit Life on lower California Street, both by Welton Becket & Associates, which virtually thump the ground as they hit the sidewalks.

In this context, Bank of Tokyo is remarkable chiefly because of the lordly unobstructed banking room at ground level — the first such space in a tall San Francisco building for half a century: 40 feet high, 125 feet across, and opulently finished in white marble and stainless steel, which is visible from three sides though tremendous walls of glass.

Thus, Bank of Tokyo can be seen as an inward-looking, highly expressive building, conveying a clear impression of grand internal volumes, not merely in the main banking space, but on the sweeping horizontal office floors above. One expects splendor inside.

At the same time, Bank of Tokyo urbanely looks outward to the surrounding historic cityscape, especially the Bank of California's majestic classical monument directly opposite, to which it has been related with extraordinary sensitivity and tact.

This attempt to be a civilized neighbor, while retaining a noble individual presence, is the key to the whole design.

For California Street, as it levels out below Nob Hill toward the bay, is a formidable environment. On either side it is flanked by massive banks, insurance companies, steamship lines and other financial institutions and corporations, whose ornate, neo-Baroque palazzos — mostly dating from the 1920s — rise on mighty colonnades and arches.

These contain some of the stirring spaces in the city, including Julia Morgan's hall in the Marine Exchange, recently restored for the Chartered Bank of London. The best of these rooms is not on California, but at the foot of Montgomery, where Willis Polk's lavish marble and bronze hall for Crocker Bank puts to shame the pseudo-Modernist cliches of Wells Fargo across the street, by John Graham of Seattle, who installed useless aluminum fins on an insensate skyscraper that was already vulgar enough.

Edward Charles Bassett, senior design partner of the San Francisco office of Skidmore, Owings & Merrill, and author of Bank of Tokyo, is not an architect likely to commit that kind of error.

Although many people who do not know much about architecture have harsh words for Bassett and SOM (as the huge nationwide firm is known), accusing him, among other things, of indifference to Bay Area regional values, the truth is that — for a major modern architect with an exceptional command of industrial technology — he is in some ways an inveterate traditionalist almost too concerned with historicism in his work.

Consequently, the local office of SOM has become its maverick — not to say, schizoid — branch, split between the austere structural objectivity of the "skin and bones" glass architecture of Mies van der Rohe and a warmer subjective romanticism which blends lyrically with the existing urban grain.

The two tendencies can be discerned in buildings as different as Crown Zellerbach, a Miesian enclosure of glass in its delightful park on Market Street, and — nearby at California and Battery — the solid 14-story palazzo of John Hancock (now Industrial Indemnity), cloaked in black granite, and mounted on a splendid, but openly pictorial arcade of reinforced concrete.

Similarly, the prodigious Miesian X-bracing of the Alcoa Building in Golden Gateway is sharply at odds with the sentimentalized Hyatt-Union Square, whose restaurant overlooking Post Street is festooned with corny nonstructural arches.

But now, in Bank of Tokyo, Bassett suddenly has combined the two approaches in a veritable tour de force. He needed a big-span structure — requiring a bold and logical concept — to accommodate the lofty banking hall the client required. But there also was the historic city to respect, and just across the street, in the magnificent Corinthian colonnade of Bank of California, designed after the earthquake by the excellent old firm of Bliss & Faville, he found the inspiration he wanted.

The temple's heroic columns, of course, are not true monoliths, as they would be in a real Roman temple. They have concealed steel cores, covered by the handsome granite known as Sierra white, which is actually light gray and appears in many downtown buildings.

Could he not, Bassett reasoned, also enclose a luminous banking space with vertical elements — steel enclosed by precast concrete — which, like the staunch old columns, would be about six feet in diameter, but unlike them would run 20 stories upward through an uncompromisingly modern building?

Moreover, could not the mood of the temple be echoed — not literally duplicated — in the lines and proportions, color and texture, of the new building?

And finally, since he wished to enclose the bottom of Bank of Tokyo with large surfaces of glass, could not the venerable Bank of California be brought into view from his own great interior space as a magnificent piece of historic architectural sculpture, very much like a monumental urban stage set seen through a proscenium arch?

Out of such thinking emerged the overall concept that gives Bank of Tokyo its eloquence and sculptured richness of form.

The grand elements of the composition logically fall into place. Elevators and other utilities were unobtrusively placed on the inner flank of the site, to the east, so that the other three sides, fronting on California and Sansome streets to the south and west, and the alley to the north, could be freely developed to enclose almost completely open floors 125 feet square.

Only 16 vertical members support this open plan, four great cylinders 25 feet apart grouped in a square pattern at each corner of the building, and connected at each floor by girders 65 feet across that also clear-span the great banking space below.

Thus the whole building, seemingly so formally organized, is unusually free. The corners provide small spaces splendidly suited for conferences and executive offices, and the big central areas open for innumerable different arrangements of desks, counters and files.

Now that the basic concept was formulated, the SOM staff pitched in to give the building its fastidious final details. Of these the most ingenious are the precast concrete panels, both curved and flat, that sheathe the structural system between the long ribbons of glass.

For they are composed not only of sand and concrete but of pulverized Sierra granite, which when sandblasted to a given depth brings out the handsome gray of the stone, between bands of concrete that have simply been left white.

Yet sometimes the meticulous concrete work — technically the finest job of precasting I've seen — verges on preciosity, as in the strange little protuberances of the big corner panels just above ground level which Bassett euphemistically describes as "bosses," using an old architectural term, but which are bound to be seen as nipples.

A single great convex disc would have been more in scale here.

All this conceals an inner steel structure that is much leaner than the husky concrete forms that give the building sculptural force, just as it could also be argued that the great banking room is excessively cluttered by its suspended hoop of chrome — a much too flashy lighting fixture — which hovers above the tellers' counter, and could have been dispensed with easily.

But as one climbs the granite steps and enters beneath the powerful girder that spans the entrance only nine feet overhead, and then — quite suddenly — experiences the exhilarating central space, everywhere meticulously detailed, the fine old Bank of California comes into sight, as marvelous proof of the continuity of serious architecture in San Francisco.

At that point one cannot help remembering the spirited old Alaska Commercial Bank which made way for Bank of Tokyo, with its charming nautical decorations of ropes and anchors, sporting porpoises and walrus heads, some of which Bassett has saved — poignantly enough — at the entrance of the new building. The loss was painful, but on balance — as this new monument takes what surely will be a historical place in the city — it was worth it.

September 6, 1977

■ BOLD STATE OFFICES TO SAVE ENERGY

Three remarkable "energy efficient" state office buildings are on the drawing boards in Sacramento, reckoned to use only about 25 percent of the electricity and gas required by conventionally air-conditioned structures in the hot valley climate.

This alone makes them important enough, for if their conservationist features are not altogether unprecedented, having been anticipated in many "solar" homes, sod houses and small commercial structures, they are nevertheless the first sizable public office buildings of their kind in the world, ranging in floor area from 200,000 to 350,000 square feet, which puts them in another class than rural communes and residences of Berkeley intellectuals with solar devices on their roofs.

Yet the new state office buildings are not merely technical feats — or rather, antitechnocratic lessons. They also happen to be significant works of social architecture, not unworthy of the highest level of the enlightened private sector, but absolutely rare in governmental buildings.

In strikingly different ways, for their concepts are not at all identical, they have been designed according to real human needs of their several thousand occupants, especially the need to be more than a bureaucratic cipher, which marks a welcome break from abstract cost-accounting that in fact is extremely wasteful, and has disfigured Sacramento (like Washington and virtually every large capital) with phalanxes of authoritarian blockbusters whose crushing facades and labyrinthine interiors condemn their inmates to Kafka-esque servitude.

These fresh developments amount to a vindication of the orthodox outlook of Sim Van der Ryn, who was appointed state architect two years ago at the age of 40.

Although he and his staff actually designed only one of the buildings, he is fundamentally responsible for the philosophy underlying all three, which are the first major structures put up by the state since the Reagan administration halted construction and decided to lease ordinary commercial premises.

Yet even good architects had cause to be wary of Van der Ryn in 1975. Not only had he given up on "Architecture with a capital A," but he had ceased to practice the small-scale humanistic architecture — notably housing for college students, the elderly and migrant farmworkers — which had given him a precocious national reputation.

Instead, as a counterculture ecologist, far-out Berkeley professor, veteran of the battle for People's Park, and founder of the communal Farallones Institute which at its bases in Inverness, Occidental and Berkeley sought to relate physical environment with "biological concerns," he concentrated on recycling, frugal plumbing, solar heating, bohemian "wood butcher" construction and contemplation at Zen centers such as Tassajara Hot Springs in the uppermost reaches of Carmel Valley, where he met Governor Jerry Brown.

Van der Ryn's detractors pointed out that he had never done a large building, and not even many small ones in industrial materials such as steel and concrete. More seriously, he had not the slightest experience in running a huge bureaucracy such as the 400-person state architect's office. It not only approves all design for the state, whether by private firms or by in-house staffs of agencies such as the Department of Parks, but also has a legal right to do plenty of architecture on its own.

Yet Van der Ryn had the advantage of an acute shortage of office space in Sacramento, so the three buildings, together with two others soon to follow quickly were financed by the Legislature for a total of $90 million.

Rather nervily, he decided to do the first building himself, since he knew best what he hoped to achieve in new standards for both pleasant working conditions and economic energy consumption — objectives which he of course perceived as totally compatible. He selected a big site near the Capitol on the block bordered by Eighth, Ninth, O and P streets, which suited his intention to go lowrise — only four stories — and at the same time to wrap his building around a great skylit court, which is the key to the whole concept.

Now, such courts have appeared in many different kinds of buildings during the past 10 or 15 years, from Kevin Roche's magnificent enclosed garden for the Ford Foundation in New York, to John Portman's festive and theatrical atriums in hotels such as our own Hyatt Regency.

But virtually all of these big spaces impose heavy loads on air-conditioning systems, whereas Van der Ryn hoped to achieve just the reverse by taking advantage of a special — if not unique — condition of the Sacramento climate: the steep and rapid fall in temperature every night, when ocean breezes blow up from the bay through the Carquinez Straits to cause a drop of 30 or 35 degrees after torrid summer days.

Winter presents no problem in Sacramento, when heating is necessary.

But in summer the thermometer often tops 100; therefore Van der Ryn and his carefully picked top assistants adopted a strategy of cooling the building at night by opening the skylight, vents and other openings to trap the cool breezes. At the same time fans and other devices draw them through the building by expelling the hot daytime air, so that a natural flow would be established that could be likened to artificial respiration: out goes the bad air, in comes the good.

The spacious central court, besides serving as a social center, with its balconies, cafelike cafeteria and seating areas, trees and plants, would also serve as a reservoir of cool air, reducing the temperature, say, to 65 degrees when workers arrived in the morning.

The next problem, logically, would be to keep the buildings from heating up excessively during the day. Here common sense prevailed. As valley residents have long known, simply to keep the sun from penetrating the building directly, screening it with thick and massive construction (on the principle of old adobe buildings), and also use of awnings and other external sun breaks such as structural overhangs (as on old farmhouse verandahs), can keep buildings much cooler.

Furthermore, merely by discarding the hot luminous ceilings which today make almost all office spaces neurotically overbright, would also help considerably. "Task lighting" — which simply means lamps at individual desks that can also be directed overhead by well-designed fixtures — would make a decisive difference.

From all these considerations a very decent building promises to be built, cordially overlooking the tree-lined streets from balconies and terraces that are shaded by projecting upper floors and cheerful canvas awnings, all of which breaks up into intelligible human portions what otherwise could be a forbidding mass.

The structure is rather heavy, as Van der Ryn desired — perhaps too heavy. In purely architectural terms the facades are somewhat disordered, or even messy. Some of the details, at this late state of design, are coarse.

But little matter, for one will be able to step easily out on the terraces, or into the lively ambience of the great community court.

The second building, intended for Evelle Younger's Department of Justice, has the San Francisco firm of Robert Marquis & Associates as architects (chiefly known for excellent redwood houses), but Van der Ryn and his staff — especially the young architect-planner Bobbie Sue Hood — established the basic program for it.

Here the use of night air for cooling is again expected to be extremely effective, largely because the New York engineer Fred Dubin — one of the leading pioneers in the field — has designed the system (he has actually been advising Van der Ryn all the time).

But the most fascinating feature of this sprawling one- and two-story establishment of 350,000 square feet, much of which is just a shell for computers, is its intelligent arrangement of interior "streets" — really, lofty skylit corridors — which pass several outdoor "neighborhood" courts, the "turf" of individual agencies which they can develop as they wish, for Ping-Pong or volleyball, or flower gardens or vegetable patches.

These corridors converge at a large central court, which Marquis calls a "town center"; and although this rather pretentious nomenclature seems misleading, it may prove to be precisely that: the social core of an immense legal and judicial operation that may help to humanize it.

This building is still being refined, and I hope it turns out to have the dash and elegance, as well as the warmth, that Marquis and his associates wish to give it. Much, in all of these new state jobs, will depend on details, on good furnishing, and above all on an overall sense of architectural command — not control, but true fulfillment of the possibilities of the concept.

The last building, if all of the above holds true for it, too, could well be a masterpiece. This is the winner of the competition Van der Ryn has just conducted — by all odds the most thoughtfully conceived competition in the history of the state — in which no fewer than 41 private firms entered.

The winning design, lo and behold, is by one of the biggest architectural and engineering conglomerates in the country, Benham-Blair & Affiliates, with 11 different offices and 550 employees, whose usual clients include the Air Force.

Its concept, calling for an immense solar collector overlooking a largely underground building that is really a park, has far to go before it is great architecture. Perhaps it may never get that far, but it already shows an exhilarating way to integrate Van der Ryn's ecology with broader urban development.

October 10, 1977

■ LEVI'S CHOICE — BE GOOD OR BE GREAT

The decision by Levi Strauss & Co., purveyors of blue jeans to the world, to vacate its characterless space in the 29-story slab at 2 Embarcadero Center, and to move to a lowrise headquarters complex in a great urban park at the foot of Telegraph Hill, calls for a public vote of thanks in a city that has already gone too far toward Manhattanization.

After skyscraper construction reached a pinnacle of corporate vulgarity in the Transamerica Pyramid, the reversal of the trend by another major San Francisco company is such welcome news that it overrides my doubts — some of them very serious — about the quality of Levi's architecture at this early stage of design.

Even if the scheme were to go ahead in its present imperfect form, however, the city on balance would be the winner. The tremendous new park alone, which will probably be called Levi Square although it would be more accurate to call it a piazza or plaza, will be a magnificent civic improvement — a space as large as Union Square and Golden Gateway's Sydney Walton Park combined, with something of both their moods, formal and informal, on either side of Battery Street for two blocks from Greenwich to Union.

Not only will the open border of greenery along the Embarcadero permit spectacular views of shipping and the bay between Piers 23 and 27, but the landscaping of this raw stretch of Battery Street should also make it a gracious entry to downtown, to those driving or walking south toward the financial district.

Moreover, in anticipation of the historic district that has been proposed for this part of the waterfront, two important architectural mementoes — the little brick building known as Cargo West (supposedly a bordello during Barbary Coast days), and the larger and much finer Italian Swiss Colony warehouse — will be saved, and hopefully integrated, with the three new office buildings that will go up around the square (with housing, garages and more offices scheduled later on two more blocks on the other side of Sansome Street, along Lombard and Montgomery).

The program for all of this development makes excellent sense, because restaurants, pubs and retail shops will be installed at ground level, both on the square and on the adjacent streets, enlivening the whole area at night as well as by day, unlike single-purpose corporate premises that are dead after 5 p.m.

Thus, if this were an ordinary commercial development, it wouldn't be bad at all. But it happens to be the new home of a fantastically successful San Francisco business institution, with sales last year of $1.2 billion and a net income of $104 million.

Thus, although the citizenry must be grateful for its virtues, just as its employees must be for the company's enlightened benefit programs, there is no strong reason why the city should accept the present scheme, which in fact can be easily strengthened, or — if Levi Strauss wishes — redesigned altogether.

The design in fact is not actually its own, but was delivered to the company, as part of an ingenious real estate promotion, by developer Gerson Bakar and his partners.

With considerable astuteness Bakar saw the possibilities of the run-down area north of Broadway as far back as the 1960s; and he was able to acquire control of the four blocks that comprise the core of the Levi project and two other blocks as well.

The key to it all is the willingness of Levi to be the principal tenant in what is basically a simple rental proposition. If Levi — presumably solvent for a long time to come — goes along, there will be no difficulty in financing the whole $60–$75 million project.

This suits the corporation perfectly, for unlike many large companies that have built virtual palaces for themselves, Levi — besides eschewing an image of splendor — "does not care to go into the real estate business on its own," as chairman Walter Haas Jr. puts it, even though it currently possesses $88 million in property, plant and equipment in various locations.

Instead, Levi prefers to entrust such nettlesome matters to experienced developers such as Gerson Bakar, or to architect-developer John Portman in its long-term lease at Embarcadero Center. What makes the Bakar deal especially attractive, indeed, is his willingness to take over the Embarcadero Center space, and relet it after Levi moves to his buildings, thereby relieving the company of still another chore.

Unless this background is known, the quality of the architecture may be inexplicable. Levi's own industrial design and fashion-styling have been brilliant, but the buildings hatched by Bakar are clearly below the level of architecture by other corporations that are similarly committed to fine design in both their products and construction, such as John Deere, Weyerhaeuser, Boeing, IBM, Upjohn and Union Carbide.

Yet this was the inevitable outcome of Bakar's kind of design development, including selection of architects. This was radically different from that usually adopted by great corporations, which carefully screen leading architects from various parts of the country — as Seagram's did, for instance, before getting a masterpiece from Mies van der Rohe.

Bakar's chief experience has been in moderate-priced housing, some of it very decent, but his office construction has been mainly low-cost speculative structures on the northern waterfront done by two offices — Hellmuth, Obata & Kassabaum and M. Arthur Gensler & Associates. It might have been useful to split the Levi project between them, with Gyo Obata doing the buildings (for he has had a better-than-average record in office-building design) and Gensler providing the interior design, which is his specialty.

Oddly enough, however, Bakar pitted them against each other in an "in-house" design competition.

They are still sharing the commission, even though Obata won the first round, perhaps because his scheme for the main Levi building at the southwest corner of the site, which will house its top brass, included a large glass-roofed "atrium" — or enclosed court — reminiscent of the extraordinary interior garden, framed in rich granite and cinnamon-colored corten steel, which Kevin Roche created for the Ford Foundation headquarters in New York. Walter Haas Jr. rightly admires this great verdant space, with its eucalyptus and magnolia trees, and thousands of flowering shrubs and vines.

But there the resemblance breaks off with Levi's chief building, a six-story structure across from the Ice House, at Sansome and Union. The Ford Foundation appears externally as a cube, but is essentially an L-shaped office building that is transformed into a cube by facades of glass, ten stories high, which rise majestically on 42nd Street.

The Levi scheme is really a square doughnut, but open at its northeast corner to provide a view over the park and out to the bay. This has been done in short, choppy strokes, without much conviction, for the building steps back in weak recesses on the left of the main entry, but is given a straight surface on the right, so that the architecture seems to propel one forward restlessly, as if it were pushing one's left shoulder, into an interior space that so far hasn't been studied at all.

Another notch has been cut out of the building's southeast corner, ostensibly to accommodate the little Cargo West building, which is only two stories high, and hasn't really been integrated with the rest of the design. Maybe Cargo West could have been integrated with the rest of the building — lined up with its roof before stepping back, like a little ziggurat, in terraces that are supposed to be richly planted.

The terraces are a fine idea, for they should be accessible from the offices through French doors, and they also provide a gracious transition between the headquarters and the two subsidiary buildings.

But the terraces, too, are handled without much conviction, and are made weaker still by the strange windows of the upper floors whose proportions are at odds with the big openings at ground level, and which are curiously rounded in some places, and rectangular outlines in others.

What can be the reason for these phony, nonstructural arches? They seem to be parodies of the staunch genuine brick arches of the historic buildings in the neighborhood; and their only justification would seem to be a desire to placate the Landmarks Advisory Board, which must issue a certificate of appropriateness before the design can be built in this historic area. But the board's attitude is terribly old-fangled and pictorial, given to slavish imitation of the past rather than relying on the same principles of forthright structural expression which makes the venerable warehouses and cold storage buildings so powerful.

It was pressure from the board, indeed, that led to the phony arches of the concrete garage at Lombard and Sansome, a caricature of the wonderful Merchant's Ice and Cold Storage Building of 1896 next to it. Or at least developer Ron Kaufman, a man chary with a penny when it comes to paying architects, intimates that the board forced him to design it that way. The board, for its part, says that, bad as the garage may seem, it is superior to the earlier designs hacked out by Kaufman's draftsmen.

Now, a very important point is involved here. If we are to have officially inspired mimicry of historic architecture, forced on developers by sentimentalists in the Planning Commission as well as on the Landmarks Board, the whole area is going to look as bad I fear as the ersatz Victorianism of Warren Simmons will turn out on Pier 39 a short distance away. This may be preferable to the surrealistic car wash that was somehow permitted at the corner of the bay and the Embarcadero, but to a company as rich and powerful as Levi Strauss, whose officers belong to families that have sponsored the arts in San Francisco for generations, it is not the only alternative.

There is no reason to use brown tile that could be mistaken for 19th-century brick (even though this might be done sensitively), when one could build nobly — as the Ford Building was — in fine materials that will help to lift up our hearts as we pass these buildings for years to come. Moreover, such materials could express the true internal structure, which probably will not be concrete, but a live frame of steel. One thinks of exquisite buildings clad in copper by the Finnish master Alvar Aalto.

Similarly there is no reason to assume that the landscaping can simply be added, after the buildings are designed, like ketchup on a hamburger. The potentially marvelous plaza must not only be carefully related to the exteriors of the buildings, but also be brought into their interiors, and on to their superimposed terraces, with such wit and grace that it will all seem a complex single thing, rather than simplistic confusion.

In other words, this should be done as a great work of art, which does not mean that it should be extravagant or perverse, but on the contrary, it must be sane and civil to a degree that Gerson Bakar has never come close to achieving in buildings that are merely the outcome of financial calculations.

"Levi's don't have to be blue, they just have to be good."

Wrong. They can be superb.

November 28, 1977

■ GM'S FREMONT PLANT — THE BEAUTY OF FUNCTION

A clever European architect, Hans Hollein, some years ago published a photomontage of an aircraft carrier in an unspoiled rural landscape.

By this legerdemain the huge warship, so menacing on water, was transformed into an astounding technical palace: a megastructure more overwhelming — and in some ways more magnificent — than Versailles or Hadrian's Villa.

Hollein could have spared himself the trouble. He could have shown a photograph of the General Motors assembly plant on its 411-acre site beneath the East Bay hills at Fremont, where it suddenly looms up beside the Nimitz freeway as the biggest thing of its kind in this part of the world.

More than half a mile long (2,280 feet), and nearly a fifth of a mile wide (900 feet), the factory would not look small even in the Midwest industrial belt, where plants of such size are not only common, but often are grouped, for miles on end, in complexes such as Ford's River Rouge or GM's own works at Pontiac or Flint.

In hedonistic Northern California, however, nothing quite approaches this immense building, which is not a megastructure so much as a megamachine: a great mechanical device in itself, filled with tens of thousands of smaller machines, and like a technological cornucopia spewing out other machines at what counterculture types must consider an alarming rate.

On parallel assembly lines 45 cars and 36 trucks pour forth per hour. That's 81 vehicles every 60 minutes, or one every 44 seconds. All ready to drive off.

Whether or not it was socially just and ecologically wise for GM to have moved out here, on open agricultural land, when it abandoned a small and obsolete Chevy plant in Oakland in 1963, thereby depriving a poverty-wracked inner city of much needed jobs, there's no denying that GM's great new facility expressed the evolving scale of a regional metropolis.

It belongs to the superscale of the freeways and BART, the jet terminals and container ports, the new medical centers and expanded universities.

The GM plant's bigness alone — 2.66 million square feet of floor area under a single roof, in which 6,500 employees earn $131 million per year — is not so important as the fact that the damned thing is beautiful.

Designed by GM's engineers in Detroit, whose notion of "architecture" is pitilessly revealed by the silly little office building they plunked down in front of the factory's majestic facades, this is modern engineering art at a very high level, freed from cliches because it makes no pretense at being fashionable.

It has a job to do; this has determined the proportions and clear composition of the long walls of steel, extending half a mile in a steady rhythmical pattern on the industrial plain.

These heroic facades were painted a gleaming white, but they have since darkened to a creamy tone, giving the long horizontal lines — emphasized by upper and lower bands of dark windows that travel from end to end — a grand sober strength.

This in turn makes a splendid pedestal for the vertical display of stacks and vents on the roof. There the fantastic uprights express the functional divisions within, such as the paint shops, which are topped by exhaust tubes of stainless steel.

These are icons of industrial civilization: the plainspoken vernacular of mass production design which cannot really be described in the lexicon of traditional architectural theory. Like the container cranes of Oakland, the dynamic beauty of this utilitarian architecture is what, in Le Corbusier's phrase, ordinary "eyes don't see."

Perhaps it is easier to perceive the implications — the glory and the terror — of a purely technological environment inside the enormous factory.

Here one is truly inside the belly of the whale.

The work force is a microcosm of blue-collar America. White and black, old and young, hip and square, they weld and bolt, lift and adjust, checking paint, fitting doors, guiding fenders into place. Ten or 15 percent are women.

Sometimes they sing or joke. Occasionally there is a whiff of pot. There is a certain edge between salaried nonunion management and UAW wage earners. Somehow in the midst of all the technology, a Bible study group has a little prefab structure sitting on the factory floor, with a "cathedral" interior, in which they intone hymns and pray during breaks.

The vast structure contains all this in a two-level show.

On each floor, 20-foot-high steel columns, spaced 45 feet apart in either direction, support trusses that raise the height of the space to nearly 30 feet. Beneath the powerful march of steel overhead, the machines flow past on parallel assembly lines, in a system that carries 1,119 cars and 453 trucks at different stages of completion at any given moment. It is literally beyond individual comprehension. Only the computers know fully what is going on.

The process originates in the Midwest, where parts are loaded on freight cars that eventually are brought into this factory as mobile warehouses.

Conveyors and other machines bring these components to the moving lines, where an IBM card programs each car in a balanced sequence, so that time differences between say, bumper or fender installations of different models, are evened out into a steady passage of work.

The engines and frames are assembled on the lower floor, while car bodies and truck cabs are put together above, swinging up and around through paint shops and upholstery stations. Then — in technological copulation — these tops are suddenly dropped by giant handling apparatus to the level below. They always land on the right chassis, though each commenced a similar journey nearly half a mile away.

Much nonsense is circulated in the art world today about "happenings," nonevents which amuse a frivolous public that has never progressed much beyond childish games.

But here, in the great factory, is an authentic aesthetic event, with machinery that reduces most so-called kinetic sculpture to the status of toys.

By paradox, among the public that needs desperately to understand the art of the engineers, it is only children — and their elementary school teachers — who see this extraordinary display of American creative strength. They come every weekday, in school buses, to ride wide-eyed through the factory on "elephant trains." Their parents should come along, too.

March 27, 1978

■ AN ARCHITECTURAL JOY IN SILICON VALLEY

The most spectacular recent success story in Silicon Valley belongs to the Qume Corp., which makes electronic printers many times more rapid than the fastest automatic typewriters, and since 1973 has moved upward architecturally from a remodeled Hayward garage to the Bay Area's finest new industrial building.

Situated off Trimble Road, between Highways 17 and 680, in San Jose, it's the first large factory anywhere to have its own interior garden: really, a skylit, landscaped "street" that runs the 400-foot width of the building, separating the tall, single-story assembly line area on the north, from two stories of equally open office space on the south.

Consequently, at the very place where the technological environment is usually most tyrannical, deprived of natural light and any other intimation of the organic world, the center of Qume's hard-working operation is filled with greenery and the refreshing presence of water that courses from a fountain, past planted beds and sitting areas, through channels and pools.

At the very heart of the building, the shrubs, flowers and nearly full-grown ficus trees — about 15 feet tall — enfold a sunken cafeteria area, which has some of the mood of a garden restaurant. But one doesn't have to be in this oasis to enjoy its outreaching mood. The trees are elating to anyone glancing down from the offices, or across the work stations of the two-acre factory space, and there is another line of ficus trees and shrubs bordering the other side of the assembly lines, in front of a translucent northern wall, so that workers putting together the exquisite printing machines have greenery in view whenever they look up.

These amenities — plus a high standard of furnishing throughout the building and a parklike setting outdoors — do not prevent the $10 million establishment from being "economically competitive."

Qume sells its printers like crazy (most of them are marketed under other labels such as IBM) in spite of the difference in cost between a first-class building and a typical Silicon Valley tilt-up concrete shell.

It's hard to detach the cost of the extras from the overall price of the project, because the goodies have literally been built into the entire design, but from President Robert E. Schroeder down, Qume's management thinks it was worth paying a premium for a place that would be "a joy to work in" and "a source of pride" to the company.

Not everyone in Silicon Valley feels that way. It's easy to forget, amidst high-sounding talk of smokeless electronic industry, how fiercely competitive and often ruthless this part of the economy can be. Labor is largely semiskilled and turnover is high. A large proportion of the work force is dark-skinned or Spanish speaking. Subcontractors and jobbers feel the weight of the giant multinationals pressing upon them.

Thus many electronics plants — if not R&D facilities and headquarters offices — are rudimentary affairs, relieved by lawn outside, but grim within. Even IBM's immense manufacturing facilities beside Highway 101 (in contrast to its resplendent Santa Teresa software labs a few miles away) are dreary affairs hardly helped by bad exterior art.

The difference at Qume may be that the company's chief officers are so young, ambitious and close to day-to-day operations. The real creator of the business — called a "technical genius" in the field — is engineer David Lee. He developed the first "daisy wheel" printer for Xerox, an astonishing circular device a couple of inches across that, in its latest evolution, prints 55 characters per second, forward and backward, against 15 characters for the fastest automatic typewriters.

Inventor Lee found backing for his own company six years ago from Sutter Hill Ventures of Palo Alto, who installed Schroeder — an administrative and financial whiz — as president. Lee and Schroeder were then both 35 years old, and they quickly assembled a team mostly as young as themselves.

In 1974, they moved from their garage to an old Dixie Cup warehouse in Hayward, which they merely patched and painted before starting to make their own printers. Schroeder's wife Ann picked the colors, and she has been concerned with the aesthetics of the firm ever since. (Schroeder's previous experience had been with Cummins Engines, the great Columbus, Ind., manufacturer of diesel engines that, led by Irwin Miller, has not only made its home city an architectural showplace but has built some of the most beautiful factories in the world.)

By 1978, Qume had annual sales of $100 million, and decided to build architecture that would be worthy of the Cummins tradition.

The name Qume, by the way, means nothing. It was meant to be "meaningless but memorable" by a company that could not predict the full scope of its future activities, but wanted to sound "positive."

The building isn't meaningless, but it is certain memorable. In its 30-acre parklike setting on the featureless industrial plain, with the East Bay hills in the background, the building expresses its own strength in long, sweeping horizontals, indented at entrances, and further enriched by color to break up what otherwise might have been daunting masses.

The tremendous facade of the office section, facing south, is divided into two symmetrical parts, with a modest entrance between them that is perhaps not assertive enough. But the whole composition expresses clarity and quiet strength, with projecting sunshades drawn as long, uninterrupted surfaces that do not detract from the monumental lines of the whole. Too often, solar-protective devices clamor for attention, rather than effacing themselves as part of the architecture, but that mistake was not made here, where soft gray and beige colors enhance a feeling of calm, and gently frame the cool silvery window strips of reflective glass.

The real entrance to the building is from the parking area on the west side, where a curving garden wall — painted the same strong blue as the steel exterior sheathing of the industrial areas — sweeps toward a friendly entry at the end of the interior "street."

The street itself is identified on the outside by its translucent walling — also used for the skylight — of Kalwall panels. This remarkable material comes in 16-foot lengths that impart a rhythmic consistency to the building's modular composition; and it enables the center of the building not only to be filled with light, but to remain comfortable in all weather. Natural light warms the building most of the day (with only a pickup from the air-conditioning systems under extreme conditions), and yet the Kalwall's insulating qualities also keep the interior cool.

It consists of a four-inch-thick laminated plastic "sandwich" with a fiberglass core, ribbed with black aluminum stiffeners, that give it the appearance of a high-technology Japanese shoji screen.

Inside the garden is all radiance. The company might replace the concrete fountains, done by the architects, with a first-rate fountain sculpture; but otherwise, apart from some orange chairs in the cafeteria, the whole design is hard to fault. The steady processional march of the steel colonnade, painted a light blue so as not to overwhelm the interior mood, and not to clash with the richer blue of the walls, is interpenetrated by magnificent ductwork — painted different shades of red and lighter red and orange. All this adds up to a wonderfully optimistic feeling of unimpeded space and logical colored forms.

The open office plan is particularly refreshing. Everyone has the same decent, if not luxurious desks and chairs, from Schroeder and Lee to the receptionists. There are no closed-off offices at all, although there are conference spaces, where doors can be shut. The officers are out in the open, and seem accessible to everyone.

The manufacturing and warehousing spaces are even finer because of their 18-foot ceilings, and the splendor of the equipment that is everywhere in action.

It is a major work of art by the Palo Alto firm of Hawley-Peterson, with Charles A. Peterson as partner-in-charge, and the young architects John Duvivier and Curtis Snyder heading the design team. Duvivier has since started his own practice, and I wish him good luck, for he is obviously a very good architect.

Is there anything wrong in this technological Eden? If any fault is to be found, it is perhaps with the fine grooming of the building. Although manufacturing procedures are meticulous, the social areas are not well-kept, possibly because the work force — largely from humble backgrounds — has little experience with architecture of this quality. The cafeteria and coffee-break areas are littered, and so is the pleasant little outdoor eating area, on a sandy beach beside a man-made lake.

Perhaps Qume's top leadership, bought out last year by ITT but still in charge of the company, will have time to think of such details, even though they are busy developing new gadgets such as "floppy disk memories." At any rate, in spite of their need for security, they will hold an "open house" in January which should not be missed.

November 12, 1979

■ IBM'S NEW PALACE OF TECHNOLOGY

IBM's gleaming monument to technocracy, silver and immaculate, comes into view as a vision of controlled order beneath the Santa Teresa hills, where cattle still graze. It sits on Bailey Road just west of Highway 101's fumes, noise and pathetic housing strips on the southern verge of San Jose.

The contrast between the splendid utopian isolation of the Santa Teresa computer programming laboratory and the nearby squalor of unprogrammed America is one index of the importance of IBM's new technological palace.

Another is the National Honor Award it received last month from the American Institute of Architects, mainly because it is one of the most fascinating displays of reflective facades, achieved by shining aluminum and mirror glass, yet created by the modern environment.

The laboratory in fact is unique. There is no architecture quite the same as the group of eight cross-shaped towers, "plugged" into a 680-foot base that conceals a massive battery of computers. It is the first facility in the world expressly designed for research and development of computer programming, a "science" scarcely 20 years old, which in its own right has become a highly marketable commodity.

Like the computer itself, programming systems are constantly evolving and must be protected, mainly against corporate espionage, by elaborate security.

Hence the need for specialized buildings, accommodating no fewer than 2,000 programming experts, in an isolated setting — more like a fortified monastery than cloistered universities such as Oxford with which IBM likes to compare it. It can be entered only through a single main lobby, and thereafter is accessible only by means of electronically coded identity cards.

When the San Francisco architectural firm of McCue Boone Tomsick (MBT) tackled such problems, neither it nor IBM had preconceptions of what the buildings should be. The main requirement was high "creative" performance, which seemed to depend on the contentment of the scientists and technicians, an interesting group which can be described as an egalitarian elite, mostly in their 30s, perhaps half of them women, and a number of them from minority backgrounds.

Almost all asked for private offices with views, as well as cable terminals at their desks to give them instant access to the computers.

This led to the basic plan of the buildings, each shaped like a Greek cross, with utilities and shared spaces at the center, and private offices and small conference rooms — about 60 percent with spectacular views — in the projecting arms of the cross.

The offices are each only 10 feet square, but they seem roomy enough, thanks partly to the carefully designed desks, filing cabinets and other furnishings, which — although not unusual at this level of corporate architecture — are surprisingly handsome.

But what of the buildings themselves? Their brilliantly polished surfaces, almost compulsively taut and refined, are unmistakably patrician architecture of the 1970s, seemingly impervious to time or personal touch even though aluminum does weather, especially under smog conditions such as exist in the Santa Clara Valley.

For the moment, however, the smooth walls of metal and glass appear unaging. Ordinary human considerations seem beyond the realm of the hermetically sealed, puristic facades that are so deftly jointed that not the slightest projection mars their prismatic forms.

Grouped asymmetrically around the great formal plaza that is the roof of the vast computer center on the first floor, the arms of the towers reflect each other's gleaming images in an endless interplay of refined shapes — slender verticals of silver light that shift as the viewer's position changes, in an ever-changing game of abstract aesthetics.

There is more to the game, which — like the computers — is governed by absolute mathematics, in this case an Euclidean diagram of 45-degree angles. These are plainly visible in the severe paving of the plaza, which lines up all the buildings on long diagonal coordinates that could have been ordained by Descartes. On these strict axes, every view, every change of light, is rigidly held within great angular patterns, triangles within greater triangles.

And the buildings, as they touch on the 45-degree axes, form rectangular courts which — in a remarkable surprise — are filled with color. Eight beautifully modulated tones, taken from the spectrum of the rainbow, are integrated in the total design, red related to orange, and orange to yellow, green to blue and blue to a greener blue that the architects call teal.

These matched and contrasting colors suddenly appear in the openings between buildings, their reflections caught in the silver surfaces of the other facades, so that their effects are constantly repeated and enriched.

For this tour de force we must thank Gerald McCue, principal designer for MBT, who was then also chairman of the architecture department at the University of California at Berkeley, and now is head of the Harvard Graduate School of Design.

He has always been a careful architect, but never before has McCue achieved such unexpected poetry. As he explains, the extraordinary optical effects owe much to his admiration for the reflective sculpture of James Prestini, in stainless steel or nickel-plated aluminum.

The superb Prestini in the library at Santa Teresa, by all odds the finest piece in an outstanding art program at the laboratory, shows the same endless reflectivity as the buildings themselves.

Certainly IBM marks a new level in the work of McCue Boone Tomsick. The same idiom of aluminum and mirror glass has been used with even greater refinement by other designers, notably the exquisite New York architect Richard Meier, but he did not have to face the same stringent earthquake requirements that MBT encountered at Santa Teresa.

Some seismic problems were solved with great brilliance, for example the chamfered corner piece of the buildings, which set up rich strips of light, but are actually breakaway panels that will fall if the taut facades move during a tremor, thus protecting the rest of their delicate surfaces.

In spite of such refinements, the whole project in some ways is troubling. The location itself, which not only usurps hitherto unspoiled land, but also extends the sprawling urbanization of the South Bay, raises doubts.

Although IBM occupies only 50 acres of a magnificent 1,180-acre site that was part of the pioneer Bernal Ranch, it stands aloof among the surviving orchards and grazing land. Its presence is less arrogant when the winter rains turn the hills a lush green, but it takes on a harder isolation when they are baked a tawny brown in summer, cut off abruptly from the land, and imposing on it a strict geometry that becomes harrowing in the noonday glare of the great elevated piazza.

Had there been more planting and trees, like the cottonwoods in the courts next to the buildings themselves, the immense central space might have been less forbidding. But the computer room underneath prohibited deep planting beds in this location, so that the straight walkways are unshaded, as are the bright paved surfaces they lead to, with the glass-and-metal buildings flashing on all sides.

There is always a sense of unrelenting control, of tremendous unseen power that makes ultimate decisions. But, of course, this power is directly below, in the guarded computer facility.

In the last analysis, the intricate machines may rule all.

True, they are beautiful — painted a cool IBM blue in their artificially chilled atmosphere — with their reels silently spinning as data are organized. At one end of the room, a glass wall opens on a sunken court, but because of the power of the contrived environment — in the highest sense an artificial environment — the greenery looks like a machine-produced picture of nature, in which every organic value has somehow been analyzed, systemized and programmed.

June 26, 1978

■ A 27-STORY COLLECTION OF ARCHITECTURAL ERRORS

For a case history of how to screw up a $135 million office building on an important downtown site, take a look at the nearly completed 100 First Plaza.

It's a 27-story mistake, or rather a collection of mistakes, misbegotten from the muddled base and malformed midsection to the 65-foot spike sticking out of its squashed top, facing the Transbay Terminal at Mission and First streets.

Usually, architects compete for top billing in a project of such size and prominence, but this baby is so strange that no one will step forward as father of the bastard.

Neither of the design's chief progenitors — Richard Keating, who was then head of the Houston office of Skidmore, Owings & Merrill and now runs its operations in Los Angeles, nor Jeffrey Heller of the San Francisco firm of Heller & Leake — wants his name attached to the result of their ill-fated liaison.

You can't blame them. Theirs was a shotgun marriage.

The bitterly incompatible architects were brought together by Texas developer Michael Barker in 1984, midway in a tortuous design-review process that lasted two years and required no fewer than six different designs under constantly stiffening downtown planning controls.

By the time Heller was called in, four undistinguished schemes by Keating — far below the level of his best work — had been turned down by the city planners.

The nebulous grounds for rejection were that they did not meet San Francisco's "contextual" urban design criteria, which is another way of saying they did not satisfy the planners' notions that new towers should parody romantic "skyscrapers" of half a century ago.

The ostensible model here, particularly for the base, was the handsome Art Deco Shell Building of 1929, a block away at 100 Bush Street. Architecturally, they are much further apart.

Unfortunately, the planners — with their penchant for pseudo-historic "hats" — would not accept the Shell's finely modeled flat roof, and insisted that something like a sky-bound oilcan be placed on top of 100 First Plaza. Keating, accustomed to laissez-faire Houston, was incensed by such interference.

Meanwhile, businessman Barker was having fits about his financial agenda.

He and his partners and moneylenders had $31 million "exposed," as they say in the real estate trade, and they stood to lose a bundle if the project were delayed interminably by City Planning Director Dean Macris.

The Downtown Plan has made Macris the design czar of San Francisco, assisted by his department's resident aesthetic guru, Richard Hedman, recently retired, who played the role of Rasputin.

Enter the nimble Jeffrey Heller. He has since had his own differences with Macris, but at the time Heller could be described as the planners' darling.

His assignment from Barker was to ease the ordeal of design approval in the same way that the politically adroit lawyer, William Coblentz, was enlisted to smooth the building's passage through Dianne Feinstein's City Hall.

Not only had Heller deciphered arcane provisions of the Downtown Plan more expertly than any other architect in town, but as a confirmed anti-Modernist (who has since quieted down a bit), he had swallowed whole the planners' gospel of chopping up buildings and overdressing them in a wild variety of colors and conflicting materials, under the delusion that humanism is a mess.

Anyway, that is how 100 First Plaza would turn out two designs later, in what Keating — who may not be Bernini, but on the national scene is a far more accomplished designer than Heller — has called a "sordid" surrender to bureaucratic taste.

Heller absolves himself of the charge.

Producing model photographs and dates, he claims that his office contributed only "massing studies" in white cardboard, and that even those proposals were violated in the last scheme, when he says his only service to Barker was to help make the presentation to the Planning Commission.

He has even written a formal statement to The Chronicle decrying the building's faults.

Still, that has not stopped him from appearing in a promotional film that Barker shows to prospective tenants, giving the impression that Heller was not a part-time consultant but a principal designer of the building.

Keating, who is conspicuously absent from the movie, says that he would like to remove the Skidmore, Owings & Merrill name from the construction sign at Mission and First streets.

(The San Francisco office of the firm, by the way, is a quite separate design group from the Houston branch, and had nothing to do with the project.)

Putting the blame on Heller and Hedman, Keating concedes that he lost interest after Barker — far from guiltless in this debacle — cut the budget when the downtown rental market was collapsing in 1985 and his unforeseen legal and architectural fees were piling up.

Barker admits that the building was cheapened.

Granite surfaces, for instance, were replaced by less costly concrete panels and off-the-shelf glass curtain walls — on a building that Barker promised, almost to the end, would be largely clad in stone.

In the end, apparently, the working drawings were simply cranked out by Keating's former minions in Houston after he moved to the Los Angeles office of Skidmore, Owings.

Yet Keating can't get off that easily. Some of the most unfortunate features of the building, for instance the crass modeling of the lower floors, were present in the earliest design, and stayed to the end.

So that's how 100 First Plaza came into the world.

It is the city's first major building to have been wholly governed by the coercive Downtown Plan, as well as by other restrictions imposed by the supervisors and the voters, although it was exempted from the increasingly absurd "beauty contests" that adjudicate building permits under the strictest downtown antigrowth regulations in the country.

That does not mean the process is all wrong.

It is simply that the design controls are too rigid and that the planners have been allowed to lord it over architects.

Otherwise the plan is filled with admirable innovations, such as mandatory developers' allocations for housing, transit, art and usable open space (and, in this case, Barker's necessary purchase of 40,000 square feet of "air rights" that protect a historic building on Second Street). Most important, the strict height and bulk limits are excellent.

Consequently, 100 First Plaza is less oppressive, as a view-blocking, sun-denying object in the cityscape, than the mammoth International Style highrises that were perpetrated before the plan took effect in 1985.

Compared to those goliaths, 100 First Plaza is a midsize building. However, it also is worth noting that at a height of 382 feet (or 447 feet including the spike), and with 490,000 square feet of floor area, it would have loomed very large in the skyline of 1960.

It also could have looked a lot less chaotic, even decent, if it were carefully detailed.

The protruding and receding facades, stepping back clumsily as they ascend, seem pummeled out of reddish putty.

But the choppy floor layouts, which as prescribed by the plan diminish from 23,000 square feet at the base to 7,000 feet at the top, provide an exceptional assortment of interior spaces. The angular bay windows, although badly framed, offer sweeping views from a large number of offices.

From a distance, say from the Bay Bridge, the light reddish color and picturesque massing of 100 First Plaza may seem pleasant enough.

At closer range, however, the restless surfaces turn out to be not in a single tone of coral, for instance, but a motley of conflicting pinks, like gowns at a Texas wedding, clashing in a profusion of ill-matched materials: polished granite, painted metal and two contrasting finishes of the same precast concrete, heavily sandblasted to make the stone aggregate emerge and lightly blasted to a bland smoothness.

One of the first rules of architecture is not to combine active forms and busy colors, but to settle for one or the other, which the designers could have taken to heart on the vulgar base, with its stingy Mission Street colonnade.

Stonework may be a dying art, but here the granite veneer, as the French say, has been murdered, sawed in tiny pieces, as if a multiplication of cuts were a virtue.

To make the base fussier still, a dash of greenish granite has been thrown above the main entry, like stray pieces found in the stone yard.

Strips of dead-white precast concrete run up and across the first four floors, like a mad grid, breaking off without reason and starting again. This will look worse when graphics for shops, restaurants and a bank are added to retail premises on the first two floors.

Higher up, all four sides of the building aggressively jut outward and slice back in patterns that Barker says were suggested by Hedman to enhance "verticality."

Triangular prows, or "noses," of blackish glass run up the centers of the facades, nearly to the top of the building, where they are abruptly cut off, instead of being integrated with the topmost floors.

Flanking these protuberances are mean little "beaks" of bay windows that also rise almost the full height of the building, then meaninglessly cease.

It is a pathetic attempt to emulate the soaring lines of Timothy Pflueger's magnificent Pacific Telephone Building of 1925, a short distance away at New Montgomery Street, which, unlike this mess, is clad in a single, calm material, white terracotta.

Looking at such a masterpiece, Barker and his architects might have learned how to do better corners than the weak glass surfaces angling backward at the corners of 100 First Plaza.

The skimpy metal frames of these cheap curtain walls, more suitable for a suburban highway strip than for downtown San Francisco, are tinted pink. The almost identical frames of the "noses," a few feet away, are painted white.

And then comes the top. Before he struck out, Keating tried several schemes, including a shameless crib from a triple-roofed tower by Philip Johnson in Houston.

Then he proposed a pitched roof, but the planners said that there are now enough pitched roofs and pyramids south of Market Street, and someone (probably we will never know who) glanced toward another Hedman-influenced building at New Montgomery and Market streets, where a "pickle-sticker" from a World War I German helmet surmounts a malproportioned clock tower. So now we have a second pickle-sticker.

February 15, 1988

■ EIGHTEEN DECENT FLOORS OF ART DECO REVIVAL — THEN POW!

The Art Deco revival, beloved by yuppies at Jazz Age dress-up balls and by almost everyone else who prefers style to substance, finally has produced its first San Francisco highrise.

Capped by still another of the Post-Modern "hats" that litter the skyline at the behest of our coercive city planners, the 24-story office building at 505 Montgomery Street turns out to be a very strange facsimile of 1920s design.

Up through the 18th floor, the gray granite-clad shaft is suave Deco, or something close to it, and a very creditable addition to the cityscape. Then — Pow! — a totally unrelated, very un-Deco, but quasi–Second Empire mansard of silvery metal and glass has been piled on top of the building, adding six more floors of rental space.

As if this were not enough, a gleaming 100-foot spire, thinning to a needle, is simply stuck on the top-heavy tower, looking rather like a Moderne cigaret lighter.

Why anyone, least of all the once-great Modernist firm of Skidmore, Owings & Merrill, should have thought such pseudohistorical parodies could stand comparison with the city's wonderful romantic "skyscrapers" of half a century ago is baffling.

Timothy Pflueger's Pacific Telephone Building of 1925 and his medical-dental building at 450 Sutter Street, finished in 1930, are often described as Art Deco, but they are essentially Modern buildings enlivened by very original ornamentation. They are also beautifully ordered, with consistent vertical lines from the bottom to their flat tops.

The point is, they were not trying to imitate the past but to inaugurate the future. And it is worth noting that because of the architecturally subliterate notions of City Planning Director Dean Macris and his guru bureaucrats, Pflueger's buildings could not be built the same way today.

By paradox, however, 505 Montgomery Street was actually designed in 1984, a year before the draconian Downtown Plan took effect. Even then, however, the city planners had "interim controls" that could hold up projects for years.

Skidmore, Owings & Merrill, already turning Post-Mod, willingly went along.

So the building was chopped into two parts. At the 19th floor, without any transition except some skimpy granite finials, the uppermost six stories slant back, as if sliced with a knife, stepping up in tiers in the center, tapering straight back on the ends.

The steep, vaguely 19th-century shapes — a little like the Napoleonic roofs of the Louvre — are no more true mansards than Philip Johnson's and John Burgee's weird Victorian roof of black-tinted glass only a block away, at 595 California.

Viewed together, say from Portsmouth Square, it is hard to decide which is the odder confection, or whether Skidmore, Owings & Merrill, once above such things, may not have cribbed Johnson's idea.

At this stage, it is impossible to say and doesn't matter much because both designs show contemporary architects ransacking historical forms they don't fully understand and don't really feel.

Skidmore, Owings & Merrill's mansard is "cleaner," as architects say, but also is festooned with the spire, stuck on without any architectural preparation for a drastic change in form, that outdoes all the other rooftop protuberances that the planners have attached to buildings, making them unusable by helicopters in an emergency.

This "communications spire" is 505 Montgomery's *pièce de résistance* and, taken alone, the shiny aluminum tube (painted with a remarkable metallic paint called Duranor) can be seen as an ingenious period-piece sculpture concealing an altogether modern antenna.

Yet it is primarily there for looks, in a cheeky reference to great American architecture of six decades ago.

According to Larry Doane, the senior Skidmore, Owings & Merrill partner who headed the design team, 505 Montgomery Street attempts nothing less than to capture "the spirit of such classic Art Deco landmarks as the Chrysler Building or the Empire State Building in New York."

Whew! Apart from the fact that those supertowers of 60 years ago are 1,000 feet high and more — and that the ascent of the needle-pointed Chrysler Tower, especially, is beautifully developed over the last 300 feet of its rise in great fan-shaped forms of silvery metal, diminishing in graceful curves until it narrows in a single magnificent line that pierces the sky — those structures' power and refinement, their fearlessness, confidence and joy, cannot be simulated by this stumpy, disjointed parody of the real thing.

This is not to say that Skidmore, Owings & Merrill hasn't done well with other aspects of 505 Montgomery. It is not an affront to the city on the scale of another parody of the Chrysler Building — the nearly completed jukebox of a Marriott Hotel at Fourth and Mission streets, where the Art-Deco fan shapes are done in silver mirror glass.

Maybe it would have been better (although less profitable) to have dispensed with the top of 505 Montgomery. At close range, seen down Montgomery or Sacramento Street, where the uppermost six stories and spire are out of sight, the shaft has an urbane dignity.

A strong sense of order is established by the five-foot width of both the smooth masonry uprights and the windows of gray-tinted glass. The tailored stonework is far superior to the average speculative dreck on this edge of the financial district, the proportions surer than Skidmore, Owings & Merrill's adjacent Bank of Canton, in reddish granite, whose lines are matched by 505 Montgomery's in a subtle and sensitive way.

The handling of the base is admirable. Done in lighter granite than the walls above, its mood is patrician but cordial. To either side of the lofty central portal, set off by vertical strips of stone that move inward from either side toward the bronze doors, are spaces for a bank (now under construction) and a high-ceilinged store that is still to come.

Their large windows, nicely framed, are surmounted by wonderful grills of gray-painted aluminum — Art Deco's preferred ornamental metal, which was excitingly new in the 1920s.

The curving and zigzagging patterns at first may be puzzling, but they turn out to be logos of "505," the building's address, with the first "5" reversed, in a playful visual game that recalls the zest and wit of Art Deco at its apogee.

Credit for these virtues, I'd say, should go largely to Steve O'Brien, the project designer, and Skidmore, Owings & Merrill's highly talented graphic designer Debra Nichols. If they have done well with the exterior ornamentation, they have teamed up inside to create a stunning tour de force of an entrance hall, 25 feet high, whose lavish materials could have looked flashy but here are controlled with extreme refinement.

The walls are done in polished Rosso Levanto marble, a deeply veined burgundy surface, in which there are flowing traces of green. The floor, also highly polished, is inlaid with the same Rosso Levanto and five other varicolored marbles, set off by a border of a polished granite called absolute black.

All this is complemented by metalwork of the utmost beauty in "nickel silver" — actually an alloy of 10 percent nickel, 25 percent zinc and 65 percent copper, which gives it warmth — that has been used for the sconces and elevator doors, and combined with lovely African mahogany in the elevator cabs.

The "505" theme is repeated, played with, leavening the richness with humor, and it would be richer still if the cast-plaster ceiling, painted a flat gold for reasons of economy, had been finished in gold leaf as the desig-ners wished.

The only mistake is to have put up three creamy paintings of the 1920s by the late Robert Boardman Howard, which must have been enchanting in the Telegraph Hill dining room for which they were meant, but here are overwhelmed.

Yet for once, in this extraordinary space, Skidmore, Owings & Merrill's boast of recalling the Chrysler Building does not seem a pretense. Had they only started out freshly, without preconceptions, as William Van Alen did at the Chrysler in 1928, they could have been closer to lasting significance, perhaps to greatness. But that would require freedom which, in Post-Mod San Francisco, architects no longer possess.

April 25, 1989

Oakland Harbor, Oakland, California, 1978. By Pete Breinig. Courtesy The San Francisco Chronicle.

IV. Architecture of Transit

■ LET'S BUILD A SPLENDID BRIDGE!

The proposed $65 million San Mateo-Hayward Bridge, like the present crossing which was completed in 1929, will be one of the longest structures in the world, measuring more than 11 miles from end to end.

Because of the magnitude of the bridge, which will be visible over great distances of the southern bay, its appearance — not merely to those viewing it from afar, but also those crossing it — is of the upmost importance to this part of California.

Yet even though the Golden Gate and Bay bridges have set the highest standard of visual splendor for the people of this region, fine appearance evidently was not one of the objectives of the utilitarian state engineers — the same engineers responsible for the Richmond-San Rafael Bridge — who have once again produced a lamentably mediocre design.

The one possible justification for this mediocrity is low cost, but this technologically old-fashioned bridge may well cost $5 million too much.

Obviously a different kind of bridge should be erected, but before the alternatives open to the state engineers are discussed, their own scheme must be studied in some detail.

The new bridge will closely follow the doglegged route of the old lift-span crossing, which veers southward as it negotiates the main ship channel near the San Mateo shore.

By far the longer portion of the dogleg is the eight-mile, low-level concrete trestle which will serve as the approach from the Hayward shore on the east. The design of this causeway is far from distinguished, but nevertheless competent; and its main shortcoming — the retention of the small 30-foot interval between piles which was considered feasible back in the '20s — is justified by the engineers on the basis of economy.

This arrangement allows them to leave the old decaying piles inside and between the new ones, rather than going to the expense of removing them (for if they were out of line, they would have to be removed as a menace to navigation). Thus the old wooden piles will remain beneath the trestle, like rotting teeth, until they finally disintegrate.

The new trestle, in any case, is already under construction, having been rushed ahead in something of the manner of a potentially controversial freeway.

The approach is not of crucial importance, however, for it can be used in connection with many types of high-level bridges, including single-decked spans, rather than the proposed double-decker if only the links with the main span are slightly changed. At present these links are designed in much the same way that the approaches of the Richmond-San Rafael Bridge split into two levels as they join the high-level structure.

And it is precisely this double-decker that requires total redesigning.

This tremendous structure, two-and-a-half miles long, will ascend gradually in a series of 300-foot spans, finally attaining a height of 135 feet above the water as it crosses the ship channel in a very substantial main span of 750 feet.

Even from the single, poor drawing of this design which the state engineers have thus far released, its structural premise is easy to understand. The zigzag trusses, tying together the upper and lower decks, could be imitated with an Erector set. So standard are these structural forms that the engineer in charge, Norman C. Raab, concedes that the trusswork could be virtually "ordered from a shop."

Now, quite apart from the structural efficiency of such a system, which conceptually is not much different from that of several famous 19th-century bridges, it is also easy to see what such a concept means in visual terms to anyone crossing on the lower level.

Very simply, it denies the traveler the exhilarating experience of passing high above one of the loveliest bays in the world by crudely fencing him in on either side, and placing a barrier between him and the sky.

This is closer to the oppressive confinement of a tunnel than to the open delight of a fine bridge.

The Richmond-San Rafael Bridge, Mr. Raab's *chef-d'oeuvre* until he tried his hand at this one, has already performed this perverse trick of shutting off the view for half the people crossing it. That the engineer should have been allowed by the Bridge Authority to repeat this folly is a disgraceful lapse of responsibility on the part of his superiors.

Why did Mr. Raab adopt this concept? A captious critic might point out that the state engineers have long hated views, and have perversely erected needlessly high barriers on the sides of most of their bridges. This is not for purposes of structural stability, but ostensibly for the sake of safety. A motorist dreamily glancing at the sunlit waters might drift into a crash.

But who knows if this is true? Bridges throughout the world have lacy, almost transparent balustrades which permit generous views of the passing scenery. One wonders if they have less impressive safety records than our half-blind spans.

But the engineers have another safety argument. Twin decks, carrying traffic in opposite directions, without question would prevent head-on collisions.

Yet head-on collisions may be effectively prevented by other means, such as median strips which embellish well-designed freeways.

Still, the engineers could answer in turn: Yes, but that would make a wider — and therefore more expensive — structure. For twin decks, each carrying three lanes of traffic, do not require the broader supporting pier that a single six-lane roadway would.

If bridge design is approached traditionally, as is lamentably the case in Mr. Raab's bureaucratic bailiwick, then this theory is sound enough from an economic point of view, although surely not justified in any aesthetic sense.

For nothing is more magnificent in a bridge than a ribbonlike roadway, sensitively drawn across space in an effortless gesture. There are bridges around the world which prove, in both steel and concrete, that this is no more expensive to achieve than Mr. Raab's maze of heavy girders.

As early as the 1930s, a group of brilliant German bridges showed the formidable strength, beauty and economy of ribbon structures built of steel plate girders. Vertical stiffeners divided these horizontal girders in delicately etched surface patterns, as in the masterpiece built at Siebenlehen in 1938. By 1944 American engineers had produced a comparable design for the Tennessee Valley Authority in the span over Fontana Reservoir in North Carolina.

An analogous concept in steel might have been admirably appropriate for the San Mateo-Hayward Bridge, and may yet prove to be the most handsome and economical solution to the problem of its design. The United States, of course, is the pre-eminent steel-producing nation, and it has usually made good sense to employ this wonderfully strong, light and flexible material in large bridges in this country.

Up to now its chief rival, concrete, has been generally considered too heavy for high-level crossings above large bodies of water, if only because it requires much more extensive foundation work.

At least this is still Mr. Raab's thinking, for he states that "unless there are hillsides or cliffs to provide natural abutments for each construction, concrete is feasible only in small spans of about 100 feet."

How preposterous this notion is today, how outmoded is Mr. Raab's appreciation of concrete as well as his appreciation of steel, can be seen in the remarkable bridge of prestressed concrete (an altogether different material than traditionally reinforced concrete) which is now being erected over Lake Maracaibo in Venezuela.

This daring design by the Italian engineer Riccardo Morandi won an international competition over several impressive rivals, including a concept in steel submitted by U.S. engineers. Its central spans of 771 feet each are seven times longer than Mr. Raab considers practicable in a high structure, and, indeed, are longer than the main span of Mr. Raab's own bridge.

But Mr. Raab never seriously considered the use of prestressed concrete — never even prepared an alternative design in this material to see if it might have proved cheaper. He might have been surprised to the tune of $5 million. This is the cost of his Paleolithic viewpoint.

October 17, 1961

■ COLOSSAL BOONDOGGLE:
SAN FRANCISCO'S AIRPORT MESS

All that is maddeningly incompetent, stupidly complacent, brutally insensitive and almost incredibly extravagant in San Francisco — a city that perhaps did "know how" to build in William Howard Taft's time, but would be hard-pressed to erect a decent municipal doghouse today — is epitomized in our "New Era Airport," which in fact is one of the most old-fangled, inconvenient and wastefully designed air facilities in the nation.

As a gateway to San Francisco, it should be blazoned with the inscription of Dante's Inferno: "Abandon all hope, ye that enter."

For if this is the best we can do in the way of large public works that, precisely because of their staggering cost, are supposed to serve long-time needs, we had better give up hope for the future environment in this part of the world.

Rather than inaugurating a new era, this sprawling assemblage of malconceived and coarsely executed structures is already obsolete. Almost certainly the entire terminal — which even in its unfinished state measures about a half a mile from end to end, and may yet be extended farther — will have to be extensively rebuilt if not totally demolished when the supersonic jets go into operation.

Yet by rough estimate the city has thus far sunk nearly $45 million in terminal and parking facilities alone, and the end is not in sight.

The Public Utilities Commission — a veritable citadel of mediocrity — is cheerfully prepared to spend as much again, or more, to complete the "master plan," which to me is not a plan at all, but a gross improvisation at the taxpayers' expense.

Surely this colossal boondoggle warrants a Grand Jury investigation, such as the one which yielded such fascinating information concerning the genesis of the late Charles Harney's multimillion-dollar beauty, Candlestick Park.

But the public is entitled to know who, precisely, made the efforts which saddled the city with the most unwieldy airport of its size in the country, and why a comparable metropolis, Washington, D.C., obtained at substantially lower cost a resplendent terminal in every way vastly superior to our own.

Above all, we should find out what is wrong with the building procedures of the city government, and try to set them right before more damage is perpetrated.

For in recent years we have been suffering from an onslaught of architectural butchery that might be likened to a St. Bartholomew's Day Massacre, administered by self-righteous hacks.

The airport, in truth, is merely one of a series of so-called civic improvements — the Geary Street expressway is another, and so is the new Hall of Justice, which is the most unjust building in town — which are really public excrescences.

What sort of mentality leads to these civic disasters, anyway, even though the structures are designed by a variety of architectural and engineering firms?

Because the airport is really a collection of poorly related buildings, some of which have been extensively modified by different hands over the past decade, it illustrates perfectly the kind of thinking — or rather, the lack of thought — which results in consistent banality.

The airport's history goes back to 1927, but its dramatic expansion took place after World War II when, in terms of passenger volume, it became the fourth-ranking terminal in the United States.

To serve this ever-increasing traffic, the main terminal — now the "central" terminal between the recently completed south terminal and the still unbuilt north terminal foreseen in the master plan — was dedicated in 1954.

For reasons that remain cloudy, this significant commission was entrusted to a little-known, aging architect of the old school, William E. Day, who was unable to see the job through, and had to receive help from the equally conservative firm of Loubet & Glyn.

The heavy structure these worthies produced is a monument to pseudomonumentality. Perhaps the best description yet offered for its nondescript architecture is "Century of Progress Modern" — a hopelessly dated pastiche dragged out of the '30s.

But the building had the additional disadvantage of being extremely expensive: It cost $14.1 million at a time when construction was much cheaper than today. This is only one of the large sums which have a way of creeping into the history of the airport every few years.

Another disadvantage was that it proved hopelessly inadequate for travel in the jet age. Over the space of a few years it has been remade again and again. Its courts have been enclosed. Its fingers have been extended, and extended again, so that the longest now reaches out something like a tenth of a mile.

These improvements, generally executed more cheaply than the original building itself, have nevertheless come to $5 million to date, making a total of nearly $20 million, which would seem a rather stiff price for a bewildering, cluttered structure which is a torment to the traveler who is trying to catch a plane.

The interior renovations still to be executed by architect Edward B. Page may give it a somewhat more acceptable appearance (if the airport authorities can be persuaded to control the shoddy commercialism of the concessionaires) but at present it has the civic dignity of a penny arcade and the architectural substance of a tent show.

Would it not have been logical, when it became obvious in the late '50s that a different solution would be needed for the airport's total requirements, to have scrapped this white elephant instead of throwing good money after bad?

This would appear to have been one of the alternatives open to the new consultants, Welton Becket & Associates, when they took over the job in 1957 and were asked to develop the master plan.

If they ever made such a recommendation, it has been lost in the files of the bureaucracy; and there is every reason to believe that, had such a suggestion been broached, it would not have been very enthusiastically received by the Public Utilities Commission.

Instead these Los Angeles architects, who did a much more creditable job at their own city's airport than at ours, simply adapted a concept of the traffic engineers, and decided to wrap a tremendous, curving tripartite terminal around the most enormous parking structure in the world.

As a paper exercise in curvilinear geometry, this diagrammatic site development may appear ingenious.

As a three-dimensional reality, however, it is a traveler's nightmare, in which he is compelled by the design itself to negotiate enormous distances, either through the vast morgue for automobiles or around it, walking hundreds — even thousands — of feet through dreary passages which were built as cheaply as possible because they yield few revenues from the ubiquitous concessionaires whom the airport management has foolishly allowed to crowd the main terminal structures.

As a civic design, the Becket master plan ruins the entire approach to the airport, for the garage will swell over the infield like a gigantic tumor.

Almost surely a much better solution to the parking problem could have been achieved, and this airport — like Dulles in Washington, or Kennedy in New York, or Orly in Paris — could have been approached on landscaped parkways.

Beyond this, however, the garage — like the terminals — does not seem to be much of a bargain in terms of cost, although its private operators may find it a very good thing. Its first segment, with a capacity of 2,850 cars, will cost $10 million when completed, and there are two more segments to come before the ultimate capacity of 8,000 cars is reached.

So far as I can see, the garage has a single advantage: It is being built in stages, and if it is decided to rebuild the entire terminals complex, it may be possible to integrate this immense concrete structure with some radically different terminal design.

But sooner or later — probably sooner than the Public Utilities Commission dares to contemplate — the terminals will have to come down, not only the original, elephantine main terminal which should have been destroyed five years ago, but the even more unfortunate south terminal designed by the Becket firm which was opened last fall.
April 20, 1964

■ ARCHITECTURE IN TRANSIT: BART

During the 1975 holiday season, as an unexpected gift to disgruntled taxpayers, the Bay Area Rapid Transit District's silver trains have finally begun running late at night and on Saturdays, gliding into stations that now give some idea of how well they may perform if the 75-mile system ever starts to operate at full capacity. Whatever the virtues and shortcomings of this wildly uneven group of 38 stations which have been designed by no less than 15 different architectural firms of very mixed abilities, their faults seem almost negligible when compared with the disastrous mechanical breakdowns that still prevent BART — half a decade behind schedule and hundreds of millions in the red — from providing swift and reliable service every day of the year.

For even though BART's most dangerous problems seem to have been solved, such as the opening of doors while trains are traveling at full speed, stoppages remain frequent, shutting down the entire system for an hour or so at a time and causing a good deal of nervousness among passengers stuck in the tunnel beneath the bay. But at least the brakes appear to work now, so that the luxurious air-conditioned cars — furnished almost to airline specifications with upholstered seats and carpeted floors — no longer roll past the 700-foot platforms without stopping.

Nevertheless, because the automatic controls can't be trusted, intervals of two stations must be maintained between trains. No train leaves a station until assurance is given by telephone that the tracks are clear ahead. This method is about as efficient as having an aged brakeman on the last car, swinging a red lantern. Travelers are thus accustomed to long waits on the platform: a minimum of 12 minutes, but often more, instead of the 90-second headways between trains once loftily promised by the engineers.

All this is not by way of banter at the expense of hapless technocrats, but crucial to any discussion of the architecture of the stations themselves, which are basically the work of the same engineers who perpetrated BART's technical calamities and crushing expense. Although BART's publicity makes much of the diversified team of architects, some with considerable reputations, who ostensibly designed the stations, these worthies discovered soon after they were hired that their job was mainly to apply finishes and install entrances to structures whose basic configurations had been frozen years before.

BART, in fact, has always had not 15 different architects, but a single faceless master designer: Parsons, Brinkerhoff, Tudor, Bechtel, a consortium of three enormous engineering bureaucracies which set the parameters for station design back in the 1950s. At that time supposedly preliminary concepts for prototypical stations were published to help sell the voters the largest local bond obligation in history, amounting to $793 million.

But the crude sketches, which took almost no cognizance of the personal experience of a traveler beyond his simple physical movement from place to place and still less notice of the tremendous impact the stations would have on the surrounding urban fabric, somehow hardened into very nearly final designs. Apart from relatively minor features, such as the opening of light wells in underground stations and capping of some elevated structures with rather silly roofs, the finished stations of the 1970s bear an eerie resemblance to their ghostly predecessors of 20 years ago.

Sic transit gloria mundi, or at least the potential glory of Bay Area transit.

Yet when this is said, it must be granted that — by the standards of older systems — BART's stations, like the gleaming, malfunctioning trains themselves, appear positively opulent. But, then again, the Bay Area is not the Bronx. There may be more marble in Moscow, more granite in Montreal, and for all I know more mosaics in Mexico City, but nothing like this array of stainless steel, high-performance escalators, closed circuit TV, special lifts for the handicapped, and — most striking of all — lavish allocations of space.

There cannot, for instance, be many more elegantly detailed — or, for the present emptier — concourses than in the very finest BART stations, such as Skidmore, Owings & Merrill's (SOM) Montgomery and Powell street stops in downtown San Francisco. Some 80 percent of BART's passengers pass through these big multilevel facilities, which serve the financial, shopping and entertainment districts of the metropolitan core.

Eventually they will be joined by thousands of commuters from outer San Francisco neighborhoods who now use surface trolleys and buses, which were supposed to be replaced already by new vehicles of the Municipal Railway (now officially called Muni). Unfortunately that violence-plagued organization is even more badly managed than BART and more woefully behind schedule, so that its new trains — which are just undergoing preliminary tests — will certainly not begin running on the intermediate level, just above BART's, for another couple of years.

Perhaps SOM's stations will then come into their own, with large crowds following directional patterns of the fine terrazzo paving and admiring the round columns (of which I'll have more to say later) sheathed in stainless steel, as well as whole walls of stainless steel and hung luminous ceilings — almost as suave as an office building's — which now extend in seemingly endless perspective, like a de Chirico anxiety painting, with their festive multicolored concessionaire's booths closed, and many of the pay telephones removed from their handsome mountings, for want of business.

But SOM's was only one of many approaches to BART station design, even though it is by all odds the most polished. Unlike Washington, D.C., where Harry Weese is unifying the whole system in a consistent structural and spatial idiom whose monumental power is by no means inappropriate to the Baroque national capital, BART has carried on a Bay Area tradition — dubbed "humanism" by local regionalists — of staging an architectural free-for-all. In political terms this is also called splitting the pie.

Quite deliberately, with the blessings of BART's officialdom, each of the 15 firms has gone off on its own tack (within the limits, of course, of the largely decorative role assigned to them by the engineers). There are certain standardized elements common to all the stations, to be sure, such as the quite decent stainless steel information booths and refuse containers, done by the late Tallie Maule when he was BART's in-house architect. So, too, are the escalators and all of the fare collection equipment, including ticketing and change-making machines which at first are baffling to operate, even for people who can read, but on which IBM nevertheless did a very creditable job of physical presentation.

Most of the standardized graphics, especially the directional signs by Ernest Born, are also extremely civilized, even though the suspended signs, fitted with bulbous swivel joints because of seismic code requirements, should have been studied more carefully. The maps are pleasantly legible and have been well-mounted in many different ways throughout the system, sometimes outstandingly well, as in SOM's luminous piers that also contain concealed utility lines.

Apart from these common features, however, it has been every architect for himself — good, bad and indifferent — and often with a vengeance, as if to exemplify Mies van der Rohe's dictum (paraphrased slightly) that one can't "invent a new kind of transit architecture every Monday morning." But the Bay Area architects have done their damnedest to try. Each of them has concocted a different warning strip for his platform edges, for example, none of which approaches the distinction of Weese's standard granite detail in Washington.

One wonders what BART might have been had an architect of stature been invited, like Harry Weese in Washington, to participate in its planning and design from an early conceptual stage onward. For surely, this vast project reveals nothing so much as the prevailing uncertainty of the architectural profession, which is further aggravated when even gifted practitioners use trivial gestures — overblown spaces, melodramatic roof structures and bewildering assortments of surface materials — which clamor for admiration but leave one with the impression that the architect has attempted to pit his oversensibility against insensate engineering, and lost.

Now that the damage has been done, it is painful to consider how much better BART might have been if its fate had not been sealed so early by the engineers. Curiously enough, there was a fascinating last-ditch effort in the 1960s to inject serious conceptual thought into the diagrams of the technocrats. Don Emmons, partner in the preeminent "regionalist" firm of Wurster, Bernardi & Emmons, had been named chief architectural consultant to BART. (Mark the ineffectual title: He was never a supervising architect with strong independent powers.)

Emmons had relatively little experience in civic design on the order that a mammoth transportation system required, but he nevertheless realized that BART had committed colossal errors of omission. To his great credit, he engaged a young group of theoretical architects from the University of California at Berkeley, led by Christopher Alexander, to investigate what might be done even at so late a date. Their recommendations should now be a permanent part of architectural literature.

The Alexander team called for a complex set of linkages between the "closed" system of the transit line and the "open" cityscape so that the two could interpenetrate in a broad variety of spaces and structures: plazas, buildings, kiosks.

The research group also freshly examined BART's arbitrary design assumptions, including the fixed lengths of platforms and concourses, dimensions which had been largely culled — for no clear reason — from ancient subway systems elsewhere in the country.

In particular, the researchers questioned the necessity for the tremendous mezzanines in underground stations which now provide such forlorn vistas. They also publicly raised an issue — on practical grounds of ease of circulation and actual safety in case of panic or disaster — that had privately concerned the station architects for aesthetic reasons: Why, if BART's engineers were "the finest in the world" (as they were dubbed by their flacks), could they not dispense with their forest of columns, and instead clear-span the stations?

This was too much for the engineers. At their behest, the searching young architects were dismissed. But Emmons himself, weary of his ride on the tiger, and under attack in the press, resigned afterward. (He was replaced — if that is the word — by a new architectural "special advisor": the elderly John E. Burchard, dean emeritus of humanities at MIT.)

The city of San Francisco, alarmed by the timid engineers of the major stations, asked Professor T. Y. Lin to review their designs. His verdict was that they could be clear-spanned for a fraction of the extra $3 million each that BART insisted column-free space would cost. ("Take away a zero," said Professor Lin.) Nevertheless, the columns remained.

The public found itself confronted by a bureaucracy as arrogant, obstinate and in some ways more brutal than the state highway engineers who have devastated large parts of California. Only a town with exceptional environmental awareness such as Berkeley was able to oppose BART with some success. Understandably reluctant to split its increasingly multiracial community by an elevated structure running down its main street like a "Chinese wall," which would have had the added disadvantage of blighting its business district, Berkeley easily proved that BART's estimates for the undergrounding of its part of the system were outrageously inflated by engineers who could scarcely explain their own stubbornly defended figures.

The citizens of Berkeley voted to pay the comparatively modest cost of undergrounding themselves, and have never regretted it, and their central station by Mahar & Martens turned out better than most, set in a pleasant little brick plaza with a domed skylight capping its main entry. But this was a rare victory.

Unlike Berkeley, most places along the 75 miles of right-of-way — far too many miles, incidentally, for the initial phase of a regional system — lacked the sensitivity and political know-how to resist designs that epitomized the conventional wisdom of a previous generation. Every community receives the architecture it deserves, as Lewis Mumford has said, and that, alas, is what the Bay Area has been given by BART.

December 1975, *AIA Journal*

■ THE EXPENSIVE ERRORS IN THE FERRY BUSINESS

The white space frame of the Larkspur ferry terminal — the first sizable structure of its kind in the Bay Area — was intended by its architects to be a "symbolic" building, expressing the same technological optimism as the "jet age" ferries capable of reaching San Francisco in 32 minutes, and proclaiming a new standard of excellence, aesthetically and functionally, for urban water transportation throughout the world.

And certainly the lucid structure, immaculate and radiant as a vision of Buckminster Fuller, makes a striking sight as it comes into view across the waters — or at low tide, across the fragrant mudflats — of the degraded stretch of the northern bay between San Quentin and 101.

Compared with the extensive commercial and residential development that is now transforming the slummy Larkspur shoreline as a result of the new ferry service, the terminal is obviously a serious work of advanced architecture, courageously free of the woodsy traditionalism so dear to Marin residents that can already be seen in the office buildings rising just beyond on Wood Island.

Yet the fine first appearance of the terminal is bitterly deceiving.

Like the almost incredibly overpriced ferries themselves, so trim in profile, so erratic in performance, whose cost of $15 million for three vessels — one of which doesn't run — was three times more than expected, and whose skittish turbines consume enormous quantities of gas that will be infernally expensive in the future, the superficially handsome terminal building has also become a symbol of how much can go wrong in big bureaucratic technical fantasies, largely financed by the feds, but paid for by all of us.

Originally budgeted at $4.5 million, the terminal complex — including extensive channel construction, dredging, pile-driving and platform work to support the elegant superstructure — finally was bid at $13.9 million.

For this overrun Kaiser Engineers, supposedly experts in estimating large jobs, would seem to deserve more blame than the architects, Braccia, DeBrer & Heglund, a firm that has since broken up and reformed, with Jacques DeBrer — the highly talented chief designer — moving to Robert Marquis & Associates, where he continues to do ambitious work.

Ultimate responsibility for the financial fiasco, however, must go to the satraps of the Golden Gate Bridge, Highway, and Transportation District. Floating on a Niagara of bridge tolls, this insouciant and extravagant bureaucracy is reminiscent of BART, making all sorts of PR claims that can't be fulfilled, and malgoverned (as BART used to be) by nonelected directors who are virtually unanswerable to the public.

Yet when the Larkspur terminal is seen at its best, in bright summer weather, with sunlight playing over its beautifully articulated triangular frame, 192 feet long on each side, and lightly held aloft at three points, the architecture does seem to deliver all we had a right to hope for.

The three-sided form makes sense because of the configuration of the docking facilities, which are meant to take two ferries at a time — one loading, the other discharging passengers — while the third side, sheltered by the great canopy of the roof, provides a gracious entry for the large crowds who someday can be expected to use the system.

Not only did architect DeBrer hit upon the happy idea of the space-frame structure — which can be described, with some simplifications, as an exceptionally light and efficient system of multidimensional trusses — but he also detailed the rest of the composition with admirable consistency, continuing the triangular structural theme (itself made up of small triangles) in three-sided paving, planter beds, seating areas, and even chamfered turnstiles and other minor elements that are extremely well thought out in formal architectural terms.

The ticket booth, restrooms and small staff kiosk have all been deftly integrated in this angular scheme, enhanced by mirror-glass facing (an easy surface to clean) which provides a delightful play of reflection in the light softly filtering through the Plexiglas domes of the space-frame roof, some 35 feet overhead.

The cheerful colors — white and strong blue — add to an appropriate nautical effect.

All this holds true, however, only on fair days. In cold, rainy weather — of which we had a spell last week — the unenclosed space frame (covered only on top) is invaded by stiff breezes that sweep across the water, or down from Tamalpais; and the terminal becomes a veritable Temple of the Winds.

A few inadequate glass screens do nothing to mitigate passengers' discomfort, which might not have been too serious if the ferries actually departed, as planned, every 15 minutes. But they happen to leave 40 minutes apart, which can be a mighty long wait with the rain in your face.

Even on sunny days, when the wind blows, it can be seen that an expensive mistake has been made by not shielding the waiting area; at $1.2 million for the space-frame alone, it is the costliest sun-shade on earth.

Architect DeBrer explains that the bridge authorities did not ask for an enclosed structure; and if they had, he would have designed an altogether different structure, for a space frame of this size would encounter serious wind problems — necessitating a much heavier building — if it were, say, walled with glass.

Perhaps DeBrer would have come up with something on the order of the three-sided maintenance building a short distance away which is not nearly so convincing as the terminal itself. Although detailed, again, with considerable skill, it is really a silly shape for a workshop, and more reasonably should have been square.

What to do about the exposed terminal? Ferry Chief Stan Kowleski says that his own staff will design temporary screens to go up beneath the space frame in wet weather, for he confidently assumes that he has "the in-house talent to do the job."

I advise against it. The district's hacks can't even put up a decent suicide-prevention barrier on the great Golden Gate Bridge itself, which they have disfigured with chain-link fencing.

In fairness, DeBrer should be given a chance to correct this mistake, which he can do at low cost and with much more skill.

After a visit to Larkspur, it is good to take a ferry ride to San Francisco, not merely to have a drink on the blue water, but to examine the design of the vessels by naval architect Phillip F. Spaulding of Seattle.

Without having the rakish lines of yachts, these aluminum-hulled little ships are neat enough; and, as in almost all nautical construction, their hardware and instrumentation are handsome. The interior furnishings by Walter Landor & Associates, however, fall far below this level. They stop just short of schlockiness, although perhaps they reach it in the pseudoteak plastic laminate bars. But they display the ineffable blandness of commercial art, with which the same designers create marketing devices for banks, breakfast foods, beer, and the buses of both Muni and the bridge district.

After this rehearsal of failure, I'm happy to report that the bridge district at last seems to be doing a better job on the San Francisco ferry terminal that is going up on the Bart "breather" platform just south of the old Ferry Building.

Here the architects, Environmental Planning and Design Associates, whose chief designer is Roland B. Mays, have wisely eschewed a Great Architectural Statement, and instead have come up with a modest building that shows a direction the entire ferry system might have taken.

In a sense Mays had no choice here. The colossal outlay at Larkspur wiped out the chance of any luxuries in San Francisco, just as it has apparently erased all chances of building any kind of terminal in Sausalito for the time being.

But he has come up with a structure in concrete, spanned by light steel trusses inspired by the metal and glass covering of the old Ferry waiting rooms. Mays hoped to cover the lofty slanting spaces, 27 feet high at their topmost point, and 17 on the lower side, with a festive roof of glass. Instead, for reasons of false economy (since a glass covering would not have cost much extra), it will be opaquely enclosed in steel.

The rest of the building, however, can be opened and closed according to the weather by movable glass walls. Some aspects of the design may not stand up to exacting scrutiny: the superstructure sits rather awkwardly on the concrete colonnade; the proportions are squat — at least on the side of the pier facing the water, where the roof seems more like a lid than an emphatic top of a building. It is hard to gauge the success of rather plain materials and finishes at this early stage of construction.

But if it is not a poetic building — as Larkspur had a chance to be —

it is sane transportation architecture, in which large crowds will be accommodated comfortably; and there is an aesthetic and functional lesson in this not only for the bridge district's bureaucrats, but for everyone still beguiled with inflated notions of Yankee know-how and technocratic infallibility.

October 31, 1977

■ A POETIC CONQUEST OF SPACE

By now the Golden Gate Bridge is recognized everywhere as a classic work of structural art. The great reddish web of steel, profiled against a panorama of hills and sky and open sea, has become as profound a symbol of its time and place as the Parthenon or Notre Dame. It's our closest equivalent to a cathedral, if only because it expresses the American will — our national ethos — with a grandeur, grace and almost mythic strength that earlier civilizations reserved for shrines.

That a technical feat should be an emblem of spiritual aspiration, comparable to religious architecture, is not so strange when the bridge is seen as a poetic conquest of space. Many medieval bridges, such as the Pont D'Avignon, were designed with chapels to celebrate the safety and beauty of the arched crossings. Famous bridge builders, such as the monk-engineer Benezet at Avignon, were sainted for their pious labors.

In that historical context, the Golden Gate Bridge must be counted a miracle. Flung up against winds and tide, shaken by earthquakes in the midst of construction, the clear span of 4,200 feet was an act of faith, at a time when people still believed in machines and the idea of progress. In the depths of the Depression, the bridge demonstrated that an amalgam of Yankee know-how, fearless enterprise and free thought could solve any problem, surmount any obstacle, with the intelligence and energy that carried the nation forward on Walt Whitman's Open Road.

The bridge thus is best seen as a community achievement at a particular moment in history. No other monument better sums up the closing phase of the industrial age, even though Rockefeller Center, Boulder Dam and the Bay Bridge — a formidable local rival with twin main spans of 2,310 feet each — were built at almost the same time.

None of those mighty projects quite matched the bravura of this bridge of bridges. The Golden Gate's main span, carrying lighter loads on its single deck, is almost as long as the Bay Bridge's pair of double-decked suspension spans. At more than four-fifths of a mile across open water, it represents a quantum leap beyond its nearest rival, the 3,500-foot George Washington Bridge above the Hudson River, whose original single deck, of unparalleled elegance, linked New York and New Jersey in 1831. The George Washington itself had more than doubled the 1,595-foot Brooklyn Bridge, completed in 1883, which easily eclipsed all previous metal suspension spans going back to the early 19th century.

The Golden Gate capped this series of heroic accomplishments, and the wonder is how long its supremacy has lasted. Spans of more than 5,000 feet are being planned in Japan and elsewhere; and thanks to high-strength steels and other new materials and new techniques, it is theoretically feasible to increase the distance to 10,000 feet or more.

Nonetheless, the main span of the Golden Gate after 50 years is still the third longest in the world. It was surpassed only marginally in 1964, by only 60 feet, by the 4,260-foot Verrazano in New York, which may have been stretched to set a record. Not until 1981 did the Humber Crossing in Britain achieve 4,626 feet, inaugurating a new phase of bridge building with huge towers of reinforced concrete rather than steel.

Yet those powerful 510-foot uprights are not so lofty as the Golden Gate's, which at 746 feet above water level remain the tallest bridge towers ever built. That's because the Humber estuary does not accommodate big ships, and the bridge's clearance is 89 feet, whereas the deck structure of the Golden Gate, clearing the channel by more than the official figure of 220 feet (it's actually closer to 235 feet), admits aircraft carriers and other very large vessels.

But statistics mean less than the incalculable beauty of the bridge. And this turns out to be much more than sound engineering.

Much of its glamour seems due to the sweeping natural splendor of its emplacement. Yet Ansel Adams — no friend of technology in opposition to nature — said that the bridge improved the Golden Gate. The entrance to the Bay offered a "rather dull vista," he told me, before the tensed form of the bridge turned it into a spectacular portal; and his photographs prove the point.

The grand symmetry of the bridge seems almost perfectly wedded to the irregular site. This is all the more remarkable because the placement of the towers and the massive cable anchorages, especially on the southern side, was mainly dictated by geological considerations.

A stringent budget also affected aesthetics. The bridge's most serious flaw is the cumbersome triple-trussed arch framing Fort Point beneath its curve. The arched form is decent enough — far more handsome, say, than the cantilever section of the Bay Bridge — but it introduces a contradictory structural system where it is least wanted, interrupting what should have been a single smooth leap toward Marin. The arch was a thrifty expedient, to keep the main and side spans from growing even longer. If the bridge were built today, it could be easily lengthened, and the arch and its bulky piers omitted, or replaced by slender, widely spaced supports.

But at a distance the arch becomes almost a trifle in the majestic trajectory across the Gate. The main cables, 36 inches in diameter, are astonishingly fine for the enormous job they must perform. They lift in absolute confidence to the tops of the stepped-back towers, whose four rectangular openings diminish in size as they ascend, increasing the sense of height.

Then the cables swoop downward in a tremendous catenary, with a gathering impression of speed, almost touching the deck at mid-span, just short of the railing, before flying upward toward the opposite shore. There is no sign of strain or hesitation, only an unswerving statement of strength and decisiveness — the mark of a thrilling bridge.

This is perhaps the most exhilarating architectural experience ordinary people will ever enjoy; and it seems a pity to inform them that experts in such matters find the "sag" of the cables too deep and the roadway too low, although its height was unprecedented in a structure of this size.

Good engineers in the 1980s would almost routinely hang the main cables higher above the deck at mid-span, improving the proportions and emphasizing the extreme slenderness of the hanger ropes and the beautiful detailing of the clamps and connectors.

Another feature that can be criticized is the thick stiffening truss of the deck, 30 feet deep, which today could be replaced by a far less obtrusive aerodynamic structure tapering to thin edges.

In the 1930s, however, the heavy trusswork was not only prudent but indispensable. Wind stresses were not fully understood. At the end of the decade the disaster of the daring 2,800-foot Tacoma Narrows Bridge — "Galloping Gertie," which shook itself to death in a moderate wind — justified the conservatism of the Golden Gate's designers.

If anything, they underestimated the bridge's flexibility. Torsional problems appeared very early. In 1951 the span was briefly closed after it was slightly damaged in a storm. To dampen excessive movement, the truss was further stiffened by cross-bracing between its lower edges, changing the cross section from an inverted U into a rectangular form that engineer Charles Seim likens to a shoebox, although the lid could be torn off if it were not fastened as securely as the deck, which has recently been lightened by a new asphalt-surfaced steel roadway.

All this, and much more, underlies the structural drama of the bridge, everywhere intensified — glorified — by its romantic "International Orange" color, the inspired contribution of bridge architect Irving F. Morrow.

Having built hardly anything on his own before this, although he had worked for leading architectural firms, the sensitive and rather shy designer was recommended by artist friends to the overpowering chief engineer Joseph B. Strauss. Morrow may have been hired because he would work for low fees and looked like a man whom Strauss could master.

Instead, Morrow's magnificent charcoal rendering had a major effect on the finished design. The stepped-back forms of the towers had already been roughly determined, possibly by Strauss himself with the help of an earlier architectural consultant. They had nothing like the opulence of Morrow's decorative details, including the Art Deco brackets of the tower portals, which disguise structure but do amazing things with light and subtly enhance the scale of the entire span and its approaches.

The ribbed surfaces of the seemingly solid tower crossbars, for instance, conceal X-bracing beneath, which handles the structural loads. But the ornamental furrows create a soaring effect. Morrow continued this theme on the great concrete piers and the underpinnings of the towers, subtly softening ponderous forms. The open railings permit generous views of the bay, in contrast to the crude barriers of the Bay Bridge. The lighting standards were models for their time. The tall, curving toll booths, now being replaced, were beauties.

Yet the bridge's color is Morrow's noblest legacy. Variously described as a kind of vermilion, it is largely a mixture of orange and lamp black, which produces the burnt reddish-orange that responds so eloquently to changing light, in sunshine or mist, from soft dawn to violet twilight.

The success of Morrow's sculptural and painterly architecture almost precludes the question of whether the bridge might not have appeared still stronger, purer, more "honest," if rational engineered forms of the basic structure had been allowed to speak powerfully for themselves, without Morrow's operatic orchestration.

But there's no denying that the unjustly half-forgotten architect merged function and decoration in an extraordinary way. Precisely how he worked can be glimpsed in a rare show of his drawings, as well as correspondence and documents concerning the bridge, at the San Francisco chapter of the American Institute of Architects, 790 Market Street, until June 8.

By sorting out the roles of Strauss, Morrow, the superb engineering staff, intrepid work crews and a host of other talented people who designed and built the bridge, we are slowly arriving at an accurate historic record of the whole vast undertaking.

There was never any doubt that the masterly design was largely, if not entirely, the work of other hands than the chief engineer's. The question since the 1930s has been, whose?

The 50th anniversary has been an occasion for much squabbling over who did what, most recently in a kindly meant but misleading book, *The Gate* by John van der Zee (Simon and Schuster), which must be read with the utmost care.

Van der Zee has a double purpose. He not only is bent on denigrating the feisty, unlovable Joseph Strauss, an indomitable promoter who tried to hog credit for everything, but also has tried to elevate a rather obscure figure, Strauss' subordinate design engineer, Charles Alton Ellis, to the empyrean of structural art as the principal creator of the bridge, even though he never did anything else of nearly the same distinction.

The exhumation of Ellis is praiseworthy, since he was clearly an excellent engineer, but van der Zee's claim is made at the expense of the able Clifford E. Paine, chief assistant to Strauss, who before his death in 1983 told Harold Gilliam that he actually designed the bridge.

There must be truth in both these versions, but it cannot be the full truth. As van der Zee concedes, an infinitely great "genius" first proposed a 4,000-foot bridge for the Gate in 1925: Leon Solomon Moiseiff, one of the searching engineers of his generation, who later became the foremost member of the bridge advisory board and saw the design process though to the end, under separate contract to the Strauss engineering firm.

A concept of much grandeur seems utterly beyond the capacities of men like Strauss, Paine and Ellis. Yet each in his own way helped to make the idea a reality; and when the story is put in final perspective, by someone without an ax to grind, Strauss especially may fare better than his detractors suspect.

This difficult man, far more than anyone else, got the bridge built against daunting odds. His role was analogous to that of the "building bishops" of the Middle Ages, like Maurice de Sully at Notre Dame, who were not designers but who made the crucial decisions, and took tremendous risks, to create the cathedrals. Even if the Golden Gate Bridge does not last 1,000 years, much less "forever," as Strauss vowed it would, he should always be thanked for that.

May 22, 1987

■ A WORK OF ENGINEERING ART ON THE BAY

If you have correctly surmised that most "environmental" sculpture — palmed off by museums as modern art — is simply mindless junk, you owe yourself a trip to the greatest architectural sculpture show on the shores of the bay, performed by the colossal container cranes of the Port of Oakland.

They are astonishing machines, some of them A-frames 230 feet high (or as tall as a 23-story building), which can swiftly travel hundreds of feet down the long wharfs. They have revolutionized worldwide shipping since they were first developed 20 years ago by the Paceco Corp. (the old Pacific Coast Engineering Co.) of Alameda.

Oakland's giant gantries have simultaneously bankrupted outmoded, ill-managed ports such as San Francisco's (which belatedly bought a few container cranes, but lacks backup facilities). After the huge Port of New York, Oakland is the second largest container-handling facility in the United States, and the sixth busiest in the world.

It provides 69,000 jobs with an annual payroll of $1.14 billion in a city that has little else going for it economically. This suggests that the enterprising port officials, who also created the pleasant (but architecturally so-so) Jack London Square on the estuary, might take over the rest of Oakland, and put it all in the black.

Certainly they know how to run the thriving, tremendous port: a technological city-within-a-city whose chief monuments are the 16 great cranes, spaced at heroic intervals on the new concrete wharfs.

Together with the strikingly beautiful container ships moored alongside, these towering structures are perfect illustrations of the plainspoken nobility of pure industrial design — the impersonal art of engineers — which, as Le Corbusier complained long ago, are "what eyes don't see" in aesthetically illiterate modern society.

Motorists stalled on the Bay Bridge near the toll plaza rarely look southward a few hundred feet to what might be the mightiest composition in the whole harbor: the four towering A-frames of the SeaLand docks, whose steel frames, painted a hard black, present a formidable group of tall, changing profiles as they hoist their long booms to the vertical so they can change position beside the ships.

The A-frames are the more spectacular of the two main types of "Portainers" (as container cranes are called in the shipping industry). But the second, low-profile type, at 100, 120 or 125 feet only half the height of the A-frames, are equally interesting, and in many ways equally beautiful. Painted a strangely lyrical white, these work the docks farther south and west, in the flight pattern of Alameda's naval air strip, which made lower structures mandatory.

Each of the two types has advantages, and most ports have both nowadays; while both can be modified in an almost infinite variety of subtypes (which include some refinements that only engineers can understand), the principal difference between them is easy to spot.

The bridgelike boom of the A-frame is simply lifted when it would otherwise interfere with the masts or stacks of a ship, whereas the boom of the low-profile crane moves forward and backward, in deft reaching movements, on a horizontal axis within its supporting frame.

Otherwise they function similarly, if not identically. When the boom is in position above the ship, a "trolley" carrying the hoisting mechanism moves out above the containers stacked on deck or in the hatches.

With great rapidity — it is routine to move 250 containers in a single eight-hour shift — the container is lifted (in new models, two can be lifted at once); the trolley moves back, above a waiting vehicle or freight car, lowers the container, and resumes the operation. In loading a ship, the procedure is exactly the reverse.

At all times of day this dynamic technological tableau is thrilling enough, as the remarkable container-carrying vehicles, like enormous lumber carriers three and four stories high, barrel past on rubber tires beneath the cranes.

But at night, when banks of floodlights are turned on, transforming the wharfs into enormous stages of brilliance, the effect is overwhelming. Ship after ship moves into place, and the different kinds of cranes do their work.

It is worth studying the port at closer view, going down the raunchy old sailor's strip along Seventh Street (which can be reached easily by the Nimitz freeway or from the foot of Broadway) and following the BART elevated structure before the tracks go beneath the bay.

On the way, as if to prove how brutal and weak the architectural profession is these days, in contrast to the elegant strength of the engineers, it is worth looking at what may be the worst public building — and that's saying plenty — in all of Oakland: a mammoth concrete post office facility that resembles a block house on the Siegfried Line. I don't know who the perpetrators of this beauty were, but when priests commit mortal sin on this order they are unfrocked, and something similar might be done with architects [Note: it was perpetrated by Stone, Marraccini & Patterson.]

But then the industrial landscape takes over, and it is magical. Outside the Doran Co. works, which makes ships' propellers, there are always some of the superb solid bronze screws — quite reddish in the sunlight — and, to me at least, reminiscent of Brancusis.

Then the cranes appear on either side of the road. To the south is a haunched series of white low-profile frames made in England, serving United States Lines, American President Lines and other companies.

To the north a triad of Matson Line A-frames, painted gray and — in what is the real glory of the port — two new modified A-frames whose tops taper inward on all sides, painted immaculately in white. Every detail of these exhilarating structures — the lofty cab of the crane-operator nearly 200 feet overhead, the machinery house on the back of the boom, the stairs spiraling upward with extraordinary delicacy beside the massive legs of the great moving structure — adds up to an unforgettable picture of a world that is still rapidly evolving.

For the cranes are still being refined in innumerable ways. Their control systems are being computerized, so that the crane operator will no longer be a driver and lifter, but a "crane commander" who directs automated mechanism. These include touches as light as sensors, which will monitor the movements of ships as they lift and roll in the tide so that the movements of the crane will respond more quickly than if they were controlled by humans.

All this may lead eventually to unmanned — virtually unpeopled — sea terminals. But it seems unlikely, even if this were more practical or desirable, that these wonderful machines will ever cease to be part of a profound human experience, in which — like all fine art — they lift up our hearts.

This art even has a history. Down the estuary, on Alameda Island, the first container crane, created in 1958 by Paceco for Matson Lines, still stands. Now owned by Crescent Wharf & Warehouse, it is still in profitable use, still lovely — if such a word can be used for anything so strong, on the wharf just behind the Del Monte plants on Buena Vista Avenue. It should be declared a historical monument, for this is where it started, designed by engineers such as Murray M. Montgomery and Charles H. Zweifel, unknown except to other engineers. They gave us this structure, now painted a rather unfortunate green, but transformed to powerful black when seen from the east, against the afternoon sun. It should be saved, and painted white.

February 27, 1978

Way down in nethermost Oakland, at the foot of 16th Street, there is a railroad station so beautiful that even people who don't care much about architecture realize it once had something to do with civic pride.

Only 76 years have passed, not long for a classical monument, since the Beaux-Arts palazzo was completed in 1912 as a gesture of the Southern Pacific's (SP) confidence in the future of the city.

The three great arched windows, surmounting balustrades, cornices, architraves and Baroque escutcheons, perfectly symbolized Oakland's boosterish optimism and growing prosperity during the great age of railroading.

The building, like the surrounding neighborhood, has taken a beating since then. Battered, begrimed, betrayed even in ordinary maintenance by the SP since the 1950s, and abused just as badly after Amtrak took over in 1971, the station has been held together in recent decades only by the integrity of its construction and the fineness of its materials.

Yet it is essentially sound and can easily be put to right, even though pipes have burst and roofs leak so that the interior walls are crumbling in places and are everywhere soiled. It is hard to ruin a steel-framed building faced in Sierra granite and top-grade terra-cotta whose lofty waiting room is paved in California marble and furnished with great benches in solid oak.

Not that yahoos can't try.

Now that Amtrak and the Port of Oakland are thinking of building a better-located passenger station on First Street, across from Jack London Village, the challenge is to save the venerable station from being ruthlessly knocked down like an elderly person mugged in the street. [Note: the 1989 earthquake damaged the depot beyond repair.]

That fate will be all too possible once the SP transportation company, now merged with the Denver & Rio Grande, again gets its mitts on the monument. The SP still owns the property, leasing the building to Amtrak for a nominal charge. The SP's record in historic preservation is bleak, and the company is reportedly interested in "developing" the site.

The Oakland City Council had the wisdom to declare the station an official landmark in 1984, but even if it is placed on the national registry of historic monuments — which the SP may oppose — the building might still not be safe against a coalition of high-rolling Oakland pols and SP bottom-liners.

In other words, it is up to the people of Oakland — and of west Oakland in particular — to see what a treasure they have at 16th and Wood streets and to put it to a healthy new use.

Such a restoration will take money, especially if a few historic structures around the plaza, like the SP Hotel, are restored with the station. But railroad architecture on this order is priceless today.

Almost nothing is left in California to compare with the 16th Street station. Oakland's crude old Western Pacific depot of 1909 at Third and Washington streets, converted to a variety of commercial uses, does not approach its quality. There are some outstanding Mission Revival stations, notably the marvelous union terminal in Los Angeles. But as far as early-20th-century classicism is concerned, the genuine article, not the diluted pastiches of the 1930s at Stockton or Sacramento — the Oakland station is the only thing of its kind this side of Denver or the Pacific Northwest.

Designed by the Chicago architect Jarvis Hunt (1859–1941), who also did stations in Kansas City and Dallas, the building itself — exclusive of tracks and trestles — cost the SP $370,000. Equivalent to perhaps $30 million today, the outlay was all the more remarkable because this was not the main terminus for travelers to San Francisco, which was down at the SP's Oakland ferry pier at the foot of Seventh Street, but an uptown transfer point for East Bay passengers.

That had an important effect on design. The SP's electric interurban lines ascended to a raised platform behind the station above the main line tracks. Another SP electric line stopped directly in front of the station amid the greenery and handsome lamp standards of a landscaped square.

A lesser architect than Jarvis Hunt might have made a mess of these converging systems. But he combined them in a design of calm efficiency, in which there is no conflict between modern practical needs and Beaux-Arts formal elegance.

Dominating the composition is a splendidly ordered facade. The station measures 270 feet across, counting two side wings that include baggage rooms, a boiler house (topped by a delightful classic chimney), and other utilitarian spaces. What matters, however, is the massive central block, which has a strength that is almost Roman.

To emphasize its prominence, the slightly lower wings are set back a few feet so that the main facade emerges in all its power. Its almost unadorned side walls, in an accomplished display of fine masonry, perfectly frame the three colossal round-arched windows in the center — opening about 25 feet high — that impart an eloquent note of welcome.

Some time in the past, perhaps in the 1950s, the original glass was either replaced or, as far as I can tell, coated with a blue sun-resistant film that mars the whole effect, but that can be easily rectified. In any case, it cannot spoil the modeling of the arches, which are scooped out in concave niches that give them monumental depth. The central window lifts above a metal canopy, held by heavy chains and blazoned with scroll-like decorations, that shelters the main entrance (whose present cheap doors are relatively new and will have to be replaced).

The tall side windows, rising from richly sculpted bases, are finer still. Beaux-Arts design is often dismissed as a derivative art of historic formulas, but like all classical systems it leaves ample room for originality. Here Hunt came up with stone "fountains" that virtually pour out of the building as sculptural abstractions.

Like the entire base of the building, where hard use requires resistant materials, they are done in "Sierra white" granite (also used extensively in the San Francisco Civic Center), which is not really white but a silvery gray. It has been superbly matched by the grooved terra-cotta surfaces above, gray-flecked to resemble granite, which were cast to Hunt's designs by the ceramics firm of Gladding-McBean when it was at the peak of its craft. In morning sunlight, the facade can go golden.

The palatial mood continues in the waiting room, 116 feet long and 66 feet wide, which lifts about 40 feet to a coffered ceiling. The plaster ornamentation, once again, is very original within the Beaux-Arts discipline of scale and proportion. The materials have largely held up under grievous maltreatment, not least because the marble pavements have been carried six feet up the walls as wainscots.

Light floods in through the three great windows. Somehow this essentially European architecture, quite French here, has created a very Californian space.

On the south wall, set beneath the Southern Pacific sunset emblem, the Golden State is celebrated in a painting of Emerald Bay at Lake Tahoe. On the north wall is a painting of Mount Shasta, beneath a clock that stopped long ago. That was probably around the time that the three great spherical lanterns, suspended by chains which used to be raised or lowered from the attic above the ornate ceiling, also ceased to work.

How Oakland can make time run again in this noble room is a question that has several possible answers. The most promising, to me, would be to create a museum celebrating the history and aspirations of the city's black community, which in fact got its start here more than a century ago when Pullman porters and their families settled in Oakland. Congressman Ron Dellums' octogenarian uncle, C.L. Dellums, was president of the Brotherhood of Sleeping Car Porters and became one of the stirring figures in Oakland history.

Today there is a small but fascinating museum of local black American history that is inadequately housed in the red brick Carnegie library at 5606 San Pablo Avenue. It needs room to grow. So does specifically black American art, now getting some attention in the Ebony Museum in a Victorian at 1034 14th Street, but obviously in need of expansion and encouragement that can probably best come from the Oakland Museum.

The Oakland Museum is one of the great works of Modern architecture in the Bay Area, a building that is also a green and flowering garden. Now is the time for West Oakland to begin to flower, too.

January 2, 1989

Wurster Hall, University of California, Berkeley, 1989. By Saxon Donnelly.
Courtesy Regents of the University of California.

V. Schools, Jails and Churches

■ THE RIGHT ARCHITECTURE FOR AN ACROPOLIS

To visualize the potential unity, order and richness of the American environment, which is now so tragically marred by disunity, disorder and poverty, one must go to our more handsome colleges and universities. For it is on the campus, as virtually nowhere else in the country, that architectural permanence, rational organization of diverse activities, generous provision of open space, liberal respect for the arts and sciences, and — in some ways most significant of all — freedom from the automobile and from advertising, can be seen acting together to provide an organic milieu for civilized life.

In this sense, the finest passage of cityscape in America is probably Harvard, and in the Bay Region, the grand old quadrangle at Stanford (but not, unfortunately, the hodgepodge of mediocre newer buildings which surrounds it).

I am not advocating that these academic complexes should be literally duplicated in downtown San Francisco. I am merely pointing out that the campus, at its finest, embodies principles of design which may be fruitfully employed throughout our civilization, and particularly in redevelopment areas where whole cityscapes are to be created at a single stroke.

A cheerful case in point, modest in scope and purpose, but powerful in its possible role as guide to civic design elsewhere, is Foothill Junior College in Los Altos Hills.

Here, on a splendid 122-acre site, has arisen a group of some 40 buildings, all constructed of the same materials, sharing the same basic structural concept, and comprising a harmonious — but richly diversified — whole that is unrivalled in this part of the world.

This is a major work of architecture and planning, possibly the finest design yet devised by the distinguished office of Ernest J. Kump (who did the college in association with the firm of Masten & Hurd); and everyone who is disturbed by the tawdry confusion of most new construction would do well to make a pilgrimage to this little Acropolis for reassurance that all is not lost.

An Acropolis it certainly is: A hilltop consecrated to the most lofty values of the society which built it. Although Foothill is called a "junior" college, it is really a community college which goes far beyond academic and vocational instruction in its functions. The San Francisco Symphony, for example, gave a rousing performance before a sell-out audience on the campus two weeks ago. The handsome theater is frequently filled by Peninsula playgoers. The library eventually should serve most local needs for books.

Foothill, then, is a multipurpose cultural resource, receiving heavy communal use by day and night; and thus it is a formative influence on the whole surrounding community, and not just on the 3,500 young students who will regularly attend classes.

It is to the credit of the architects, especially Kump's chief designer Arthur Sweetser and landscape architect Peter Walker, that they saw the college in this light from the start, and gave the design problem such thorough study that they came up with a solution admirably suited to the present and future needs of the community.

The site development especially is excellent. All of the buildings are organized around related landscaped courts, ranging in size from intimate patios to formal outdoor assembly areas. Except for the monumental gymnasiums and swimming pool, which were thoughtfully placed on an adjoining knoll and are reached by a footbridge spanning a little valley, the entire complex of classroom structures, library, auditorium, student center and faculty offices is set on the gently rolling top of a low hill. One must leave the automobile at the base of the hill in one of several lots which have been carefully distributed and landscaped so that the hundreds of parked autos nowhere seem too oppressive.

And once he walks on the curving paths to the top of the hill, toward the broadly sheltering roofs of the redwood buildings, which come into sight one after the other in beautifully organized — but visually very free — sequence, the pedestrian is in a world that belongs to him alone.

There is no noise, but there are natural sounds. There are no gas fumes, but there is the smell of grass. There is no senseless clutter, but there is vitality and variety, reinforced by stirring vistas of higher, surrounding hills.

Yet there is also impressive unity, and this has been achieved — as it must be — by consistent architectural control of space and materials.

Space — or rather, lucid mastery of space — is the supreme content of architecture, and here space has been handled in a searching, extremely original way. Although the buildings vary greatly in size and function, they share a harmony of form that is the direct result of their interior spatial organization. Ever since the '30s, when he built the first "cluster" schools in California — composed of unified groups of classrooms — architect Kump has experimented with what he calls the "space-module" theory of architecture. That is, his buildings are made up of rather large, unobstructed volumes — identical, or closely related, column-free spaces; and they are therefore not based on the small divisions in plan which characterize most modern buildings.

At Foothill the "space-module" is 60 by 68 feet, which is large enough to accommodate four classrooms. This unit governs the dimensions of all the buildings, large and small, except for three octagonal lecture halls which are used as foils for the other structures. Some buildings are composed of a single module; others — such as the library and the gyms — contain several modules.

But what gives this system even greater unity is the way the steep, hipped roofs, covering single or multiple spaces, share the same system of proportions (and incidentally conceal vents and other mechanical excrescences within their generous forms). Everywhere there is a sense of calm strength, and a welcome absence of pretension.

A deliberately simple palette of materials further enhances this effect. The roofs are uniformly shingled with redwood shakes. The walls are of rough-sawn redwood, or in the low faculty office structures, warm brick. The great V-shaped piers which support the roofs (and thus provided column-free space within) are all of the same pebbled concrete aggregate.

Thus Foothill can serve as an example of the way our raw environment may be developed, quickly yet on a grand scale, without leading to confusion and tawdriness. Buildings such as these, to be sure, would be inappropriate in a city, where they would appear impossibly rural. But the lessons they contain, showing the value of consistency, simplicity, order and care, might well be heeded by those modernists who mistakenly assume that these qualities are incompatible with true vitality and humane innovation.

December 25, 1961

■ A WINNING PAVILION AT SANTA CLARA

When Jesuits create an architectural image, they do it boldly. Just as the order's home church of II Gesu in Rome, built between 1568 and 1575, established the model of compelling Baroque splendor for the Counter-Reformation, the padres of the University of Santa Clara have helped to open an era of radiant, seemingly weightless, air-supported structures — a pure architecture of light and space — in the fiberglass roof of their new recreation and sports pavilion.

Like most radically innovative buildings, this one has serious faults, including leaks and terrible acoustics. But on balance it is a triumph.

To anyone interested in the vitality of uncompromising modern design, the translucent Leavey Activities Center — the first great air-and-fabric structure in this country, and second in the world after the U.S. pavilion at the Osaka World's Fair in 1970 — warrants an architectural pilgrimage to the once sleepy campus of fake Spanish buildings off Highway 17.

Today the 3,500-student university, much improved academically, is alive with a fresh, healthy spirit.

Ordinary students, jogging and working out, as well as the excellent Bronco basketball team, are cheerfully on view in the $5 million center, completed in 1975, which really consists of two adjoining air-bubble buildings.

The larger dome encloses the Toso athletic pavilion, clear-spanning a 4,600 seat basketball arena and other facilities in a lordly space that measures 310 by 210 feet.

The smaller and lower dome, 135 by 130 feet, is the demountable covering of an Olympic-sized swimming pool, surrounded by a garden, which is open to the sky from April to November.

The buildings are technically and economically significant in so many ways that there is a temptation to describe them in material terms of cost (only two-thirds the price of conventionally roofed buildings which would have amounted to $7.5 million) or even in terms of weight (an astounding 37.5 ounces per square yard above the basketball court).

But their chief value is their immaterial, elating architectural presence, at once modest yet strong — even powerful, which breaks fearlessly from the past, but nevertheless respects the older campus environment.

Their low profiles, billowing gently above landscaped earth forms that contain the play areas, do not rise above the traditional buildings near them (unlike unfortunate recent additions such as the highrise Benjamin Swig Residence Hall). And they mercifully screen ugly industrial structures bordering the campus on the southeast.

Thus Leavey Center is not merely a technical feat, but a complex work of environmental art. The design team responsible was headed by Paul Kennon of the Houston firm of Caudill Rowlett Scott and by the brilliant New York engineer David Geiger, the foremost authority in this new field of construction. Associated with them were Palo Alto architects Albert A. Hoover & Associates.

Although the exterior of the domes is quietly impressive, it is the wonderful display of light and space on the inside that makes them so special. The curving roofs are so lightly flung up, kept steady by diagonal networks of slender steel cables veining their luminous skins, but literally floating on air, that they seem scarcely supported at all.

But of course they must be. This becomes immediately apparent as one enters the revolving doors (which serve as air locks) of the main building, and hears the noisy blowers pushing five pounds of air pressure per square foot against the great covering.

The high sound level of the blowers might be unbearable in an ordinary building, but there is always plenty of sound in a sports facility, which can be deafening even in ordinary gyms when excited fans cheer. Nevertheless the blowers could have been much quieter, if not altogether silent, if dampeners, acoustical membranes, and other superior equipment desired by the architects had been installed.

This would have cost another $100,000 perhaps, which the university simply didn't have.

As it is, Santa Clara got a monumental bargain because the quality of the soil in this location, infiltrated by a high water table, is close to the consistency of Jell-O. Steel or concrete would have required extensive foundation work for this reason alone. Also, Santa Clara is a seismic zone, where heavy structures must be beefed up, so flexible air-supported coverings offer unusual advantages in earthquake country.

But it is the spiritual quality of the architecture that counts most: the exhilarating play of space, everywhere enhanced by brilliant colors — red, orange, yellow, blue, green — that set off major features of the building against a muted background of beiges and grays, and rich carpeting of purple.

The detailing is unusually fine because it is closely related to functional design. The yellow blowers, for example, are strongly identified, and so is the red trusswork of the high platform above the basketball courts, supporting upturned floodlamps (which are only needed at night because of the wonderful natural daylight) and catwalks for television crews during important games.

But these handsome trusses are also a fail-safe device which will hold up the great roof in case back-up mechanical support systems fail during a power outage. The roof would descend gently, taking two hours to deflate completely, although it would fall quickly if vandalized or hit by a plane. But so might any building.

All this adds up to a heartening impression of *mens sana in corpore sano*, as the young people circle the room on the running track, practice baseball or tennis in netted enclosures, play Ping-Pong or racket ball, or simply relax at the end of the great room which is landscaped and terraced as a garden.

Or they can take a swim in the pool, which has a different quality of refreshment and repose, possibly because it is so lushly planted. Here, incidentally, the roof fabric is not Teflon-coated fiberglass, as in the main space, but vinyl Dacron — a cheaper and far less attractive material.

At first air-structures were not thought of as architecture at all. They were introduced without fanfare as temporary shelters or storage buildings. Then the military used them for radomes in the Arctic and elsewhere. Next came recreational uses, such as enclosures for tennis courts.

The big change came at Expo '70 in Japan, when the New York firm of Davis, Brody & Associates, competing for the U.S. pavilion commission, asked engineer Geiger to come up with a structure that couldn't have been built a decade earlier.

The rest is history. Strictly speaking, Santa Clara was not the next fabric structure (a smaller building preceded it in Tennessee). But it was the first large, permanent and architecturally splendid structure of its kind. Conceived in the early 1970s before the full severity of the energy crisis was known, and now consuming $70,000 annually in gas and electricity, it is nevertheless a worthy forerunner for the colossal Silverdome in Pontiac, Michigan, the largest indoor stadium ever constructed.

This incredible building, also engineered by Geiger, is 560 by 760 feet, seats 80,500 people at Detroit Lions football games, and is 200 feet high from the playing field to the superb covering. It is technically more advanced than Santa Clara's in every way, and shows the full economy of air-structures when they reach gigantic dimensions.

Larger than the New Orleans Superdome (430,000 square feet to 420,000), the Michigan Silverdome cost only one-fourth as much — $42 million against $160 million. Mechanically it is much cheaper to operate. The cost of extra energy is more than offset by savings in artificial illumination and heating. And construction took only two years, compared to four for the Superdome.

Still more refined concepts are under way, in college athletics — pavilions being built in Florida, and much bigger ones — immense industrial structures and sports complexes new being studied here and in Europe with proposed spans of 1,000 feet or more.

One could even cover Candlestick Park.

Beside them, Santa Clara will seem primitive, but it came first, and it will last as long as architectural history lasts.

January 23, 1978

■ FINDING FORM ONCE AGAIN ON THE FARM

Glory be, there's a new wooden building down at The Farm, as folks used to call Stanford, and it makes plenty of sense.

For the first time since the magnificent 19th-century buildings went up around the Old Quad, the likes of which we'll never see again, a distinguished out-of-state architect, Harry Weese of Chicago, has had the chance to offer a lesson to our local worthies. He has shown how to build thoughtfully in the warm Palo Alto climate for the extraordinary human community — at once informal and exacting — that constitutes a great university.

The Terman Engineering Center — this antitechnocratic work of art is an engineering building — has adjustable wooden shutters that can be pushed aside in winter to let the sun in, or drawn in summer to keep the interiors shadowy and cool, setting up a seasonal architectonic rhythm on the relaxed but elegant facades.

Moreover, the building is also ventilated by fresh air, blowing through open windows, and upward through corridors, stairs, and air wells to open skylights in the roof, rather than by air conditioning behind sealed glass in a structure crammed with costly mechanical apparatus.

Still more important as a humane architectural principle, windows are provided almost everywhere. Except in a few specialized spaces such as the auditorium, the building is wonderfully open to the outdoors, its L-shaped form enclosing a garden and sunken pool on two sides, and quietly facing the rest of the new engineering and science complex on the others.

There are no windowless interior compounds. Instead, secretaries, students, research assistants and professors can look up from work, out over trees and grass, to distant hills. These are only some of the many acts of courtesy in a building that everywhere displays exquisite consideration for the people who actually use it.

The Terman Center marks a radical turnabout for a university which, since World War II and after a long decline, has become an architectural disaster area.

A building of such unassuming strength would be rare anyplace in these days of boorish macho design and technological overkill. But it is downright remarkable to come across postwar architecture of such intelligence at Stanford.

Since 1945, when it emerged as a major world university, Stanford has raised $417 million — with no less than $230 million going for new construction and renovation alone — in an expansion program that undeniably produced tremendous scholarly benefits, but deeply harmed the nearly unspoiled campus.

Stanford is not the only famous school that has sacrificed a great architectural birthright. It has played what might be called a Big Game with UC Berkeley in architectural butchery, for which a blunt ax would be an appropriate trophy.

Cal's brutal postwar buildings, including its new College of Environmental Design, have been individually bigger and uglier; but destruction on The Farm has been more tragic because Stanford started with so much more.

Conceived on an incomparable 11,000-acre site by the masterly landscape architect Frederick Law Olmsted (who also worked at Berkeley), together with the fine Boston firm of Shepley, Rutan & Coolidge, Stanford entered the 20th century with the noblest campus design since Thomas Jefferson's University of Virginia.

At the end of the mile-long Palm Drive, perhaps the finest ceremonial approach in our country, the grand unities of the Old Quad (still all right on the outside of the buildings, but partly ruined by interior remodeling) show how mighty a concept this was.

The steady processional beat of the great arches, the sureness of scale, the wealth and sobriety of the buff-colored sandstone masonry, all powerfully linked together — beneath an array of red-tiled roofs — by the long perspectives of the arcades, brightening and darkening in sunlight and shadow, add up to an overwhelming impression of civilized order and intellectual purpose.

This 19th-century medievalism — "Richardsonian Romanesque" — is the soundest kind of regional architecture, as well as modern university design, brilliantly suited to setting, climate and future expansion. A continuum of such cloistered spaces could have been, and in fact was meant to be, extended across the parklike campus.

It was too good to last. As Paul V. Turner wrote in his study of the campus, the grand design was abandoned soon after Senator Stanford's death in 1893. It was not killed by lack of money, but by provincial vulgarity, epitomized by Mrs. Stanford and her dim-witted brother, Ariel Lathrop. The fine East Coast design team was replaced by local practitioners, who have been in charge of the campus ever since.

By 1941, when the aging classicist Arthur Brown Jr. perpetrated Hoover Tower, a lot of bad buildings had gone up, hardly related to one another except by yellowish color and red tile roofs.

But it was after 1945 that the worst damage was done. Before Stanford discovered that it could raise money by other means, large tracts of open space were consumed by an architecturally appalling 71-acre shopping center and other commercial development on land that should have been sacrosanct. This includes the foothills, where the 655-acre Stanford

Industrial Park with its "smokeless" factories generated traffic congestion, noise, air pollution. There was also, to complete a chain reaction of devastation, the new freeway.

Comparable destruction, or worse, was inflicted on the central campus by institutional planners, "old boy" architects and administrators. But guiltiest of all, intellectually, was the famous faculty which, if it interfered at all, meddled only to make mediocre buildings worse.

What resulted was an eerie exercise in historical parody. The handsome stonework of the early buildings was echoed, or aped, in reinforced concrete, often so crassly that one wondered how trustees and donors, who presumably know the value of a penny in running their corporations, ever approved such odd concoctions.

The strangest is John Carl Warnecke's hulking undergraduate library, which has something of the consistency of congealed mustard. An assortment of out-of-scale tile roofs was wildly plunked down on a weakly uncertain mass, which is further disfigured by pictorial tapering uprights that ostensibly recall the honest arches of the Old Quad.

In the vicinity of such construction almost anything should look good, but no such luck. Confronting the library is an authentic dog by Skidmore, Owings & Merrill — the pompous and ponderous Law School — which is surmounted by still another ungainly red-tile roof.

All this is by way of preamble to the predicament confronting Dean William M. Kays of the College of Engineering in 1973, when four important alumni, the electronics magnates William R. Hewlett and David Packard and their wives, endowed a much needed new facility. This new unit, costing $9.2 million in all, would provide the Engineering School with a library, auditorium, classrooms and lounges, in honor of a beloved campus figure, Provost Emeritus Frederick Emmons Terman.

Dean Kays, a feisty type who landed in the first wave at Normandy, assaulted Stanford's entrenched architectural misconceptions as if he were on Omaha Beach. Against the die-hard resistance of the campus bureaucracy, he bypassed its list of architects, and after a nationwide search selected Weese as his designer.

They hit it off immediately, not least because Weese — who did an extraordinary wooden-louvered U.S. Embassy in Ghana, and had much experience in energy-saving, ecological design — agreed that if one couldn't give up air-conditioning in Stanford's balmy climate, one should perhaps give up modern architecture entirely.

This was all before the full seriousness of the energy crisis was felt, but Kays and Weese anticipated it, in the same way that they opted for a wood-framed structure when runaway construction costs made steel and concrete extremely expensive in the mid-1970s.

Weese and Kays did not win all the battles. The architect never wanted fluorescent light fixtures in offices, but preferred simply to provide plugs, including overhead outlets, so that the occupants could individually decide what kind of lighting they wished. This could be floor lamps or desk lamps, or Japanese paper lanterns hung from above.

And the building is comfortable. Even on the hottest days last August, when the building was first opened, everyone worked pleasantly enough, as breezes were drawn into the building by a natural system of airflow. The doors to the corridors have inserted louvers, through which air follows a series of logical modest devices, until it is vented through movable skylights that anyone can control with cables attached to small reels.

It all came together as a triumph of common sense. Because this is really a substantial building of 150,000 square feet, seven stories high, and used for many different activities, the lowest parts of the structure were framed in concrete — the rectangular columns rotated 45 degrees to give a slender, diamondlike effect. Above the frame is wood: laminated beams of fir and hemlock, mounted and clamped to fir columns. The shutters are cedar. The infill is brushed stucco of a soft brown, almost beige, that lives happily with the older campus environment.

The building alone cost $50 per square foot, at the same time that lunkhead nearby structures were costing $70 or $80. But the real value has been in the restoration of humane architecture to Stanford, as the university approaches its second century.

February 20, 1978

■ A CAMPUS THAT WENT ASTRAY

The devastation of the once magnificent campus of the University of California in Berkeley is nearly complete. In the wake of an incompetent, brutal and extravagant postwar building program, the last open spaces — pathetic remnants of one of the finest natural sites in the world — are being filled in.

Since the campus was largely unspoiled in 1945 (when only a few bad mistakes had been made, such as the intrusion of the stadium at the foot of the hills and putting the radiation lab on the upper slopes), it has taken just about 30 years for bumbling administrators, meddling regents, an apathetic faculty and — above all — so-called modern architects to ruin most of the rest.

Because there was no real expansion plan, not even a large-scale study model of the Multiversity, but only rudimentary maps of where new buildings could go, the parklike environment was mercilessly uprooted, bulldozed, paved, fenced and ultimately crushed beneath a phalanx of hulking pseudomonuments.

Taken individually or as a hodgepodge whole, these cheap-looking, but in fact rather expensive bureaucratic blockbusters add up to an educational disaster — for buildings teach us either right or wrong things — as well as an architectural calamity.

With the important exception of the urbane Student Center by Vernon DeMars and Donald Reay, which is a planning triumph even if the buildings arranged around the great plaza are not very distinguished in themselves, not one of the new structures has any clear or gracious relation to the others.

They have merely been slapped down haphazardly wherever land was made available. Even when done at the same time by a single firm, they exhibit wildly conflicting idioms and incompatible materials, in a porridge of Modernist cliches.

The pitched tile roofs and ersatz traditionalism of the Hertz music complex, for instance, confront the insensate, squared-off, flat-roofed block of the Kroeber Hall of Art and Anthropology, both concocted simultaneously by Gardner A. Dailey & Associates, who did two more big buildings elsewhere on the campus — Tolman and Evans — which have not the slightest connection with these.

What may be worse, some of the new buildings are parodies of the splendid Beaux-Arts classicism of John Galen Howard. The biochemistry labs by Wurster, Bernardi & Emmons at the northwest corner of the campus and John Carl Warnecke's Campbell Hall, another science building close to the Campanile, both wear outsized red-tile roofs like hats. Their crude detailing shows how far academic architecture has declined in Berkeley since the early 20th century.

Howard's meticulously scaled and richly organized compositions — California, Durant and Wheeler halls, the Campanile, Sather Gate, Doe Library and his masterpiece, Hearst Mining — had many different purposes and basic forms; still they were all strongly unified, given grand monumental harmonies, by a beautifully sustained classical vocabulary, by consistent proportions, by the same fine materials such as stone and bronze, and by the same lofty cultural purpose.

What is more, the spaces between Howard's unified buildings were treated as rich and dignified entities. Since then a variety of landscape architects have cut them up, replacing grass and bricks or flagstone paths with blacktop in patterns reminiscent of children's train layouts.

Before environmental crimes of this magnitude, it doesn't do much good to assign blame, even though it is clear that the late William Wilson Wurster, dean of The College of Environmental Design and powerful chairman of the campus planning committee, presided over the debacle. He now has his monument in the most coarsely technocratic and — so far as its neighbors are concerned — ill-mannered of all the new buildings: Wurster Hall. Designed by three members of the faculty, Joseph Esherick, Donald Olsen and Vernon DeMars, it is the building in which a good share of California architects and planners are educated.

But if Dean Wurster and the campus' chief architectural bureaucrat, the recently retired Louis DeMonte, made policy (or failed to), it was implemented by a couple of dozen leading Bay Area firms, many of whom are pretty good at putting up redwood houses, and who describe themselves as "regional humanists."

What price humanism now?

Because the cultural cost is beyond estimation, the financial price may have relevance. But the campus bureaucracy, which several weeks ago was asked for construction budgets since World War II, can't provide even a round number. Since at least $150 million was spent by 1965, when I last made a count, twice that much would seem a fair guess.

Now that there's no more room on the central campus, and the city of Berkeley has balked at further expansion, whatever future buildings go up must be crammed into unfortunate sites.

This has already occurred directly north of Wurster Hall, where a 50,000-square-foot addition to the School of Optometry — a long overdue and worthy project — has been shoehorned into a totally inadequate location.

In itself the new building is a decent enough essay in concrete by Mackinlay-Winnacker-McNeil, in some ways superior to the old optometry building, which is one of the poorer, later Beaux-Arts structures, done when the classical movement was running into the sands.

The addition is modestly framed in concrete, without any of the heavy structural antics of Wurster across the way; it looked better before bulky balustrades and sunscreens of laminated wood, stained a strange gingery orange, marred its terraces and broad window openings. The well-defined terraces, plus a landscaped berm and sunken court, give it a protective margin.

Nevertheless, the site is so confined that this good-sized four-story structure can't help banging against the blank sidewall of the Hertz music auditorium on the west, and looming over some of the most charming redwood buildings that have survived on the campus: the faculty club by Maybeck, Howard, and others; the equally delightful women's faculty club (now desexified like the men's and open to all) by Julia Morgan; and between them the captivating log cabin — made of trunks of redwood trees — that was long the Senior Men's Club.

Oddly enough, this treasure was scheduled for demolition — a notion that was wisely overturned by conservationist protest.

When the campus bureaucrats wanted an Engineering Center, comparable to the new Thomas Engineering Center at Stanford, containing a library, auditorium, conference rooms, offices and other needed facilities, it did not occur to them that these facilities might well be distributed elsewhere in the vast engineering complex on the north side of the campus. Or that — horrors! — one of the university's massive parking structures might be torn down to provide a site, and that Sierra Club faculty members walk to work or take a bus.

Instead of rethinking the whole process which had landed them in a position of unavoidable vandalism, the administrators deprived the College of Engineering of the only open space in its midst. The site they picked is hemmed in by Gardner Dailey's egregious Evans Hall, a monstrous math building and — on a forbidding podium that no one ever uses — the fortresslike Davis Hall by Skidmore, Owings & Merrill.

Here the University, after irate disputes among students, faculty, staff, and top bureaucrats, instructed architect George Matsumoto to erect — or rather, to hide — a nonbuilding; a landscaped, terraced structure that would be a garden, on the order of the Oakland Museum.

A buried structure was impossible because another big building was needed, and it was prevented from descending very far by a maze of underground utilities, serving the surrounding engineering labs that are really industrial operations.

Much as Matsumoto tried, the building kept popping out of the ground, growing bulkier and unfriendlier.

In some ways the faults of the other buildings will be partly rectified, for their high bases will now be masked by the new building's terraces, ramps and stairs, which make up for sharp changes in level. But it will all result in a loss of pleasantness, the blocking of views, the proliferation of concrete, the eradication of any sense of calm and repose.

And now, as a new 100,000-square-foot building for business administration is proposed, there is talk of putting it on Observatory Hill, or of razing the beautiful row of old residences on Piedmont Avenue.

What is needed here is a bold and fearless decision to build not for today — or worse, according to the stupidity of yesterday — but for tomorrow, in a great, discreet, courteous building that will show some understanding, after so many years, of what a university should be.

April 24, 1978

■ INVENTIVE, GENEROUS DESIGN FOR
SAN FRANCISCO SHERIFF'S LOCKUP

Jails by definition are not happy places, but the great, curving glass facade of the new sheriff's facility at the San Francisco Hall of Justice — a work-furlough dormitory rather than a traditional jail — is going to be an architectural delight when it is completed in 1993. Maybe the 400-bed facility will not exactly overjoy the inmates, although this overnight lockup will hardly be a tough joint.

For a jail, the interior has been designed inventively, even generously, in "new generation" circular living spaces, or "pods," with individual rooms on the perimeters. Such arrangements, administered by single officers at central posts, are becoming standard in the more civilized Bay Area counties.

So are work-furlough programs, such as San Francisco's, in which offenders are free to hold outside jobs during the day.

But the exterior makes the building unique. To thousands of motorists driving past on Interstate 80, to and from the Bay Bridge, the tremendous undulating wall of glass — 300 feet long and 60 feet high — will appear as a spectacular work of art.

Softly glowing by day, gleaming gently at night, the translucent facade has been conceived as a colossal light sculpture by environmental artist Douglas Hollis, working in company with architect Gregory Williams, who heads the design team composed of the firms of Williams & Tanaka and Del Campo & Maru.

The architects hit upon the original curving shape of the building, but it is Hollis, one of three artists brought into the design process at the insistence of the Arts Commission, who has refined what had been a crude facade, verging on vulgarity, into a magical surface of white "fritted" glass.

This specially manufactured ceramic glass should be extraordinary. In texture, it will be somewhat similar to the clouded glass of Helmut Jahn's great United Airlines terminal at O'Hare Airport in Chicago.

At O'Hare, however, the glass is etched in exquisitely proportioned geometric grids. Hollis has opted for a wild, swirling composition that plays across the whole front of the building, scarcely kept in check by the silvery aluminum window frames.

Flowing over the architecture, the cloudy patterns of the glass, subtly laced with dark gray, will suggest fog or mist rolling over the city.

The facade itself, billowing and receding in three successive surges beside a wide bend of the elevated freeway, should enhance this effect of a moving atmosphere, playing over a triad of circular forms.

These arcs, coming into sight one after another, are meant to be seen at freeway speed, recalling the "kinetic perspectives" of David Alfara Sequieros' building-wide murals in Mexico that were expressly painted to be seen from moving cars.

Hence the three arcs widen, from 40 to 46 to 52 feet, as the building goes west to east on the long triangular site, headed toward the bridge, developing a baroque dynamism in front of the dull, inert Hall of Justice.

That is the architectural idea. Because one cannot see inside, the facade may seem to be merely a screen that disguises the correctional facility within (of which passing motorists will be hardly aware). But it also screens off much of the Hall of Justice looming beyond.

A philosophical problem arises here. To mask the real nature of a jail, even a furlough dorm, which at a distance might be mistaken for a slightly flashy office building or, heaven forfend, a roadside motel, violates the Modernist dictum that architecture should tell the truth about itself.

Our never-take-a-chance city planners wanted the new building to be "contextual" — that is, a blocky pseudo-historic clone of the Hall of Justice, which is by all odds the ugliest and the most unjust public building in town.

The planners were rightly slapped down by the Arts Commissioners, led by feisty Anne Healey and former Planning Director Rai Okamoto. The commission also set a new city policy so far as public art is concerned, requiring it to be an integral part of the building, not a tacked-on decoration.

Consequently, the building's art allowance of $600,000 was diverted to early conceptual design, and Hollis and his fellow artists — Carl Chen of Santa Monica and Vicki Scuri of Seattle — seized the chance to be artist-architects in many places inside and outside the building.

Instead of an ordinary parapet to hide unsightly mechanical equipment on the roof, for instance, Hollis created another interplay of curving forms to complement the curves of the facade below. In a stunning optical phenomenon called a "moire" effect, he has devised a perforated double screen of galvanized steel that will loop around the roof in three connected circles, swooping upward and downward between low and high points of 6 and 16 feet.

A wavy, mysterious rippling, like the shimmering of watered silk, will be produced by the doubled bands of gleaming metal, as if by magic.

It is worth explaining the trick. The metal ribbons will be perforated in identical geometric patterns, but they can never line up exactly. More precisely, they can never be seen at precisely the same head-on angle, and the beholder instead sees a continuous, strangely kinetic three-dimensional surface.

The technique has often been used by graphic designers and constructivist sculptors — Naum Gabo, for one. So far as I know, however, moire has never been tried before in sculpture at such monumental dimensions on top of a building as long as a football field.

If it works — and I think it will be a zinger — Doug Hollis, a San Franciscan who is just becoming known internationally for works such as his "Rain Column" water sculpture in the Rincon Center atrium, will have made a major contribution to public art.

Chen, the Santa Monica artist, also has done original things, playing elegantly with reflected natural light in two tall, circular atriums to be capped by rotating skylights, slanting at the angle of the sun, which will house mirrored "heliostats" — sun-catching devices set just beneath the outer glass. These heliostats' — long, slender reflectors, like vanes or louvers, will incline upward or downward as they circle to track the sun throughout the day.

Both the skylights and the heliostats will be computer-controlled, so that their moving forms — 20 feet in diameter — will be high-tech kinetic sculptures in themselves, poking up behind the moire screens on the roof and transmitting natural light nearly 50 feet downward through the cylindrical atriums.

The warm glow of ambient light, mixed with light flowing in through Hollis' freestanding glass facade, will enter the inmates' accommodations through security windows and glass-block walls, making this architecturally one of the most innovative correctional facilities in the country.

The closed living quarters — six superimposed two-story "pods" — will be stacked in three drumlike interior towers, with bedrooms ringing central social spaces where inmates will eat, watch television or simply relax. They will also find relief in the adjacent atriums. One space, comfortably furnished, will be for visits from families and friends. The other, more interesting aesthetically, will be a meditation room where prisoners can find solitude and spiritual solace.

The third artist, Scuri, is less daring technologically than Hollis and Chen and seems closer to traditional crafts than to advanced contemporary art. Her main task has been to pave the outdoor plaza, the main lobby and other public spaces, a considerable floor area, which she will cover with patterns conceived as large geometric rugs.

The geometry is not purely abstract, for the individual concrete pavers, 18 inches square, will each describe a seven-pointed sheriff's star, buff-colored, within a field of black.

The symbol delights Sheriff Mike Hennessey, a rare arts lover and fine gent among law enforcement officials. Yet sample castings of the pavers appear very crude in comparison, say, with the resplendent pavements of the new San Jose Convention Center by the Danish artist Lin Utzon.

They do not compare, for that matter, with the work of Hollis and Chen in this very building whose architecture has been so much improved since the artists were given a direct role in design.

It is the first time that San Francisco has gone so far in this direction.

If the finished building does not in every way fulfill the promise of the models and drawings, the city at least will have made a start toward reintegration of the arts and architecture, once inseparable but estranged in modern times.

April 8, 1991

■ CATHEDRAL PLAN — A GOOD START

The bold originality of the preliminary design for the new St. Mary's Cathedral is cause for civic rejoicing — and also for undisguised relief — in a city which only six months ago had every reason to fear that this major monument would be simply another huge architectural cliche, marring the skyline of the Western Addition, not far from the Jack Tar and the Federal Building.

Instead, San Francisco now has a clear opportunity to erect one of the significant religious buildings of the century.

The cross-shaped superstructure of shell concrete, an extraordinary feat of modern building technology, will soar 180 feet — the height of an 18-story tower — from an emplacement of great potential majesty.

Not only will the exterior be a formidable symbolic presence in the cityscape, but the vast luminous space within, through which colored light will filter downward from an enormous overhead cross of glass, will also possess rich liturgical meaning. The square plan, moreover, has enabled the architects to place the altar almost in the center of the building, thus breaking down the historic Roman Catholic division between the clergy and the people, and making this church — in Archbishop Joseph T. McGucken's phrase — "the Cathedral of the ecumenical council."

The cathedral, indeed, may be properly described as revolutionary both in religious and structural concept. Although fine central-plan churches were built during the Renaissance and Baroque periods, none was based on this modern unifying premise, which brings the sacrament openly into the heart of the congregation. Yet St. Mary's also has spiritual roots as old as Christianity. If the Church itself, in ideal Biblical terms, should be "a seamless garment," the integral unity of this structure of concrete is an admirable expression of wholeness.

Structurally, of course, the tremendous hyperbolic paraboloidal shells — upended saddle-shaped membranes of concrete and steel — could not have been technically achieved in any age except our own. So far as I know, these are the largest shells of this type ever proposed for an actual building (as distinct from theoretical design exercises); and in this respect, too, the cathedral will take a worthy place, as a work of engineering alone, in the city which built the Golden Gate Bridge.

For the daring of this concept — and it is essential to note that it is still little more than a schematic concept which obviously requires much refinement — we are indebted to Pietro Belluschi, dean of architecture at MIT, and the masterly Italian engineer Pier Luigi Nervi.

These eminent figures in modern architecture came to bolster the efforts of the distinguished and conservative architects to whom this splendid commission was first entrusted, Messrs. Angus McSweeney, Paul A. Ryan and John Michael Lee.

Apparently these gentlemen, good parishioners who had never dealt with so complex a problem, soon found themselves beyond their architectural depth, and then — to the credit of the archbishop and his associates — Belluschi and Nervi were called in.

In a remarkably short time they have done brilliantly, but careful study of the models, especially the overall site model showing the cathedral's position at the heart of the Western Addition redevelopment area, shows how much remains unfinished in this design. The cathedral can easily be spoiled by slipshod detailing and — what is worse in a structure whose final effect will depend so critically on technical refinement — by coarse execution.

Probably the models should never have been shown publicly at this stage of the design, but public interest made this impossible. The square pedestal of the cathedral, for instance, from which the soaring shells will emerge, is still undergoing revision, which it certainly needs.

At present the superstructure sits awkwardly on this dull base, and some meaningful structural relation between the two must be developed, so that the entire structure flows upward as a dynamic entity from ground to sky.

The top of the building also requires some reconsideration. According to architect Belluschi, the spire, shown as a solid form in the model, will be redesigned as lacy openwork. Perhaps it could be dispensed with altogether, for it seems to me an inconsequential afterthought which adds nothing to the emphatic Christian impact of the immense cross below.

But more than this, virtually every architectural detail of this large building is still to be considered: the doors, the glass for the 180-foot-high lateral windows and for the translucent roof, and the furnishings which must embellish both the corner chapels and the towering central vessel.

This vast interior, furthermore, must be sensitively handled if it is not to overwhelm the individual worshipper. Its lighting, for instance, can either help to exalt the individual, or crush him.

Even the exterior sheathing of the great shells, for which white marble is now being considered, may end up as some different material. Although San Francisco is in large part a white city, marble is a reflecting material that does not always live happily on large surfaces in sunny California, and it should warrant the most exacting study before it is used on a colossal scale in the cathedral.

The site development of the surrounding area also presents many vexing problems. The Redevelopment Agency, director M. Justin Herman assures us, is doing its best to clear the view to the south, and if this tremendous vista is opened, it will be the most important example of large-scale civic design in San Francisco since the creation of the Civic Center. Unfortunately, at this late date, Mr. Herman can do nothing about the torn outlines of the redeveloped cityscape on the other sides of the cathedral, which — as I feared long ago — is turning out to be a hodgepodge of competing architectural forms.

The cathedral should be strong enough to hold its own against even the ungainly towers which will arise on the east and north, but the architects will also have to make sure that its own immediate setting is not badly compromised by unfeeling design and economic niggardliness.

Indeed, it is here that one can detect where the Belluschi-Nervi design ends, and — one suspects — the discarded McSweeney-Ryan-Lee notions may begin. To either side of the splendid entrance piazza, for instance, a parking lot has been installed, as if this were a gigantic religious supermarket. The cathedral may indeed be a safe way to Heaven, but it is not a Safeway, and those excrescences of blacktop must be removed.

At the rear of the Cathedral, the maladroitly organized dependencies of the archdiocese — including clerical quarters and a school — should be thoroughly re-examined. What is wanted here is a mood of spaciousness and wealth, not of cramped barrackslike accommodations.

In the development of the site the landscape architects, the gifted young firm of Osmundson & Staley, who are responsible for the very creditable roof garden of the Kaiser Center in Oakland, should be able to do much if the church wishes them to.

And this is where Archbishop McGucken's continuing responsibility becomes unmistakable. As His Excellency remarked last week, with what the old church chroniclers would have described as "the candor of a dove," his first reaction to the Belluschi-Nervi concept was something akin to "fright."

The archbishop is now enthusiastic, and rightly so, for his new cathedral should place this archdiocese in the forefront of modern intellectual and liberal Catholicism.

But as Pietro Belluschi wittily observed, let us hope that "the fear of God" remains with everyone connected with the execution of this great undertaking until its completion.

What is needed, first of all, is the clarification of the status of both Dean Belluschi and Professor Nervi in the whole project. The public — and I refer not merely to the Catholic lay public but to the city as a whole — has the right to know who will retain control over the vital phases of design. And with Belluschi in Cambridge, Mass., and Nervi in Rome, one can only wonder if problems of liaison have been thoughtfully worked out, or if there is not some danger of failure of communications.

These suggestions are offered not in a carping spirit, but in a slightly heady mood of surprised delight. For, frankly, I never expected the design of the cathedral to display such bold distinction, and if the archbishop and his staff continue in this brave direction, we must all stand ready to cry Bon Voyage and Bravo!

January 29, 1964

■ THE RESTORATION OF A TRUE SAN FRANCISCO MONUMENT

Like a vision of Byzantium, inspired by the dome of Hagia Sophia, Temple Emanu-El is the most majestic religious building in San Francisco.

Apart from the very different public rotundas of City Hall and the Palace of Fine Arts, nothing else in the city compares to the great synagogue at Lake Street and Arguello Boulevard. None of our other handsome places of worship, not even the colossal concrete-and-steel shells of St. Mary's Roman Catholic Cathedral, approach the temple's timeless grandeur and spiritual meanings.

All of us who care about architecture, Jews and non-Jews alike, can rejoice that it came through the earthquake unharmed. The temple, completed in 1926, in fact looks almost as good as new, and perhaps better in some ways.

The domed interior space, which can accommodate 1,700 worshipers, had just been splendidly restored, refurbished and, in a moving ceremony, reconsecrated a few weeks before the quake struck.

So far, only the main sanctuary has been restored at a cost of $2.5 million, and work is continuing in other parts of the building in a long-range project that will cost $12.5 million.

If it is all up to the level of the repairs in the sanctuary, it will be a triumph.

After the quake, nary a crack appeared in the replastered surfaces, colored a warm beige instead of the former dull cream, and elegantly enhanced by new burgundy upholstery, darkly gleaming cork floors, remade doors of blue leather and oak, and innumerable other details, from new hardware of polished bronze to unobtrusive speakers behind the oak pews that transmit sound so naturally that voices seem hardly to be amplified at all.

Overhead, soaring above mighty Roman arches, the unadorned sweep of the dome is an emblem of the cosmos that transcends its Jewish purpose and defines a universal space.

This is not architecture in the class of Hagia Sophia, of course, but it is worth recalling that the imperial sixth-century church of Justinian and Theodora, whose name means "Holy Wisdom," was transformed by Turkish architects nearly 1,000 years afterward into a seemingly perfect mosque.

Emanu-El, which means "God be with us" in Hebrew, also is an intimation of boundless divinity, and we have no other space in this part of the world that imparts this universal essence on such a monumental scale.

The temple also is specifically a monument to modern Judaism, and Reformed Judaism at that, which to strictly Orthodox Jews, accustomed to services conducted entirely in Hebrew, the wearing of skullcaps and prayer shawls, and separation of men and women, may not seem very Jewish at all.

Yet this is Judaism in the tradition of the Enlightenment. Architecturally, as in Enlightenment churches, its doctrine — ideally expressed — is pure illumination. And never, or at least not since the underside of the dome was marred in 1940 by asbestos acoustical tiles, which were stripped away and replaced in the current restoration, has this noble room appeared more radiant than in the Hanukkah season.

Hanukkah after all is the "Feast of Lights," named for the miracu-lous replenishment of lamp oil when the Temple of Jerusalem was rededicated in 165 B.C., and the most interesting aspect of the restoration of Temple Emanu-El has been a powerful increase in candlepower.

When the beautifully remade bronze chandeliers are turned up — there now are concealed upward-pointing lights to brighten the dome from below — the whole space glows with new excitement and vitality.

It may be too bright. In addition to the added voltage of the chandeliers, a ring of theatrical spotlights, aimed downward at the pulpit and the Ark of the Covenant, has been inserted at the crest of the dome.

Liturgically, these overbright lights may seem an improvement, especially to younger members of the changing congregation. Encouraged by the young intellectual rabbi, Robert Kirschner, a former rock guitarist who is 37 years old, the new generation at Emanu-El has wished to enliven the services, which have long been formally organized and rather ornate.

Architecturally, however, the circle of spotlights is the one serious mistake of an otherwise flawless restoration. At the crown of the dome, the flow of curving space is interrupted at the very point that it should continue unimpeded — calm, unified, unbroken — in the display of mystical oneness that is the essence of monotheism.

A certain drama has been gained, if it were truly needed, but a corresponding solemnity has been lost. Looked at from below, the spotlights are literally dazzling, and a little vulgar.

In some ways they are as unwelcome an addition as the immense stained-glass windows to either side by Mark Adams — "Water" on the east and "Fire" on the west — that were installed in 1972–73 and unchanged in the restoration.

These splashy biblical abstractions changed the quality of light that had filtered through the pale golden, handmade original glass, which has been beautifully restored in the temple's third great window, framed by a Roman barrel vault above the balcony on the north. This part of the temple shows how subtle and elating the play of natural light had been throughout the room before the colored glass was added.

Yet nothing can deprive this domed and arching space of its magnificence. The restoration architects, Robinson, Mills & Williams, with David Robinson in charge of design, have in every other respect maintained or improved the work of the distinguished architects of the 1920s, led by the masterly neoclassicist Arthur Brown Jr., who a decade earlier designed the City Hall.

In addition to Brown, who was clearly the principal designer, the group consisted of his partner John Bakewell Jr.; Sylvain Snaittacher, a member of the congregation; G. Albert Landsburgh, a specialist in theater design who also collaborated with Brown on the Opera House; and not least Bernard Maybeck, creator of the Palace of Fine Arts and the poetic Christian Science church on Dwight Way in Berkeley, who seems in the case of the temple to have been mainly a color consultant. To follow such designers, let alone improve on their work, took some doing. Hardly any expense was spared half a century ago to make this one of the most sumptuous synagogues ever built.

The temple cost $1.2 million, when money was still money, although the congregation did not stint on luxurious materials where they were wanted: sea-green marble columns, classical Italian travertine walls and pavings, bronze portals and lamps, and — most precious of all — the Ark of the Covenant of gilt bronze and cloisonne enamel, a tour de force by English craftsmen, beneath its monumental canopy of creamy travertine and emerald marble.

Yet Arthur Brown achieved the temple's ultimate grandeur with essentially humble materials — cement stucco over a steel frame — by reliance on classical massing and Roman volumes: arches, pediments, massive vaults, another range of arches, from the nobly proportioned forecourt to the dome of russet tiles, which is as high as the dome of Hagia Sophia and which can be seen for miles across the cityscape.

Unlike Hagia Sophia's incomparable masonry shell, mounted on pendentives, Temple Emanu-El is a double-domed structure. The topmost outer dome, framed by steel ribs, covers a seldom-visited but astonishing room enclosed by redwood planking laid in straight lines on a curving surface. The inner dome, directly below, is not structurally a dome at all, but an angular steel frame from which the plaster domical shell is suspended above the sanctuary.

So it is not the altogether lucid and logical structure it first appeared to be. That is what separates the provincial masterpiece from the greatest domed architecture in the world: at Florence, at Rome, in the London of Christopher Wren.

But the space created is true, as any philosophy that may be demonstrably false can be aesthetically true, like the philosophy of Plato. Temple Emanu-El, in much the same way, belongs to us all as a work of art. A dome by its very nature orders and unifies space. To experience that unity at its most humane, upholding canons of humanism that go beyond any separate creed, you cannot do better than to attend a special service January 13, when the congregation of Emanu-El — close to wealthy Presidio Terrace — will be joined by the congregation of the Third Baptist Church of the Western Addition, to celebrate the birthday of Martin Luther King.

January 1, 1990

VI. Retail Shopping

■ WRIGHT'S JEWEL IN MAIDEN LANE DEFACED

Of the many ambitious projects which Frank Lloyd Wright conceived for San Francisco, including the famous concrete "Butterfly Bridge" to span the bay, and a design for a slab skyscraper which would have been a generation ahead of its time, the Master was able to execute only a single commission — the little V. C. Morris Store in Maiden Lane — in this city which prides itself on aesthetic discernment and cordial support of the arts.

Although it would be enough to establish the reputation of most architects, the Morris Store, designed in 1948 when Wright was about 80 years old, is not one of his major works. it is not even a completely new building, but a renovated old one which Wright's clients, the late Mr. and Mrs. Morris, did not own, but leased. The cramped site on a narrow back street also curtailed the scope of the project.

Within the limits of their resources, however, the Morrises allowed the architect maximum freedom. Indeed, they allowed him to demonstrate — in the midst of our crass business environment — how gracious, how decent, how truly civilized a modern mercantile establishment may be.

"Every great architect," Wright once declared, "must be a great original interpreter of his time." The Morris Store is his interpretation for what a shop — admittedly, a highly specialized gift shop which caters to discriminating individuals — ought to be in the middle of the 20th century.

Therefore, even though the handsome little building occupies a noteworthy place in the series of curvilinear designs (including the Guggenheim Museum) which culminated his long career, the chief importance of the Morris Store resides in its social premise. Here, on one of the rare occasions when he was confronted by a commonplace, small-scale urban problem, the Master responded with a solution that was simultaneously modest and rich, forthright and profound, at home in its surroundings and yet brilliantly individualistic.

The very brilliance of Wright's deeply personalized architecture has too often thrown into shadow the broad social objectives which were always implied in his work. For in spite of his passionate individualism, so deeply rooted in the 19th-century romantic image of the artist as a

Rincon Center, San Francisco, California, 1989. By Steve Ringman.
Courtesy The San Francisco Chronicle.

uniquely original creator, Wright saw himself not as the author of splendidly isolated masterpieces, but rather as the supreme builder — the prophetic unifier — of a new order of civilization.

His structures, quite literally, are molds in which he hoped to shape human life; consequently their practical functions are inseparable from their spiritual intent. When both function and spirit are thus integrated in a single, consistent structural and spatial expression, Wright believed that architecture virtually assumes the properties of a living organism.

The grandeur of this concept permeated even his smallest buildings (and sometimes overwhelmed them). The Morris Store, fortunately, bears the weight of this philosophy lightly enough: it is an occasional poem directed against the huckster mentality which Wright hated.

"Instead of the vulgarizing display of merchandise on the sidewalk," Wright offered the passerby "an invitation to come in." The invitation took the form of a deep round arch — the only aperture in the exquisitely organized facade of Roman brick — and it is irresistible.

But before the interior is seen, the good sense and elegance of this wall must be appreciated. The beautifully laid brickwork — where in San Francisco can its equal be seen? — completely covers the nondescript front of the old structure which already stood on the site, and it also screens the interior of the shop from the ugliness of Maiden Lane, which was more unsightly in 1948 than in its refurbished state today.

The wall is simple but not plain (Wright throughout his life tried to educate Americans to the fact that civilized simplicity is not that of a "barn wall"). The richness of the detailing and the drama of the arch save it from severity. There are no loud signs: the architecture, as it should be, is the shop's only advertisement. At night the subtle lighting, including the soft glow from the interior which fills the arch, offers an example of good civic behavior which is as rare in San Francisco as in all other American cities.

And as soon as one is beneath the arch — so reminiscent of the neo-Romanesque arches which were a popular feature of U.S. architecture in Wright's youth, but so freshly used that it appears wholly modern — the spirit and function of the architecture suddenly blend with new organic richness that was not altogether apparent from the street.

The circular form of the arch, continued in a rounded tunnel of glass, is in fact an architectonic introduction to the spiraling interior — a play of space which rotates slowly beneath the luminous bubbles of the plastic ceiling — and which was the first of Wright's completed works to give an intimation of the great spirals of the Guggenheim Museum (which was designed before the Morris Store, in 1946, but finished only in 1959).

This interior strikingly reveals what Wright — fascinated by the sculptural qualities of concrete — meant when he urged: "Why not throw away entirely the implications of post-and-beam?" Instead, he offered an interpenetration of "continuous space": "Space. The continual becoming: invisible fountain from which all rhythms flow and to which they must pass."

The Morris Store is a veritable fountain of such space, rising on the great swell of the circular ramp which leads to the upper level. Every detail of this composition — the beautifully drawn line of the handrail which runs along the ramp, for example — adds delicate intensity to the overall effect. Under the store's new ownership (of which I'll have more to say in a moment), some of the details have been badly marred, even ruined, but Wright's intentions are still unmistakable. Here is a cavern of quiet — almost a sea grotto (which some of Wright's critics liken to a "fishbowl") — in which space flows like water.

But the building, after all, is a shop (and a very successful one, which provided a handsome return on the heavy investment until the Morrises grew ill in their last years), and it is interesting to note that the architecture, as Wright intended, is at once the most courteous and persuasive of salesmen. The circular niches are really showcases, just as Wright's circular furniture is also part of the sales apparatus. The ramp, leading gently upward, is an invitation to the top of the store such as no staircase could provide.

All this, it would appear, should have been obvious to the shop's new owner, the Los Angeles silversmith Allan Adler, who himself is a craftsman of some ability. When he acquired the store, in fact, Adler's announced intention was to keep the store as it was, making only the most minor changes, some of which Wright himself probably would have agreed to, such as a reorganization of the jewelry department at the rear of the lower level. Yet although Wright's staff — including his very able representative in San Francisco, Aaron Green — remained on the scene after the Master's death, no effort was made to consult them when the recent changes were made.

Wright — always sensitively respectful of materials — had furnished the interior in natural, brushed concrete which, before it was poured, had been tinted a soft beige: the marvelous Wrightian sand color. Over a decade it had been soiled in places, and could have been cleaned, but the new owner mercilessly painted it white.

The Wrightian furnishings have been ruthlessly removed from the jewelry department, at the rear of the lower level, and replaced with the most commonplace tables and showcases which could be seen in any trinket shop. Here, too, ugly green carpeting — green is supposedly flattering to jewelry — has been laid on Wright's fine paved floor. The walls have been covered with burlap, and then painted a light green which would have given the Master apoplexy.

In the most unfortunate touch of all, the new owner intends to replace the charming bed of green plants in the archway with a glass showcase, so that "vulgar merchandising" will now return to this, as to any ordinary sidewalk. Somehow, some way, the public must convince Adler of the folly of this betrayal of Wright's design.

Once, after he had finished the Imperial Hotel in Tokyo, Wright was told by *his* old master, Louis Sullivan: "At last, Frank, this is something they can't take away from you."

In his bitter indictment of mass vulgarity, *Genius and the Mobocracy*, Wright reflected: "I wonder why he thought 'they' couldn't take it away from me? 'They' can take anything away from anybody."

September 25, 1961

■ AFTER THE CITY OF PARIS

John Carl Warnecke & Associates, architects of the Neiman-Marcus store which will replace the doomed City of Paris at the southeast corner of Union Square, has announced that the new building will be "done in the spirit of the old structure."

In particular it will have an "important" interior space that, happily enough, will be covered by the same wonderful skylight of colored glass — the glory of the present rotunda — which will be salvaged before demolition begins.

This is virtually all we know about the proposed design, except that the main entrance will be moved up Geary Street to the corner of Stockton, in order to line up with the diagonal of the square.

Otherwise we are completely in the dark so far as the quality of the new building is concerned.

Anxious San Franciscans, however, need only to glance at the skyline, where the new Federal Building, the Hilton Tower, the Chinatown Holiday Inn and other major structures by the Warnecke firm now figure prominently, to gain some inkling of the kind of architecture that may be in store for them on Union Square. [Note: Warnecke lost the City of Paris commission to Philip Johnson, but this appraisal of the firm's work remains remorselessly accurate.]

At best, of course, Neiman-Marcus could — and should — give San

Francisco a finer building than the decent old monument it is going to destroy.

At worst, and the Warnecke firm's design for the mammoth Tishman Building on lower Market Street reveals how bad that really could be, such an approach to design — for all the talk about creating an important new space — might merely amount to punching a big hole in an ill-conceived structure and clumsily mounting the old skylight above it.

Warnecke has built a number of creditable buildings, all rather small, chiefly schools, and mainly in redwood. Nothing he has done since is better than the Mira Vista Elementary School of 1951, across the bay in Richmond, whose broadly gabled roofs climb a steep hill with considerable vigor and charm.

But then, like other redwood regionalists who did well enough in the suburbs, but had little experience in the big city, he expanded his office and started to work on a much larger scale, in steel and other industrial materials, in San Francisco.

What followed was a series of weakly designed and executed, but undeniably big buildings, which were made doubly unfortunate because of the importance of their sites.

The first of these calamities was the brutal Federal Office Building, with its fake portico, which in 1959 utterly disrupted the classical order of the Civic Center.

Warnecke & Associates shared the commission with other firms, but took credit for design.

Far from being an emblem of democratic government, it is a symptom of maladies that infect it: uncouth officialdom, bureaucratic tyranny, heavy-handed misuse of industrial technology and chilling indifference to individuals unlucky enough to spend time within its thick frame. Anyone who finds the exterior oppressive should venture within, especially to the clerical compounds on the upper floors, and sample personally the labyrinthine, harshly lit and cheap looking (although in fact fairly expensive) U.S. government environment.

Across town, another public space — Portsmouth Plaza, where the American flag was first raised in San Francisco — also suffered irreparable harm in 1971 when Warnecke's firm, this time in company with architect Clement Chen, erected an odd concoction called the "Chinese Cultural Center," which is nothing more than the Redevelopment Agency's euphemism for a Holiday Inn with a spare room for Chinese artifacts.

This bulbous slab, from whose roof nonstructural ventilation ducts emerge like tumors, exhibits just about every mistake that can be committed in civic design. It arrogantly turns a narrow side to the square, squirting a very mistaken bridge across Kearny Street into its center, depriving the tiny playground of light, and almost incidentally, ruining the Kearny Street vista toward Telegraph Hill.

If this were not enough, the Holiday Inn has also ripped open a hole in the eastern flank of the square, which was once staunchly filled — as the side of a square should be — by the old Hall of Justice. The loss of this neoclassical palazzo seems especially lamentable because at modest cost it would have made an excellent cultural center for Chinatown.

On the site of still another destroyed classical monument, the templelike Fireman's Fund Insurance Building, across from the even finer (and magnificently preserved) temple of the Bank of California at the intersection of California and Sansome streets, one of the best emplacements in the financial district, the Warnecke firm designed one of its least convincing towers in which Great Western Savings is the main tenant.

Here a nostalgic, but perhaps justifiable local motive — the San Francisco bay window — was simulated, if not parodied, by alternatively projecting bays of dark glass, which appear tacked on — or rather, glued — to the face of the building. This strangely characterless curtain wall seems to unroll upward like so many lengths of Saran Wrap, and there is a slickness about the whole building that makes it unworthy of its solid neighbors, the banks, insurance companies, shipping lines and corporation headquarters that front on California Street.

An even worse tower, because it is much bulkier and heavier, is the recently completed Tishman Building on lower Market Street, massively blocking the view at the foot of Battery Street, which is worth a glance if you are wondering what is actually meant by the Manhattanization of San Francisco.

This insensate skyscraper, some 40 stories tall, is about as clumsy an essay in concrete-covered steel as we have in the city.

Its striated facades, ribbed vertically by narrow bands of concrete and glass (which reduce window areas and views, but also cut down on air-conditioning loads), violate one of the cardinal principles of modern architecture: structural veracity.

This arbitrary striping of the walls not only hides but falsifies the internal nature of the building: its somewhat dense and heavy — but logically consistent — grid of steel.

But it is when this huge lump of a building hits the street in the successive thuds of its colonnade that its full banality can be appreciated.

Here again, what seems to be an indifference to architectonic sensibility is exposed in the cumbersome forms of what is supposed to be a plaza, but is nothing more than a jumble of unrelated elements squashed by the bulk of the tower: thickly modeled stairs and balustrades, a chunky clock tower that seems too short, roughly proportioned paving — all done with a dull, confused blandness.

What all of these buildings lack is architectural character. There is no discernible aesthetic development, no strong philosophical commitment — even a bold commitment with which one might disagree, but still respect — as one moves from building to still bigger building, culminating in the Hilton Tower.

The parvenu interiors of the Hilton, like those of the Holiday Inn, cannot be attributed to the Warnecke firm, but to interior decorators who have remorselessly demonstrated the taste of the management.

The Hilton exterior, however, unmistakably belongs to the same boring family of buildings which resist analysis as fine architecture because of their very absence of refinement. This 46-story shaft — one of the tallest objects in the skyline — has the look of an early schematic sketch, obviously in need of further study, for example in the lines of cantilevered floors which project in the upper facade, the windows that dribble down end walls, and the utilities blocks which sit like lumps on the roof.

Perhaps it would be unreasonable to ask more of what has become a nationwide firm, now mainly based in New York, where a 160-man staff handles Neiman-Marcus' work.

One last thing that Neiman-Marcus might do, before the City of Paris goes down, would be to donate a photographic study of the building to the architectural school at Berkeley, so that future students could see what San Francisco has lost.

For if the City of Paris is not exceptionally distinguished on the exterior, it was nevertheless carefully done according to neoclassical principles that were fully intelligible to its architect, Clinton Day, back in the 1890s. The City of Paris at that time rented only the bottom two floors as a store; the four upper stories were offices.

Clinton Day therefore knew that, because the client required tall spaces only for the store, he would have to maintain monumental scale and mood by treating the upper parts of the building as heroically as possible, without falsifying their floor divisions.

This he did with much skill, using Doric pilasters to frame the large openings at the base, and carrying their lines upward to a decisive cornice (removed as an earthquake hazard only a year ago), which gave harmony and coherence to the whole. Then, within this grand scheme, he used an increasingly rich classical vocabulary — first Ionic columns and then Corinthian — to carry his building upward in successive two-story stages.

All this is as old as the Colosseum in Rome, and we would not do it again today: but it was done pretty well in San Francisco around 1900, and it is a shame for ourselves and our children to lose it.

But the loss of the radiant, sun-filled rotunda is a tragedy, and not only the conservationists whose eyes filled with tears at the Planning Commissions' decision, but all of us know it, including Jack Warnecke's spunky daughter Margo who tried to save it.

The rotunda actually dates from after the fire, when the inside was gutted, even though the walls remained erect. While the City of Paris moved to temporary quarters on Van Ness Avenue, the whole interior was rebuilt as a department store, and the rotunda was opened for business in 1909.

The architect this time was not Clinton Day, but a superior architect — almost unknown today — named J. R. Miller. Whether he himself did the rotunda or whether it was designed by some still unidentified person in his office, it is unquestionably architecture on a high level.

The rotunda is not actually an enormous space. The beautiful ellipse of the skylight — in which the legendary golden ship of Paris floats on a snowy field of white glass — measures only 55 by 36 feet. But it is the apparent size and spaciousness of a building that give it scale and civilized presence, and here the architect succeeded admirably through richness of detail.

Probably never again will San Francisco see such a Parisian mixture of Art Nouveau and neoclassical detail so richly drawn in the manner of French department stores of *la Belle Epoque*: the lovely classical masks of the goddesses, their hair twined with vine leaves and dripping grapes like pearls, the fluted columns and lush capitals, the varying baroque outlines of the several levels, right up to the gilded sea gods who, at either end of the skylight, seem to hold the golden ship aloft.

The motto Felix Verdier put on the first City of Paris in 1850 was *Fluctuat nec Mergitur* — "It floats and never sinks" — and he chose as a symbol the ship in full sail. He thought he knew its destination, and one can only hope, after the City of Paris is gone, that the vessel will find a noble port.

August 15, 1974

The regional shopping center is an American invention of the 1950s. Not even the Grand Bazaar of Constantinople, or the glass-covered shopping arcades of the 19th century, although similar in some ways, offer true historical precedents for the immense complexes of department stores, specialty shops, eateries, pubs, movie houses, ice rinks and other commercial amusements, linked by landscaped malls, and surrounded by 50 or 100 acres of parking lots, that first sprouted at the edge of U.S. cities, like Victor Gruen's Northland on the rim of Detroit in 1952.

In San Francisco the smaller and less interesting Stonestown was designed by Welton Becket & Associates about the same time, with the Emporium's first branch as its anchor.

Suburban centers followed, such as Hillsdale and Stanford, both mainly by Becket and equally crude architecturally. But then the center developers moved outward to remote, still half-rural locations, like Concord, where SunValley opened in 1967, and Eastridge (1971) in the far reaches of San Jose, awaiting suburban sprawl to catch up with them.

Each of these very big centers (Eastridge has four major department stores and a total of 1.6 million square feet in leaseable space) not only dwarfed less-imposing competitors, for example Valley Fair in San Jose, but also revealed successive advances in shopping center design. The Bay Area, if not the front-runner in every respect, became one of the leading places for this kind of architectural innovation.

For it had become clear by the 1960s that the giant centers constituted a new kind of serious architectural problem on the order of airports or universities.

They are virtually cities in themselves, with as many as 3,000 employees, serving regional populations of half a million. In almost every aspect of design, especially their enclosed, air-conditioned malls, they differ decisively from complexes that have only one or two department stores, and sometimes none at all.

The intimately scaled, tree-shaded Town & Country in Palo Alto, to name one of the earliest and still among the finest of the smaller centers, is merely a collection of shops and restaurants carefully arranged around a parking lot.

Like the Strawberry Town & Country in Marin, or the redwood Boardwalk in Tiburon, not to speak of stagy "theme centers" like the Old Mill in Mountain View, these are toy buildings compared to the tremendous ensemble of Hilltop, the newest and architecturally most significant of the big Bay Area centers, just off Interstate 80 as it heads out of Richmond toward Pinole.

Hilltop seems as formidable as an aircraft carrier on its barren site, a former Chevron tank farm which someday will be softened by hundreds of newly planted trees. For the time being, however, the 80 acres of black-top — parking for 6,500 cars — is very raw, plainly exposing the huge building for what it is: a rectangular shell more than 1,000 feet long and half as wide, soberly walled in dark brown concrete block, that encloses 1 million square feet of easily divided, rentable space, flanked on three sides by the great blocks (approximately 200,000 square feet each) of Capwell's, Macy's and J.C. Penny. A fourth department store, presumably Sears, will go up on the north.

The whole mass has a strong and, for a shopping center, fairly unified presence, which would be stronger still if the department stores had been better integrated in the overall design, especially Capwell's, which crassly juts above the others with an expanse of orange tiles and ugly signs that are at odds with the entire composition.

But it *is* a composition, deserving of the name architecture, unlike the crude merchandising diagrams of Stonestown a quarter of a century ago, and indeed of many other centers — Eastmont in Oakland, Bayfair in San Leandro, El Cerrito Plaza — that have been perpetrated since then.

In spite of Hilltop's numerous flaws, many of which — like Capwell's and the hideous fronts of many small shops inside — were beyond his control, the architect of this extraordinary center, Avner Naggar, a 52-year-old Israeli-born, but Berkeley-trained specialist in this field of de-sign, has succeeded in elevating Hilltop — like its predecessor Eastridge which he also designed — to what may be fairly called an important level of social art.

The chief significance of Hilltop and Eastridge, in fact, lies in their spectacular interiors — especially the grand, skylit central courts 160 feet across and 55 feet high, quite separate in mood, but both enriched by sculpture and fountains — whose luxurious seating areas, sweeping stairs and ramps, and dramatically changing levels make each of them worth an architectural pilgrimage.

To appreciate them fully, however, it is best to go back 15 years, when Naggar first arrived in the Bay Area as "in-house" architect for A. Alfred Taubman, the Detroit developer who has built a modest construction business into a nationwide shopping center empire.

Taubman had then acquired an interest in Southland, a sizable Hayward center designed by John Graham of Seattle (who despite the coarseness of this job did much better in Lloyd Center in Portland, where 8,000 cars are skillfully concealed in garages that run beneath the shop-ping areas above). To see how superior Naggar's work is to the ordinary level of this cutthroat field of building, one has only to glance at additions he made to Southland, notably the very decent Liberty House store.

At the same time, the early 1960s, Taubman and his partners were building a new center of their own, Sun Valley in Concord. Here Naggar shared responsibility with John Bolles, designer of all the Macy's stores in this part of the country; and because the site was not large enough for all the parking Taubman wanted, they decided on a two-level parking structure which — as at several other centers — led to the idea of two levels of shops within, unlike the single-level arrangements typical at the time.

The result, ungainly enough architecturally, was something like a pair of single-level centers placed one upon the other, but when Naggar tackled the problem of Eastridge a few years later, he saw great opportunities in a multilevel scheme, even though he had an enormous site — a former golf course with many handsome trees, on which to work.

Before Eastridge, centers like SunValley had "dumbbell" plans: that is, a department store at each end connected by a mall. The malls themselves, at that time, were awful enough, with the worst sculpture conceivable, terrible refuse containers, WPA benches, plastic trees, and bird cages with recorded birdcalls.

But the scheme was also less profitable than it could have been: a prime consideration to Taubman (who, as it happens, was educated as an architect at Ann Arbor, and has a sizable art collection of his own).

Consequently at Eastridge they adopted a cross-shaped plan, with long malls on upper and lower levels extending 790 feet between department stores at either end, and shorter cross malls between the department stores on either side — four big establishments in all, which meant twice the previous income.

Where these malls intersected, something totally unforeseen and exciting occurred. For they did not have to meet at the same level, but could enter a great space at several different levels allowing an unprecedented confluence of movement by tens of thousands of shoppers.

Naggar, shaping the earth on the vast site to provide entrances at these different levels, varied the slopes of the parking areas — a subtle form of customer control — at intervals of six feet, so that, when the malls met at the heart of the building, he could have a third level — an intermediate floor 12 feet high — for still more shops.

All this permitted enrichment of internal space, at Eastridge a triangular composition of outwardly moving power, upward and downward, generating energy on all sides, and traveling strongly down the vistas of the long malls, interlaced with ramps and stairs, with views from level to level beneath angular skylights.

To many customers this was too powerful — even "awesome," Naggar remarked. And so when he faced the problem one more time at

Hilltop, all was softened in curves and rounded forms including the cascading central fountain, above which Charles Perry's curving sculpture of aluminum tubes has been suspended, in a popular architecture of delight.

The sculpture may not be so good as Perry's centerpiece in John Portman's towering atrium in the Hyatt Regency, but the rooms surely bear comparison, and in many ways Naggar's less costly spaces come off better. To many they both may be merely cynical, openly commercial, crowd-pleasing architecture, but they are architecture — uninhibited and filled with genuine energy, if also flashy and often superficial.

Compared to what went on before in shopping centers, that is undeniable progress. But is it enough? If Eastridge and Hilltop belong to a "second generation" of centers, and have been imitated across the country, there is already a third generation emerging — still more mammoth complexes organized about six or eight or even more department stores, in places as widely separated as Dearborn, Mich., and the Irvine Ranch in Southern California.

Architecturally, they are not merely bigger, but better. Details are more highly refined; vistas and spaces are more deftly organized, which is another way of saying more controlled. For this is above all an architecture of manipulation, creating "good time" environments in which no one has much fun, but billions of dollars are exchanged by a fascinated public. And always there are the seemingly endless tundras of parking lots, even though they can also be seen as land reserves, on which housing and other buildings may be built, and the cars hidden beneath them.

This may all come true. But the outlying shopping centers, cities in themselves, have also had a vast effect on inner cities, downtown Oakland for instance, where in many a forlorn block, half-deserted and cheerless, stores have been vacated for new locations at Hilltop, Sun Valley, Southland, El Cerrito. Here is a place to build a new kind of center, more humane than present developers dream, that will be an integral part of the City of Man.

September 26, 1977

■ THE NUT TREE — AN OASIS OF GOOD TASTE

In the desert wastes of the commercialized American roadside, the Nut Tree at Vacaville, 30 miles this side of Sacramento on Interstate 80, seems too good to be true.

But true it is: an oasis of excellent taste surrounded by a Sahara of vulgarity.

Not only architecturally, but in virtually every other aspect of design, the Nut Tree stands in a class by itself among major drive-in facilities.

If it lacks the mad, outlandish vigor of semisurrealist roadside art such as the Madonna Inn near San Luis Obispo, the ordinary motorist's Hearst Castle which for sheer exuberance makes Howard Johnson's orange roofs and McDonald's glowing arches seem tame, the Nut Tree has a sustained elegant grace that can be matched only by a few highway establishments in the whole country.

Nothing is fake. There are no pseudohistoric Disneyland stage sets. What is new is warmly and honestly new. What is old, such as the Harbison family home with its classical portico of the 1900s, is respected for its real worth.

From the lofty steel-framed main dining room to specially built rocking horses and playhouses that are freely available to children, the thriving 170-acre complex of restaurants, shops, miniature railroad, airport and parklike grounds, on both sides of the highway, is a humanely ordered environment, warmly gracious.

All this is due to an unfailingly high standard of contemporary design, unashamedly applied to commercial strategy.

This even includes advertising billboards far down the freeway. All of the displays, from the presentation of food on a plate to beautiful educational playthings in the toy shop, receive meticulous consideration. Tropical birds in the restaurant's glass-walled aviary sup from white modern bowls as handsome as the Rosenthal ceramics of the nearby diners, who sit on Eames chairs around Eames tables.

The story of how this came about, in Vacaville, goes back to 1921, when Ed and Helen Power first started selling their ranch's fruit and nuts beside the highway.

After World War II, having been joined in business by their equally enterprising children, the Powers brought in a young designer from Los Angeles, Don R. Birrell, to take charge of aesthetics. He is the main creative spirit behind the Nut Tree's design to this day.

It was Birrell who recommended the then-unknown Sacramento architectural firm of Dreyfuss & Blackford to do the buildings in a sizable expansion program that has gone on intermittently ever since.

The architects' first project was a new restaurant and an entrance canopy. Handsomely framed in steel, the restaurant — now 20 years old — looks as if it were built yesterday.

At one end, the lofty space — 16 feet high and 40 feet across — is completely walled-in glass beneath a deep overhang that shields it from

the sun, so that it is elatingly open to the planting and sculptures outside.
Such bold use of steel could have been brutal, but here it has been
softened and given a subtle regional tone by many skillful devices. Although this is a big space, many of the tables are sheltered by canopies of
cloth which make them intimate little dining pavilions.

The fabrics have changed over the years, and are now mainly prints
from Indonesia.

The precast concrete walls are enlivened by field stones of the valley —
quartzite jasper and petrified wood. Colors are muted earth tones. And, as
a background for the delightful decorative panels with which Birrell has
hung the room, the upper walls are covered with cocoa-fiber matting.

Such devices break up the scale of what is, after all, a very large series of
buildings, filled with salable art (some good, some not so good) as well as
other merchandise.

In the store areas, especially the 24-foot-high steel-framed "patio" shop
designed by Dreyfuss & Blackford at the start of the 1970s, airplane models
(the Power family is very big on flight) hang from the ceiling. The models
are especially attractive to the hundreds of customers who fly in from all
over the West — as many as 300 planes land on a Sunday — to taxi across
the tree-surrounded Nut Tree field, surely one of the most delightful rural
airports we have, with its miniature train connection to the shops and
restaurants.

Not all parts of the complex are equal in design. The Coffee Tree, a
more moderately priced coffee shop added in the 1960s on the other side
of the highway, is clearly less distinguished than the best work of Dreyfuss
& Blackford at the Nut Tree. It's an odd concoction, reminiscent of ordinary, strident highway construction, with a soaring roof that is almost a
parody of a pagoda.

But it's all commercial architecture competing in a fierce market. And
now, the Nut Tree's entire selling operation, once so original, can be
found at regional shopping centers, local stores in Fairfield or Vallejo, as
well as in San Francisco boutiques.

Consequently Birrell and Dreyfuss & Blackford are developing designs
to enable the Nut Tree to meet still tougher competition in the coming
decade. The master plan includes a motel, a resort inn, more restaurants,
and a futuristic new little railway, all silvery metal and glass. Like several of
the most imaginative details at the Nut Tree — such as the climb-in plane
for kids at the airport — it is the work of designer Roger Fleck.

Best of all, the center of the old Nut Tree, still covered by a slanting
wooden roof that goes back to the old days, will be replaced by a 40-foot-
high space frame, tall enough to hold historic airplanes.

If the best standard of the past is maintained, this could be one of the

special things in California, a highway Crystal Palace, as the Nut Tree —
with its first charming branch store now open in San Francisco, designed
by Fleck next to the Wine Museum on Beach Street — extends its operations more widely though the state.

March 20, 1978

■ THE PORT'S ARCHITECTURAL FIASCO — PIER 39

Corn. Kitsch. Schlock. Honky-tonk. Dreck. Schmaltz. Merde. Whatever
you call the pseudo-Victorian junk with which Warren Simmons has
festooned Pier 39, this ersatz San Francisco that never was — a *chef
d'oeuvre* of hallucinatory cliches — is a joke on the Port and Planning
commissions, a joke on architects John C. Walker and Bruce Moody,
which they may come to regret (for hitherto their work could be taken
seriously) and an especially bad joke on the whole unfortunate city,
which must live for the next 60 years — that's right, sixty — with this
childish excrescence, which was stupidly allowed to deface the northern
waterfront.

It's a poor joke to everyone, indeed, except to promoter Simmons
himself, who will be smiling all the way to the bank, together with as-
sorted city officials, who were involved in decisions concerning the
project (or their close relatives), who now have businesses on the 1,000-
foot-long pier.

That the scheme would be an architectural fiasco was accurately
predicted by many unhappy souls, none more despairing than yours
truly 14 months ago in an insufficiently wicked column, which, if anything, underestimated the extent of the disaster that has since occurred.

Now, there is a difficulty in writing architectural criticism about
nonarchitecture. It is a little like applying literary criticism to illiteracy.

It has been done, for example in Stalinist journals where the buildings
seem to be by veritable Michelangelos until you see pictures of them.

Lately, too, there has been an inverted critical snobbery, practiced by
mandarins of the architectural schools, which finds environmental virtue
in places like Las Vegas or Miami Beach.

This in fact is how Walker & Moody hope their designs may be
judged, as a kind of "Post-Modern" or "ad-hoc" populism — that is, the
vernacular building of mass consumption merchandising.

But these deliberately jumbled groups of contrived shacks with cash
registers and stainless steel kitchens inside bear the same relation to truly

indigenous folk building that the fare Simmons used to dish up in his Tia Maria tamale parlors bore to authentic Mexican cooking.

To understand the false cityscape, which has been erected on the huge pier, it may be helpful to think of the linear composition as the two-level central mall of a regional shopping center, opened to the air, and without the big department stores at either end.

The mall is ingeniously widened and narrowed, so that it opens in "squares" or piazzas, and closes in "streets," which enables the developer to cram a number of smaller businesses among the larger ones. A meandering pattern — seemingly free, but in fact cleverly controlled — is set up for strollers amidst this "planned chaos," so that at times they will almost lose their way among a welter of shops and eateries, but this leads them before the maximum number of establishments where wallets can be lightened.

Actually, the sales formula is simple.

Of the total of 200,000 square feet of space, 140,000 — nearly three-fourths — has been allocated to restaurants, whereas 60,000 has gone to shops.

Because the restaurants (and their bars) are so much larger, however, there are 25 of them compared to no less than 105 shops.

Some of these shops, in an adroit touch, appear to be the "ateliers" of artisans, where you can also have the good luck to buy examples of their work, such as jewelry turned out before the customer's eyes. This is not so folksy an operation as it may seem. The shop of the "Barbary Coast Blacksmith" is manned by a brawny young employee, hovering above a smoky coal fire (in a badly ventilated space that warrants the attention of city health inspectors). On order, he will turn out a souvenir horseshoe, or a crudely turned iron candlestick holder (one was priced at 40 bucks), although if you don't wish to wait, you can find the same item already made on the shelves.

It is a sort of vulgar vaudeville, in key with the tapdancers and other performers who appear on little stages projecting between shop entries, to say nothing of the incredibly old-fashioned slapstick of some clownish divers.

Is this what San Francisco deserved on one of the most magnificent waterfront sites in the world?

Lewis Mumford said that every community gets the architecture it de-serves, and I suppose that, considering the circumstances, San Francisco was bound to receive an architectural farce.

That's what the scene looks like, as one enters beside a brand-new, old-fashioned carousel — completely done in plastic — which was specially made in Italy to show us what historic merry-go-rounds looked like. (If you're interested, there's a real beauty in Tilden Park in Berkeley, which a couple of years ago was almost sold off.)

The buildings themselves differ from the merry-go-round in the sense that, on the outside at least, they are made of natural rather than imitation wood.

But the wood, in a strange trompe-l'oeil, somehow seems fake. This is partly because much of it was salvaged from the pier before Simmons rebuilt it; and although the timbers used for decking seem acceptable enough, the siding of the building appears very odd because of its old, patchy whitewashed surfaces.

Simmons thinks they are "beautiful," even though the architects admit they would prefer to clean them up with wire brushes and soap and water, so they do not look like reused chicken coops.

Wood can — and has been — salvaged from old barns and other structures very successfully. The key to doing this right is to match the old planks carefully, piece by piece if need be, almost like matching marble, in something close to previous patterns.

On Pier 39, where no time was taken for such niceties, the planks were sawed up in six-foot lengths, and then slapped up, with unwhitewashed gaps showing at regular intervals where studs had been, so that it somehow resembles imitation stone masonry. I don't know how this occurred, but it's obvious as soon as you enter.

Combined with new wood surfaced with several different stains and washes, edges with coarse approximations of Victorian molding and brackets, and topped with an occasional phony mansard roof, the reused wood simply seems silly.

Yet the crowds — already averaging 20,000 to 25,000 weekdays, 44,000 on Saturday and 50,000 on Sunday — apparently think it is fine.

"I'm a peasant," said Simmons. "I put up what pleases the peasants, and they love it."

Upon reflection, this seems not so far from Dr. Johnson's remark that he rejoiced "to concur with the common reader"; and this mass approval, which must be seen as a popular verdict on the design, makes one wonder how advanced the Bay Area may be culturally above the American outback.

According to Simmons' scouts, 88 percent of his customers are local gentry. No less than 53 percent come from San Francisco, 31 percent from the rest of the Bay Area, and 4 percent from elsewhere in Northern California.

By contrast, the sheep being sheared in the nearby pens at Fisherman's Wharf are 90 percent outlanders, with 10 percent from Northern California.

These figures, as Simmons conceded, are his own, and perhaps self-serving. But if they are only half-accurate they would be deeply disturbing, and might cause nostalgic Herb Caen to call for the cup of hemlock, in one of Pier 39's nightmarish restaurants. (If you find the cornball exteriors strange, you should see the mad interiors to know that surrealism is alive and well as a pop-art movement in the hands of Los Angeles restaurant designers.)

Is this actually what Bay Area residents really wanted on the northern waterfront? And if so, what's wrong with it? What, asks architect Sandy Walker, should have been done otherwise, especially since BCDC regulations — and conservationist pressure — prevent housing and any nonnautical businesses here? (Mass feeding and sleazy entertainment are "water related" if they occur on a pier.)

To this I would answer that public officials — especially a port commissioner such as Harry Bridges who all his life stood for higher values for ordinary people — had a responsibility for social and cultural excellence, excellence such as that of the Exploratorium in the Palace of Fine Arts, on what is after all public property.

Planning officials, high-sounding but when the crisis came, astonishingly weak, should have demonstrated convincingly that an operation such as Simmons' would choke the already crowded waterfront with thousands of cars, turning it into a monoxide alley seven days a week.

Even when his partly completed 1,000-car garage — a real brute that flower boxes won't help much — is finished, and when construction of the new Embarcadero sewer no longer obstructs circulation, what had been a relatively pleasant part of the city is going to be permanently noisy, smelly and unnecessarily restless where it should have been calm.

It will be more jammed still in the future, thanks to the Muni's decision to run four or five special shuttles to Simmons' front door, even though decent bus service for places like Hunters Point somehow can't be provided.

Things aren't helped much by the dry little five-acre park that the city compelled Simmons to install on the shoreline. He promised it would be as handsome as Sidney Walton Park in Golden Gateway Center, but it is little more than a dull strip of grass bordered by sycamores, with imitation 19th-century benches strewn about.

The views up and down the waterfront, moreover, have been blocked by a heavy pedestrian bridge between the pier and the garage (wait until it's finished to see how much it really interferes with views), which the city approved on grounds of pedestrian safety, but is nothing more than a chute to pour customers into the upper level of his project.

Even this light bridge, which could have been elegant, turned out to be an ungainly clunker, abruptly changing directions after it crosses the Embarcadero, so it cuts off views of the great urban drama of the waterfront in two directions. (The marinas created by Simmons on either side of Pier 39, on the other hand, do open up fine views of the bay.)

The ships in the distance, like the yachts in the foreground, answer Walker's question of what would have been the right architecture for this difficult site. Pier 39 should have had uncompromising architecture of our own age, meant for civilized activities beside water, just as the merry-go-round should have been a masterpiece of contemporary children's recreational design.

But this was beyond the "peasant" mentality of the promoter, if not of architects who might have known better, and now I'll go back and thatch my roof.

October 30, 1978

■ THEATRICS PACKING 'EM IN

The crowds have slackened a bit since the wild opening of San Francisco Centre, Nordstrom's new home, but the spectacular skylit rotunda is still packed much of the day.

As they say in the trade, it's a killer building.

Tens of thousands of shoppers and sightseers have come smiling through by now, standing two abreast on the already famous spiral escalators that ascend, like fantastic kinetic sculptures, through the unique "vertical" mall.

Nothing else in the retail business is quite like this downtown mix of four levels of specialty shops and eating places, enough for a sizable suburban shopping center, which are topped in an intensely urban way by four more floors of Nordstrom's best and biggest store, all opening on the dramatic central space.

People love the theatrical environment, inside and out, as if it were really architecture.

They admire the ponderous fakery of the vaguely classical facades, even though the four uppermost tiers — finished like cheap greenhouses and stepped back to avoid overshadowing Hallidie Plaza — create a top-heavy effect and throw the proportions all out of whack, squashing the lower floors.

Closer to the building, however, the upper stories vanish from view, and then the lower facades, also four stories high, come into their own, carefully organized, and decently clad in granite and "sculpted" precast concrete.

The only trouble is that they are fakes, literally false fronts, whose "windows" on the second, third and fourth levels are not windows at all.

Because the openings don't line up with the interior floors, which run right through their centers, they have been turned into blind apertures filled with muddy brown glass, as if the building were afflicted with glaucoma. By way of doubling the error, the opaque surfaces have been crisscrossed by chintzy aluminum grillwork that is a parody of bronze grills on fine old classical banks.

Never mind. Even the British spelling of San Francisco "Centre" is part of the hype.

It is basically a populist stage set that should not be taken too seriously. Even more than the huge inverted ziggurat space of the Hyatt Regency Hotel, the interior is meant to be fun while coercing buyers into spending money on their way to the top.

At San Francisco Centre, being taken for a ride is a joy. The spiral escalators, which cost nearly $500,000, go up only to Nordstrom's first level. At that point straight escalators, which cost about one-fifth as much, take over. But if the change is slightly bewildering, it adds to the spatial excitement of looking and being looked at in a towering space, 160 feet from the marble pavements of the main lobby to a retractable glass dome that, except during cleaning, will never divide in the center and retract its sides.

This flamboyant rotunda, oval rather than circular, gathers energy from its elliptical shape. To add more zip, it is slightly larger at the bottom, 88 feet long and 56 feet across, than at the top, where it measures 72 feet by 42 feet — still quite hefty dimensions.

Yet it is by no means a great domed space. It is merely a notion of the authentic greatness in, say, the powerful coiling interior of Frank Lloyd Wright's Guggenheim Museum in New York.

San Francisco Centre was never meant to be in that league. Instead of absolute confidence, it offers a profusion of conflicting lines and clamorous details, such as the strip lights on the edges of the rotunda at each floor level.

The middlebrow shop fronts on the lower levels, Nordstom's equally middlebrow displays higher up and above all the lack of authority of the dome itself — finished in tawdry dry wall below a skylight that seems borrowed from a covered swimming pool — never achieve the harmony and strength that a great lifting space demands.

But it is great show biz, a terrific performance space, in which the public is made part of the show. When the first customers burst into the rotunda, which is paved with the same parti-colored Italian marble as the Sacred Portal of St. Peter's of Rome, they ecstatically waved their charge cards, to the applause of Nordstrom's staff lining the upper floors.

For Neiman-Marcus (destroyer of the City of Paris) and Saks Fifth Avenue (destroyer of the Fitzhugh Building), ensconced in their unlovable new stores on Union Square, it is to die watching Nordstrom pull them in on the wrong side of Market Street.

Yet all of the shopping district will profit from the ingenuity of Los Angeles developer Sheldon Gordon, the man who brought Nordstrom downtown.

San Francisco Centre was his idea, long before he landed the all-important anchor tenant, and it is bound to set a style in U.S. cities.

Certainly San Francisco has never seen anything quite like his transformation of the formerly raunchy corner of Fifth and Market streets. The supposedly risky location, for which Gordon tried to schlock off a series of outrageous schemes during most of the 1980s, turns out not to have been a big risk at all after Nordstrom got into the act.

As America's hottest retail chain, Nordstrom pitched in about one-third of the Centre's $140 million overall cost. That triggered a chain reaction all the way to Macy's. The city's main shopping axis has been extended from Union Square down Stockton Street and west on Market, where several major developments — including another multilevel shopping mall at Fourth Street and a $50 million refurbishment of the Emporium-Capwell — have been prompted by Nordstrom.

Powell Street will be cleaned up, too. The scruffy blocks have been changing over the past few years, and now the whole perspective is different from Union Square to Market Street, where the massive front of San Francisco Centre, emblazoned with Nordstrom's name in gold letters five feet high, has shouldered into view.

And glory be, whatever its flaws, whether or not the centre should be called architecture, the final design has come out so much better than expected even a year or two ago that Gordon's extraordinary retail package can indeed be considered as a higher form of pop construction.

On balance, it is a victory for environmentalists who have fought since the start of the 1980s to make this an acceptable project rather than a monstrous monument to greed and relentless bad taste.

No one expected this mock-Roman palazzo to surpass the Farnese Palace in the annals of building. The architects, Whisler/Patri of San Francisco, at Gordon's behest had previously perpetrated half a dozen outlandish and oversized schemes that took a pounding from community advocates and splenetic criticism in these columns.

In roof styles alone these aborted efforts ranged from Grauman's Chinese and Victorian mansard to Pseudo-Deco and broad-eaved Suburban. The colors at times verged on kelly green and fire-engine red.

The project was also wildly oversized. Gordon originally wanted to build a highrise office complex of 1.5 million square feet, but public protests chopped it back over the years to an all-retail operation of 695,000 square feet.

The designs remained almost incredibly ugly, however, until the city planners put the screws to Gordon after an imperfect version of the final building received an official go-ahead two years ago. If built as designed, it would have been a terrible dog, but thanks to pressure from the city planning department — and presumably with a nudge to Gordon from Nordstrom's conservative executives — the whole design has been calmed down, the colors softened and the detailing somewhat improved, even though the Post-Mod planners have had their paws all over this one.

The base especially is less garish and cut up than before. The processional advance of the four-story colonnade, interrupted only by a very unfortunate arched central portal (sporting a vulgar metal logo that looks unfinished), continues down Market Street and around the corner on Fifth without a break in the 20-foot beat.

If the top four floors can be forgotten, this base is well enough composed. Taken alone, 80 feet high to its bland cornice and 250 feet across the main frontage, it lines up almost identically with the genuine neoclassic presence of Bob Lurie's nicely recycled office building at 901 Market Street (formerly J.C. Penny) across Fifth Street, and it also sits next to the worn but still handsome Emporium with a certain parvenu complacency.

The flesh-colored pancake makeup that disfigures the Emporium is at last being mercifully covered by a coat of gray and white paint, but it can't match the masonry surfaces of San Francisco Centre which, for a shopping mall, are uncommonly decent.

The surfaces become cheaper as they recede from view, but close to the street — particularly around the tall ground-floor display windows that are braced by glass mullions and trimmed in mirror-polished brass — the cladding of greenish-granite and gray precast concrete is fairly dignified.

The specially designed lanterns and hardware, once again, are of polished brass, with door pulls of stainless steel. They not only are surprisingly presentable, but will stand up to hard use and be still easier to appreciate when the dust has settled from repairs under way on this stretch of Market Street.

Inside, it is harder to say what the final quality of the mall levels will be. Only one-third of the 90-odd specialty shops and restaurants are open, but two-thirds should be ready for the Christmas rush. Gordon is holding a few choice locations in reserve, notably ground floor premises, so that he can get the top dollar for them when the mall is in full operation. My hunch is that designs will continue to be a mix of ersatz traditional, such as Brentano's bookstore with its old-fangled carriage lamps, and "with-it" new-wave boutiques that are all neon and glass.

Nordstrom's own sales floors, concocted by Seattle designers who do all of the company's interior work, are a strange melange of blandness and, in the young women's shops, for instance, artificial radical chic. My hunch is that mid-America will love it in San Francisco as elsewhere, but what seems expressly for the Bay Area are the stylish Nordstrom restaurants and food bars overlooking Hallidie Plaza (not the bogus English pub shamelessly copied from Harrods in London).

Designed by San Francisco architect Igor Sazevich, they have a freshness and high relaxed style that seems just right at the transit hub of the region. Soon the BART/Muni station's mezzanine will open directly on the lowest level of Gordon's mall, which will not be an ordinary basement, but an upscale place to eat or shop or see a movie in the underground theater complex.

Commuters are going to pour through and merge with pedestrians entering from Fifth Street or Market Street. The spiral escalators, made by Mitsubishi (but so far used only in single stories in Japan), will become a tourist attraction. The whole surrounding area, with some 5,000 hotel rooms either recently built or under construction, will be knit to-gether in a Chamber of Commerce's dream. And, flashing their plastic, the compulsive buyers will never dream that George Bernard Shaw, near-ly a century ago, prophetically called people like them "shopkeepers' slaves."
November 14, 1988

■ RINCON CENTER — OVERBLOWN, BUT IT'S FUN

If Rincon Center's architecture were half as good as its overall planning, San Francisco would have one of the best mixed-use developments of our time.

But this mock-Baroque extravaganza is ending up a lot less than that, mainly because of its wildly overdone and partly specious Post-Modern design.

In some ways it is simply a stage set, a skylit shopping mall gussied up to look like a genuine piece of a city, with offices and housing thrown in to make it appear real.

The requisite touch of history is provided by the recycled Rincon Annex post office, a monument to New Deal idealism whose Moderne facades and famous left-wing lobby murals have been kept pretty much intact, although the interior has been gutted and remade as if an Italian street scene had been shipped over and crushed out of shape.

Yet whatever its architectural flaws, the nearly complete $155 million project makes perfect urban sense on lower Mission Street.

Even in an unfinished state, with work going on in many places, and much of the business and residential space unoccupied (although it is leasing quickly), Rincon Center has imparted a remarkable vitality and new civic focus to the rapidly changing district behind the Embarcadero.

The once-bustling waterfront area, which ceased to be a working port long before the postal facility shut down in 1981, has been jammed in the past 25 years with big, dumb office buildings that lack anything like the amenities they need, much less decent places to live — or simply to pass the time of life.

Rincon Center has started to change all that. People like it.

During the past six months, since the northern part of the project opened, upward of 3,500 visitors a day have crowded into the 85-foot-high, glass-roofed atrium — carved out of the innards of the old post office building — to eat, shop, have a drink, or merely to look at the theatrical architecture.

The whole composition came into its own as an urban design two weeks ago, when the south end of the atrium was opened to the other half of the project.

People now stroll out of the atrium into an almost equally flamboyant outdoor plaza, a somewhat different essay in curving and slanting baroque geometry, surrounded by more stage-set architecture on what had been the post office loading yard.

The plaza provides the "critical mass" that was missing, even though its shops, bars and restaurants are not yet open, and the whole complex has started to hum. At lunch hour it is hard to find a place to sit.

If the atrium and open-air plaza differ markedly in mood, together they form a continuous pedestrian environment at the heart of a tightly knit superblock, bounded by Mission, Spear, Howard and Steuart streets, which measures 550 by 300 feet, and is nearly as long as two football fields.

There will be some retail premises, including a new branch post office, on the outside of the superblock, but it is the interior space that makes it an urbane oasis.

The adjoining courts are bordered by shops, eateries and pubs at ground level, topped by four big floors of office space on the north and five or six on the south, where twin, curving apartment towers each lift 16 stories higher above Howard Street.

Never mind that the cluttered highrises, whose exteriors change from concrete to glass halfway up like eggs set in egg cups, are surmounted by queer rooftop protuberances that resemble Viking ships swallowed by sea monsters, and mar the South-of-Market skyline for miles.

The funny "hats" are par for the course in Post-Mod San Francisco, but what matters most in this shrewd urban design is not nobility and refinement. Rather, foremost is a new, somewhat Disneyish notion of commercialized entertainment which is felt as soon as the atrium is entered.

Overblown, bombastic, but plenty of fun to folks who like Pier 39, it can be charitably described as an operatic stage set, or unkindly called a pseudoclassical fraud.

Confected by the Los Angeles firm of Johnson, Fain & Pereira, with R. Scott Johnson in charge of design, it is not just another imitation of a 19th-century European shopping arcade — like the Crocker Galleria — but ersatz historic architecture that never existed at all.

The jointed "stonework" is made of painted gypsum board, essentially no different from Sheetrock in tract houses. What seem to be marble columns, adorned by what look to be metal decorations and friezes, have been painted, too, by the New York trompe l'oeil artist Richard Haas.

Haas also did the bland atrium murals that dimly echo Anton Refregier's great luminous versions of California history, Marxist statements of the 1940s, in behalf of social and economic justice, that glow on the walls of the post office lobby.

That poignant space is now strangely subdued, at times nearly deserted, although it may brighten up — perhaps not for the better — when all the stamp counters and mail-handling rooms beneath the murals are recycled as boutiques.

But at least the old WPA architecture retains its integrity.

There is no such commitment in the atrium. Even the vines drifting down from planters on the upper levels are fake (although the plants on the lower terraces and balconies, to my surprise, turned out to be real). Everywhere there is an air of contrivance and parsimony, as if the design had been nickeled-and-dimed by the development group, led by a branch of the giant Perini construction company.

And it is so heavy-handed. Although the structure is not so brutally engineered as in early versions of the design — which would have crisscrossed the central space with a thicket of crossbeams from the original post office building — the exposed framing on either side could have been made far less obtrusive for a few extra bucks.

So could the huge overhead girders, required for seismic resistance, which have been unsuccessfully camouflaged by thrifty "coffers" that simulate an openwork ceiling but look woefully oversized and top-heavy, pressing down on what should have been an elating and airy space.

Countless skylit galleries, although not many in San Francisco, have been done with more grace. But that is not what draws crowds into Rincon Center from arid surrounding highrises.

People come instead for an upbeat urban place where there is an abundance of choice and unexpected delights, like Doug Hollis' "Rain Column" water sculpture, pouring down 80 feet from a small perforated Plexiglas tray into a shallow basin.

You can sit by this fountain and enjoy a quasi-gourmet lunch from an ethnic food bar that costs as little as $2.75, or savor a cafe latte, and look around. Here people-watching is a sport, and those below are in turn on view to Rincon Center's own sizable work force, mostly Pacific Bell employees in big-windowed offices who can step out onto balconies and terraces to watch the action on the mall.

This is how cities work. They cannot escape clutter and coarse details, such as the garish chevron-patterned pavements of the esplanade or, worse, the improvised ring of potted plants that surrounds Hollis' fountain (to prevent anyone from falling into a couple inches of water and calling a lawyer). The plants needlessly break the flow of space, and so do the potted palms, which look like afterthoughts.

Yet they invite the stroller onward to the sunlit plaza that has been an instant popular success.

Here the urban precepts of W.H. Whyte Jr., the foremost advocate of "usable" public space (as opposed to unpeopled, abstract plazas), have been taken to heart in a sunny, circular piazza. It is centered around an amusing little obelisk by Joan Brown, sporting blue ceramic porpoises inspired by the WPA porpoises on the creamy facades of the post office.

As a spoof of the granite uprights in the great Baroque piazzas of Rome, including Bernini's, it is an innocent piece of nonsense, part of a merry ambience that will soon be emblazoned with shop signs, banners and other paraphernalia encouraging people to part with their money.

Nonetheless, the obelisk as an environmental toy fails to govern the basically formal piazza which — in a serious gaffe by the developers — seems not to have been finished and furnished as the architects intended.

The planter beds, which should have been meticulously designed as symmetrical parterres, have been seeded carelessly so that flowers and greenery seem almost like weeds. The off-the-shelf benches have been slapped down without any relation to the space or the architecture. Still worse, the skimpy lamp standards seem borrowed from a Hawaiian restaurant.

All this is made more preposterous by the pretensions of the architecture: "triumphal arches" above the measly doorways to the atrium and the office-and-apartment complex; more mock-classical "stonemasonry" (although this time simulated in precast concrete rather than gypsum boards); and up above, finicky curtain walls of gray glass and metal that belong on a highway strip in outer Contra Costa.

Yet it is worth ascending to the model apartments in these needlessly cut-up highrises (accessible through the Howard Street lobby), which are among the most carefully planned new housing in the city, opening on terraces and balconies that, once again, can actually be used.

In a victory for the Redevelopment Agency, which struck a three-way deal with post office administrators and the developers when the land was leased for 65 years, nearly half of the 320 units are renting at "below-market" or "affordable" rates ($600 to $1,200). The roomy free-market units go as high as $3,000 a month.

The only trouble is that the southern and easterly faces of the towers, commanding magnificent views of the Bay Bridge and the harbor, are directly above the Embarcadero freeway, whose roar makes it difficult to sit out on the terraces, or even to open a window. [Note: the freeway is now gone.]

But the view from the flats on the other side, looking down on the whole project, and outward to the massed towers of San Francisco, offers a spectacular insight into the plan of Rincon Center.

The central north-south axis of the atrium and the plaza is crossed, midway down the block, by the east-west axis of the broad, glass-canopied entries leading in from Steuart and Spear streets on either side, like a cathedral transept bisecting a nave.

And darned if the clever cruciform scheme, perfect for a shopping mall, doesn't vaguely recall powerful religious architecture of the past, like a basilica on a piazza.

That was the principle that should have been honored at Rincon Center, even on a limited budget, but once again, in this insouciant city, a great architectural opportunity was lost.

July 3, 1989

VII. Hotels, Hospitals and Housing

■ IT'S DESIGNED FOR THE GOOD TIMES

Not for many a day — not since April 18, 1906 to be precise, when the
old Palace Hotel perished in flames — have San Franciscans responded
to a great architectural space with anything like the enthusiasm they have
given to the tremendous skylit court of the Hyatt Regency Hotel at the
foot of Market Street.

Designed by the Atlanta architect-developer John Portman, it is by all
odds the most exhilarating, uninhibited and altogether spectacular space
in the history of this insouciant city.

Even the legendary Grand Court of the Palace, at seven stories, was
only half as high, and its white, classical architecture not nearly so sensational in design, as this enormous triangular room that seems everywhere
in motion, deliberately charged with wild, reckless energy, as its open
galleries surge up 15 stories, their concrete undersides glowing a hellish
red, like the inside of a ziggurat in a dream, slanting inward and narrow-
ing the space above, in deep salients, until the converging upper levels are
suddenly flung parallel to one another, only a short distance apart, and
then locked together by great girders with a kind of final violence, beneath the long strip of the skylight 170 feet overhead.

That's right: one hundred and seventy feet.

This immense, air-conditioned court, moreover, towers over a veritable indoor piazza — longer than a football field at its farthest extremi-
ties — that in itself is an extraordinary work of civic art.

For the floor of the enormous room, designed with the same razzle-
dazzle as the stories above, richly planted with full-sized trees and thousands of potted flowers, and embellished with fountains, sculpture and
tapestries, is not just a superlobby for a convention hotel (although it's
that, too, of course), but also a public place — meant for crowds and
festivity — that is larger than many historic city squares.

Like plazas that delight tourists in Europe or Latin America, it is
bordered by shops and a discotheque, and bars, restaurants and cafes —
some sexy, some sedate — whose tables spill into the central space from
the edges.

From late morning onward, the paved and carpeted passages between
these areas are crowded as little pedestrian streets. Some tables emerge

Marriott Hotel, San Francisco, California, 1990. By Jane Lidz. Courtesy DMJM.

from beneath "trellises" that offer shelter from the sheer intensity of the environment, but in this case the trellises are boldly cantilevered openwork structures that show how freely Portman tosses around industrial technology.

The sense of liberation is real. One can sit and drink and relax beside a row of chrysanthemums, enjoying a mood of *dolce far niente* and — also in a very Mediterranean way — the proximity of monumental art, including the constructivist sculpture of golden aluminum tubing by Charles Perry, lifting 40 feet above its gently overflowing, black reflective pool, at the heart of the enormous room.

Perry's beautifully considered piece, just big enough to hold its own against the colossal dimensions of the space and not seem like a bar ornament (although it is actually without traditional scale and could be any size), also pits systematic structural logic — reminiscent of Bucky Fuller's geodesics, but really quite different — against the planned irrationalism of Portman's dream architecture.

This inspired collaboration between Portman and Perry, an architect turned sculptor, makes almost all other recent public sculpture in town seem amateurish and absurd, most notably the Vaillancourt Fountain just outside the hotel.

There is plenty of other art at the Hyatt Regency (all required by the Redevelopment Agency, which provided the site as part of Embarcadero Center). None is as good as Perry's, much is merely splashy and gay and some is very bad; but all of it displays the boundless vitality and confidence — the willingness to risk and optimistic refusal to play it safe — that is the hallmark of Portman's unorthodox environment.

As no other building in San Francisco, it offers an intimation of what a popular future environment might be.

And here, in spite of the hard sell of the operation (for there are few places to sit without buying a drink), Portman is at his most brilliant as a social architect.

For all the vulgar flash of the detailing — the restless paving, abrupt changes in level, the "hot" palette of red and other strident colors, spotlight glare, canned birdcalls, and the frantic pace of the whole design — there is also genuine comfort and unashamed lushness, as in the leather hassocks of the main lounge area in which the *homme moyen sensuel*, especially if he owns a credit card, feels truly at home.

People love it. Ever since the Hyatt Regency opened with a resplendent bash that showed how it should often be used on happy civic occasions, the great court — or "Atrium" as Portman has dubbed it with a strange, classical flourish — has been just about the most popular place in town.

Not merely the usual herds of tourists ready for shearing, but San Franciscans of all ages and backgrounds and, perhaps more significantly, people from the entire Bay Area, have made the hotel an incredibly successful regional recreational facility — a fun place to go — that yanks thousands of citizens downtown from the outer Richmond or the Sunset, and farther still, from the whole far-flung suburbia around the bay.

Most of these people are by no means wildly affluent. They are usually middle, lower-middle, and — quite visibly — working-class Americans, with some money in their pockets, who may come from Duluth or Daly City.

And they have a wonderful time, or rather — what is probably more true — are persuaded by the architecture and the furnishings, at every step of the way, that they are indeed having a wonderful time, just as the seemingly luxurious but in fact so-so restaurants convince them they are enjoying haute cuisine.

There are swingers and elderly couples, families, kids, and plenty of blacks and Chicanos — mostly young and very spruced up — who obviously are at ease in the hotel.

So are the schoolchildren, brought by intelligent teachers, who splash for coins beneath the Perry sculpture, like *bambini* at the Trevi Fountain, and cheerfully acquire architectural education.

How profound is Portman's lesson?

That the ordinary person admires the Hyatt Regency may mean little enough: he also likes the Transamerica Pyramid, Pontiacs, pro football, and chewing gum.

But Tolstoy asserted, with some reason, that it is a sin to be snooty toward the aesthetics of the common people. In architecture, as in literature, one should rejoice to concur, as Dr. Johnson did, with the "common reader."

But the enormous room, seductively persuasive as it may be at first sight, does not bear careful second reading.

Certainly its principal message could not come at a better time: at a moment when modern architecture has become the most uptight, buttoned-down, boxed-in architecture in history, Portman in his flamboyant hotels in San Francisco, Atlanta, Chicago and elsewhere — if not in his basically conventional office buildings — shows one way of breaking out of the box with great gusto.

There are other ways of escaping from the cliches of modern architecture, for example in the magnificent glass-enclosed garden of the Ford Foundation headquarters in New York by Kevin Roche or, for that matter, on the flowering terraces of Roche's Oakland Museum, where the truly civilized dignity and humane grace — as distinct from the clamorous pizzazz — of the potential future environment may be discerned.

And there are many ways of creating great spaces, without the building looking as if the model had fallen off the table and was haphazardly pushed together again. An example of the use of space is the vast room — nearly 400 feet in diameter — that Myron Goldsmith of Skidmore, Owings & Merrill conceived for the Oakland Coliseum.

Such buildings represent an essentially different commitment to architecture as a fine art, simultaneously serious, noble and rich — perhaps too serious for many people.

The Hyatt Regency, on the other hand, is a partial tour de force. For the quality of the building, taken as a whole, diminishes rapidly as soon as one leaves the great space, perhaps by soaring to the revolving rooftop bar, as thousands of customers do daily, in one of the garish elevators that embellish the court as pop-art objects. "Just like riding in a pop bottle," an elderly lady with blue hair told me in the Atlanta Hyatt Regency, which contains a 22-story interior space.

Once up in the revolving cocktail lounge — a maze of mirrors and red velour which, I'm told, is the most profitable bar of its kind in the world — it's possible to see how crudely put together the rest of the hotel is.

Portman can't be blamed for the motel-like rooms, done by Hyatt's usual crew of decorators, but he is responsible for the unresolved exterior, jumbled in accordian folds for the sake of bay views on the northeast, but needlessly confused and clumsily joined with the other facades that simply are weakly drawn, with insubstantial-looking concrete cladding that resembles gray cardboard.

No advantage was taken of the possibilities of the triangular site that, even though it presented vexing difficulties, might have been opened with great cordiality to the surrounding cityscape.

Eventually, when the fourth office tower of Embarcadero Center joins the hotel on the north, its third-floor terrace will lead directly to the Atrium, so that the great space will rise overhead — like Frank Lloyd Wright's Guggenheim Museum — as soon as one enters.

But otherwise the building is hermetic, closed-in with forbidding tightness, with no decent entry on Market Street (except through the nice sidewalk cafe that has just been improvised). It would have been easy to provide a handsome entrance at the intersection with California Street: the terminus of a cable car line.

This, together with the possibility of a grand eastern entrance at Ferry Park, went almost unnoticed in the design.

Instead, the main entrance on Drumm Street is cramped within the columns of the basic structure, as if it were a loading dock.

And from here to the great space three floors above, the escalator passage is handled in a meager, cumbersome, disturbing way, so that the hotel can be recognized as the convention machine, crammed with windowless meeting rooms, that it really is.

But if it resembles any machine, it is a cash register, in both shape and function; an enormously profitable enterprise in which the enormous room is the main attraction in an entertainment world, and will enable Portman to go on to bigger things, including a 50-story space under construction in New York.

It may not be "fine" architecture, but it is a fine architectural show.

In an increasingly joyless San Francisco — striving desperately, but usually artificially, to recapture the high spirit and optimism of the Victorian era, whose sense of splendor and space was never celebrated more sumptuously than in the old Palace — we should be glad to have the Hyatt Regency.

September 13, 1974

■ THE MARRIOTT DEBATE: A HOTEL ARCHITECTS DETEST AND PEOPLE ARE CRAZY ABOUT

Flashing and sparkling above San Francisco in cascades of mirror glass, like a mutant of Las Vegas, the Marriott Hotel has generally delighted the populace and appalled the architectural community.

Both sides may be right, and it is fascinating to consider the conflicting points of view — by no means limited to highbrows versus lowbrows, patricians versus plebs, or snobs versus populists — that reveal how far we are from shaping environments in a sane and effective way.

For this bogus grand hotel, by almost every measure of architectural quality, is an absolute dog: glitzy, shallow and ruthless in its manipulation of popular taste.

Yet lots of people love it. The Marriott may not be fine architecture, but it is terrific show biz. Taken as mass-cult entertainment, it is pure pizzazz.

The glittering sheath of silver mirror glass, playing fantastic tricks with light, is a zircon ten times bigger than the Ritz. Generated by pop culture, it is pop architecture whose rounded, luminous, vaguely streamlined Art Deco form was nicknamed "The Jukebox" in these columns five years ago. The design was still on the drawing boards but could be foreseen as "a giant Wurlitzer glowing in the barroom of the San Francisco sky."

The prophecy, like Jeremiah's, lamentably came true. The amber glow is somewhat less strident, the great half-rounds of glass less bombastic, than the monstrous piece of vulgarity in the drawings, but the building is still a terrible affront to civic dignity.

Arrogantly asserting its presence in the skyline, 39 stories high and a block wide from the main entrance at Mission and Fourth streets to its frontage on Market Street opposite Grant Avenue, the Marriott and its miles of mirrored glass emerge in full brutal power.

Yet there is no denying its barbarous energy. Here is a big rogue of a building, as disruptive as the Transamerica Pyramid (another popular favorite), breaking every rule of good taste, defying every principle of scale and proportion, cheaply built and crassly detailed, but brimming with raw vitality that bursts out of its reflective silvery skin.

When the sun hits the topmost fanlights of mirror glass, 80 feet across and 40 feet high, the building "comes out" in a spectacular way.

One after the other, smaller half-rounds of silver glass light up, stepping down six, four and two stories at a time, so that parts of the building are glowing while the rest is strangely dull.

Then, as the sun moves, new mirror surfaces set off curved and rectangular flashes of light, while others go to dark, like sullen gunmetal, constantly changing in the course of the day.

In early morning, sighted from the Bay Bridge, the eastern flank of the Marriott gleams silver and pink. The southern side at midday can be silvery bronze. The most extraordinary view is from the west in late afternoon, around 5 p.m. these days, when the lowering sun turns the glass into an immense shimmering mosaic of silver and reddish gold.

Yet this is a stroke of luck, a wild throw of the architectural dice.

None of the incessantly changing reflections is a finely designed event. In fact, the whole design is a mishmash that does not bear scrutiny. Without direct sun, the glass goes dead. The ponderous block-long mass, 400 feet high, breaks up into three quite separate elements, haphazardly crushed against an off-center elevator core. All sorts of trivial details clamor for notice, and the dazzling first impression dissolves in a cheap-o pastiche whose flamboyant glass surfaces are merely technical stunts.

The curved forms are slapped against the oblong top of the building, without the slightest relation between straight lines and arcs. There was a chance for true drama here, which could have been as eloquent as the magnificent Art Deco half circles of the Chrysler Building in New York, like flashing tiaras of stainless steel, that lead up successively to its needle-like spire.

But the opportunity, if it was seen, was not taken. Marriott's cost accountants — who had a large part in ruining the project — were not about to pay for sumptuous metal cladding, when glass costs a fraction of the price. This is close to the cheapest grade of reflective glass available, squalidly framed in thick, dark-painted aluminum that looks almost black and chops up the silver surfaces.

Slender, silver metal armatures to create a seamless effect would not have cost much more. The harsh juxtaposition of thrifty materials is the main reason the hotel looks terrible in poor light — in contrast, say, to the richly opalescent and far more costly mirror glass and travertine on an office building such as 5 Fremont Center, a few blocks east on Mission Street.

The Marriott's mirror glass, however, is the sun and the moon compared to the nonreflective bronze solar glass on more than 1,000 windows below. Framed like a curtain wall of a spec office building, they belong on a suburban highway strip. So do the synthetic masonry panels — done in gutless beige that is almost a cream — that cover the rest of the building.

These are lightweight industrial products made of glass-fiber reinforced concrete, called GFRC in the trade, and cast in molds like Jell-O in cups. GFRC is not the cheapest exterior material on the market (there is a synthetic stucco called "Dryvit" you can nearly put your fist through), but it saves plenty of money in supporting structures because it is so light.

Yet it is deprived of the texture of real steel-reinforced concrete, enriched with fine aggregates, that can be nearly as handsome as stone. Even at a distance this cut-rate masonry seems bland as blotting paper.

The grubby drive-in entrance at Fourth and Mission streets — a reminder that Marriott still has the mentality of a motel business — is weakly striped with neon and embellished by granite scraps that look like leftovers, set in Thiokol joints that look like do-it-yourself home bathroom caulking.

Inside, in the parvenu lobbies and lounges, including a ponderous four-story space one floor up that must be the brontosaurus of glass-covered atriums, atrociously walled in gypsum board and furnished from Grand Rapids, the Marriott is a perfect parody of a grand hotel: a Ritz of raw democracy, where doormen are costumed as Bengal Lancers.

This is an establishment where "fresh" orange juice was squeezed yesterday, and nothing else is quite what it seems, from bogus crystal chandeliers to mirror ceilings that are not polished chrome but a pasted-on surface called Mylar. In this ambience, real marble looks like plastic veneer.

No one expects genuine feeling in a hotel chain that began as a root beer stand in 1927 and now owns something like 200 full-service hotels, 180 lesser hostelries, 500 Roy Rogers restaurants and 200 Big Boy restaurants. What was wanted in San Francisco was something higher — much higher — than Marriott's usual standard.

It is no comfort to know that it all reflects the taste of the church-going Marriott family, who will not tolerate paintings of nude ladies on the premises but who personally approved carpeting that might have been picked by Beelzebub himself — acres of carpeting in a convention hotel like this, processing credit cards like a shredder, whose enormous underground banquet and meeting facilities extend a full block southward beneath the future site of Yerba Buena Gardens.

To everyone who cares seriously about buildings and the future of San Francisco, the Marriott is still another disaster of civic design. A bitter irony of this schlock architecture is that the city's public officials (advised by a strong citizen's committee) ostensibly had powerful controls from start to end.

Instead of the great building we had a right to expect on a key corner of Yerba Buena Center, we got a garish 1,500-room convention machine that is as intrusive and awful — as soul destroying — as canned music that cannot be turned off.

■ The Story of the Hotel's Design: Marriott's notion of a "flagship" hotel was shaped, reshaped and mal-shaped by San Francisco public officials as much as it was by private architects. From start to end this mammoth tourist-shearing operation was a guaranteed architectural debacle.

First, the Canadian Eberhard Zeidler had a whack at it, and then Anthony Lumsden of the Los Angeles office of DMJM, while the Redevelopment Agency and City Planning Department futzed around the drawing boards. The design — bad to begin with — was further coarsened and cheapened at every stage by Marriott's own 2,000-person design bureaucracy back in Maryland.

Even Marriott's parsimony — the building obviously was nickel-and-dimed to death during construction — might have been less damaging if this had been a beautifully composed building, instead of a hodgepodge of three seemingly separate structures that look as though they had been squashed around an elevator core, with a mirror-glass carapace clamped on the top like an ill-fitting hat.

What makes it doubly mortifying is the city's share of the guilt.

Surely, the massing could have been much improved if the city itself had not imposed impossible restrictions on the irregular site that stretches from the corner of Mission and Fourth streets through the interior of the block, alongside old St. Patrick's Church, to a stingy entrance on Market Street.

For the city's growth-control policies, inherited from the George Moscone era, dictated that the building could not be more than 400 feet high — permitting a hotel of just under 40 stories. Yet it had to contain 1,500 rooms (or so Marriott claimed) to produce enough extra revenues, beyond a huge profit, to finance various public amenities in Yerba Buena Gardens that had been largely specified by an avowedly "anti-elitist" (but in fact small and exclusive) citizens' advisory committee called Friends of the Gardens.

Cowed by these urban villagers, the apparatchiks of the Redevelopment Agency, plus their outside design consultants who were paid hundreds of thousands of dollars in fees for ineffectual if not downright harmful advice, found themselves in an architecturally impossible position.

Not only did the agency planners have to squeeze an enormous hotel under an arbitrary height limit on a confined, irregular site. Because they had incompetently allowed the broad slab of the 700-room Meridien Hotel to block the "view corridor" down Kearny Street, former Mayor Dianne Feinstein got the City Planning Department into the act and vetoed similar destruction of the view southward on Grant Avenue.

Consequently the Marriott's first architect, Zeidler, had to push the bulky form of the building this way and that — in a no-win situation — so that the stepped-down slabs would leave a bit of sky open although the Grant Avenue view is pretty much ruined anyway.

When the configuration of the building had been basically established, everyone realized that Zeidler's architecture was otherwise terrible. This nice man's mistake had been to try to please the Post-Modernist creeps in the planning department who were then forcing pointy "hats" on buildings all over town, but Zeidler's vapid imitation of Philip Johnson — someone called it "Farouk's palace" — was so unconvincing, even to the planning and redevelopment bureaucracies, that he was given a return ticket north.

Enter DMJM. The San Francisco branch of this big Los Angeles–based design factory had been expected to do the working drawings of the project and oversee construction, but now its chief designer — the gifted but very uneven Tony Lumsden — was assigned to pep up Zeidler's concept. This he did by throwing on the wild headdress of silver mirror glass. Unfortunately, he left many crucial details to be finished by DMJM's staff here, hardly a team of Michelangelos, who, I was told, put in the mirror glass backward.

Perhaps if DMJM had exerted what the pros call "second effort," Lumsden might have decisively improved things.

He never had a chance to control the interiors, although he made minor refinements where he could. The basic layouts were set by Zeidler, but when he bit the dust, the spaces were turned over to a Santa Monica firm of hotel decorators — I guess they prefer to be called interior designers — called Hirsch-Bedner. The frothing atrium fountain is by Howard Fields. But Marriott's own staff, besides monkeying with the public spaces, were totally responsible for guest rooms upstairs. Motel-like in mood, these rooms are of an architectural barbarity rare even in chain hotels.

February 26, 1990

■ RESPLENDENT PALACE HOTEL REOPENS

The Palace Hotel — no proper San Franciscan calls it the Sheraton Palace — is again open for business this morning, and it is cause for civic rejoicing.

After decades of neglect and maltreatment, the legendary establishment has been put right in a two-year, $150 million restoration and partial reconstruction that is everywhere beyond reproach. In the great Garden Court, it is nothing short of glorious.

Since work is still going on in many parts of the building, the hotel is not doing much in the way of a formal ceremony. There will be a series of "soft" openings, rather than a single terrific blowout on the order of the opening celebration in 1909.

On that evening, there was a gourmets' feast for 1,469 diners in the Garden Court and the hotel's other major rooms and corridors to mark the present Palace's replacement of the storied Palace of 1875 that survived the earthquake of 1906 but perished, after valiant resistance to the flames, in the fire that followed.

But the spirit of the *Belle Epoque*, its unashamed opulence and sublime indifference to cost accounting, can be grasped instantly in the exquisitely restored Garden Court.

This radiant space, all creamy and gold, has been returned to us as the finest skylit dining room in the country.

Upon entering through the arched portals (which were formerly closed off by doors but happily are again open to the main lobby, as they were originally), the first impression is of a lavish display of golden light.

The room is not only the most resplendent in San Francisco, but one of the largest: 120 feet long, 85 feet wide and 44 feet high from the marble pavings to the oblong dome of amber and silvery glass. There are some 25,000 individual panes in the immense translucent skylight, arranged in 692 geometric panels, and every one of them has been taken down, cleaned, mended where necessary and replaced in a rebuilt armature under a handsome new outer skylight.

The space glows, responding to the sun, as it must have when it was finished by the patrician New York firm of Trowbridge & Livingston 83 years ago.

A soft radiance plays over the crystal chandeliers, the gilt Ionic capitals of the marbled columns and pilasters, more gold on heraldic cartouches, on gleaming sconces, in gilt niches, and still more gold on innumerable other opulent flourishes — never to be taken too seriously.

The play of golden light subtly enhances the whiteness of immaculate table linen, glistens on marble pavements and picks out red, blue and golden patterns on new carpets that are somewhat overdone in true Edwardian tradition.

But the Garden Court, like all of the Palace's main public spaces, is essentially French, not English. Its extravagance belongs to the *Belle Epoque*. Although it seems Parisian, there is nothing quite like it in Paris, except for exposition halls and department store rotundas (like the City of Paris here before it was turned into a travesty by Neiman-Marcus).

A closer relation, perfect for balmy California, is with the Cote d'Azur's grand hotels, like the Ruhl and the Negresco in Nice, or better still, as luscious as nougat, the old hotel and casino architecture of Monte Carlo.

All this, thanks to American architects educated at the Ecole des Beaux-Arts, brought a cosmopolitan civility to an earlier San Francisco. Such genuine richness is so rare in the city today that it seems a miracle that architects of the present generation, largely trained in American schools, could redo the whole of the Palace, not just the Garden Court, with something like the same civilized skill.

The San Francisco office of Skidmore, Owings & Merrill (SOM) was chief architect for the entire restoration, with Larry Doane as partner in charge and gifted Stanford Hughes (who has since left SOM to start his own firm) responsible for the all-important interiors. The transformation of the Garden Court itself, in terrible shape after long mismanagement, was done principally by Page & Turnbull, specialists in historic preservation, who are conspicuous for their flexibility and inventiveness in a field where narrow zealots abound.

But it was really a group effort, in which scores of skilled craftspeople participated, and the result is one of the top restoration jobs in the city's history. What is more, since it was impossible for the Palace in its Market Street location to compete with the top luxury hotels, it has been transformed into an up-to-date business and convention facility in the upper-middle price range. There are 45,000 square feet of meeting and conference rooms, a swimming pool, health club and other amenities serving 546 relatively small guest rooms, refurbished with much verve and ingenuity.

The overall result is one of SOM's most admirable jobs in years. As soon as one stands beneath the rebuilt porte-cochere on New Montgomery Street, there is a wonderful new sense of openness. The front doors have been moved back, at the end of a low granite staircase, and suddenly one is in a lobby that had been totally degraded by Sheraton bureaucrats with Formica minds, but now has an extraordinary spaciousness.

The reception desks are not as grand as the marble counters that were still in place after World War II, yet they have their own subdued richness in mahogany paneling and polished stone tops. The foyer areas have been logically rearranged for easier check-in and access to rooms.

Then, suddenly, as the stately main promenade is reached, running 340 feet north and south, the Palace regains its historic presence as a very grand hotel.

All the major public rooms are reached from this broad concourse, which is no longer seedy, but handsomely furnished. The hardware is polished bronze. The walls are the original false "Caen stone," simulating tawny limestone masonry in plaster that has been perfectly refinished. Large old gilded armchairs — *fauteuils* and a few veritable thrones — have been brought out of storage and reupholstered. So have some massive marble-topped tables.

Straight ahead is the Garden Court, welcoming, cordial as it has not been since it was screened off decades ago. To the right is the high-vaulted Ralston Room measuring 50 by 100 feet and holding its own spatially next to the Garden Court. Farther on, toward Market Street, is the famous old Pied Piper Bar, convincingly restored in a somewhat new arrangement. The mosaic floor, long covered by grimy rugs, has been uncovered. Mahogany paneling and painted wooden ceilings make for an admirable masculine backdrop in what was the best men's bar in the city, but is now, of course, going to delight women, too.

Work on the Pied Piper Room was still going on yesterday, and Maxfield Parrish's famous Pied Piper mural had not yet been moved back from the M.H. de Young Memorial Museum. All should be ready in a day or two, and the redone storefronts on Market Street will soon be open, too. Their original cast-iron window frames have been so faithfully reproduced in dark green aluminum that it is almost impossible to tell them from originals.

South of the Garden Court, walls have been torn out and rebuilt, and several badly related dining and meeting rooms have been thrown together to form a very decent ballroom, done with none of the crassness of other recent convention facilities in San Francisco.

Make no mistake, the Palace is now in competition with nearby pseudo-palatial hotels such as the Marriott and the Meridien. What distinguishes this dignified building from the tourist traps is the consistent high level of finishes and details, as well as strong architectonic order.

When the disastrous remodelings of some of our other historic hotels are considered — the garishness of the once magnificent Fairmont lobby, for instance, or the motellike additions to the St. Francis — the citizenry must thank the Kyo-ya Co. of Japan, which owns the Palace, for a munificence which Sheraton, which only manages this hotel, probably would have considered prohibitively expensive. There are very few instances of economy, even when costs ran over budget.

Whether or not the Japanese owners come out ahead financially, at a price of nearly $300,000 per room, depends on the success of the restaurants and bars. My guess is that they will be very popular, as they were during my salad days in San Francisco. But that will take a big improvement by Sheraton, which killed the kitchen with mess cooks who can hardly pronounce, much less prepare, *faisan sous cloche*.

What the hotel needs now is a cuisine worthy of its restored ambience, as delectable as it was when we were young and in love at the Palace.
April 3, 1991

Nothing reveals the expansion of U.S. medical care more powerfully than the new scale of hospitals such as San Francisco General and Alta Bates in Berkeley. Their tremendous additions — for better and worse — are the most significant recent hospital architecture in the Bay Area.

If Le Corbusier could call the modern house "a machine for living" (with emphasis on living), these formidable establishments can be described as huge healing machines, crammed with all kinds of technology, from the TV above the bed to exquisite surgical apparatus. As public and private hospitals, however, they are very different socially.

Alta Bates is frankly an haut bourgeois institution, in some ways more like a hotel than a hospital, serving wine routinely with meals, and providing topnotch treatment. It is smaller than San Francisco General, with 311 beds against 590, but its sumptuous back-up facilities — for intensive and specialized care — are spaciously laid out, and even more admirably equipped.

In spite of their social contrast, the two hospitals are not too far apart. San Francisco General belongs to a new generation of public hospitals, with almost none of the stigma of obsolete county charity operations. Against great odds, but with surprising success, both city officials and the architects — Stone, Marraccini & Patterson — have sought to give it some of the graciousness of private community hospitals.

At the same time Alta Bates has been visibly democratized. Thanks to federal and state medical programs, as well as union health insurance plans, there are plenty of patients who are far from rich, yet enjoy the same ambience as Piedmont matrons and Berkeley professors.

Architecturally, the two hospitals are in some ways still closer.

Both buildings offer lessons in inappropriate scale — that is, the wrong kind of presence for their purpose.

Although Alta Bates, designed by Rex Allen-Drever-Lechowski, is the more original building, and not only more deftly detailed, but more luxuriously finished, its architects have striven for the same impression of monumental grandeur as have the designers of San Francisco General.

Like ocean liners moored in quaint old ports, San Francisco General and Alta Bates physically overwhelm the older hospital structures still standing near them, to say nothing of the adjoining residential neighborhoods.

Yet although they are very big, especially San Francisco General's immense new central complex which measures 430 by 360 feet, they do not crush their surroundings by their dimensions alone, so much as by the mighty scale which their architects have given them, more suitable for Baroque palaces than modern health facilities.

Scale is a term which has several meanings. In its narrowest sense it is merely an index of measurement, like the scale of a map.

In fine architecture, however, scale conveys an impression of size — not the building's actual dimensions, but what they seem to be, in relation to individual human beings, as well as to buildings near them.

This distinction is often misunderstood, not least by maleducated architects, who talk of "human scale" as if it were achieved automatically in redwood shacks, and "monumental scale" as if it resulted merely from bigness.

But a little building, even a single open room such as the ancient Egyptian pavilion of Sesostris at Karnak, may have monumental scale, and still be deeply humane.

Conversely, big lumps of buildings such as Standard Oil of California's highrises on Market Street by Hertzka & Knowles, perched on ungainly colonnades, and pierced by hundreds of measly windows, may lack any true scale at all, and yet appear inhumanely large.

Clark Davis, chief designer for Stone, Marraccini & Patterson at San Francisco General, has too strong a sense of architectural command for that kind of weakness.

He knew that his building could not escape monumentality. At the heart of a campuslike setting, his new clinical blocks would necessarily appear very large in contrast to the more finely textured old brick buildings that will remain in use for the foreseeable future.

He also realized that, because the various elements of the new buildings would have to be physically linked, unlike the old isolated ward pavilions, they would necessarily form a long horizontal mass. Originally city officials, on the doubtful advice of earlier consultants, had contemplated a vertical hospital, 18 or 19 stories high. But it would have created all sorts of functional difficulties, in addition to outraging the residents of Potrero Hill, who would have to look at it.

Davis therefore lowered its profile to six stories on the high eastern side of the site, and seven on the lower terrain to the east, where he was able to raze an old building to create a comely park.

But then, instead of seeking ways to reduce the impact of his big building, he chose to make it seem bigger through simplified, almost brutal strokes. These were very popular in architecture of the 1960s when famous designers such as I.M. Pei — influenced by the massive concrete structures of Le Corbusier — suppressed individual window openings in compositions of great power that made multistory elements appear as unified sculptural blocks.

To control sun on these great abstract facades, through use of Corbusian brise-soleils, or fixed concrete sun breaks, Davis added another monumental device that could throw shadows into deep recesses over five or six floors at a time. He also treated his elevator shafts as powerful compositional elements, bending them outward — as Pei did, for instance, in his famous atmospheric research labs at Boulder, Colo. — in great cantilevered blocks.

This abstract oversimplification of the building, through which horizontal service floors extended more than 400 feet in continuous window bands or solid wall surfaces, again emphasized physical grandeur rather than the human complexity of what would take place inside. Pei had done this, too, on an isolated site of sweeping natural grandeur before the west front of the Rockies, but Davis was designing for a San Francisco neighborhood already deeply wounded by the James Lick Freeway, and which did not need any more architectural machismo.

Furthermore, Pei's building was not whitish concrete, but a soft reddish earth color. It was much smaller in every dimension and therefore motives which appear jewellike in his architecture became ponderous in the urban hospital.

All this is a pity because San Francisco General exhibits genuine strength — for instance, the 75-foot spans of the floors recessed on the southern and northern facades, whose full power can be felt on the massive cafeteria terrace.

It's a further pity because, when one enters the building, it is obvious that Davis has carefully provided what amenity he could under a spartan budget. Only in the depressing psychiatric ward, where the patients obviously need a kinder, residential setting, does the lucid and systematic arrangement seem forbidding.

Yet for all that it must be one of the finest public hospitals in the country, with only single and double rooms, rather than the old-fangled wards. An exemplary program by the San Francisco Arts Commission has also installed sculptures, paintings and prints throughout the building, and on the open courts. Some of the art is good, some of it weak or worse, and badly installed, but nevertheless it is a great step forward.

Alta Bates also presented serious problems in urban design. Although the hospital, formerly tucked away on side streets, was expanding to Ashby Avenue, a major thoroughfare on which big professional buildings for doctors have started to spring up, this part of Berkeley is still a closely knit, family neighborhood of small homes and vociferous citizens, who hollered like hell when the hospital revealed its plans.

Perhaps Alta Bates should have simply packed up and moved to Pill Hill in Oakland, where another big structure wouldn't have mattered much. But that would have been more expensive, and less convenient to the snazzy Berkeley medical corps.

These doctors wanted serious architecture, and they got it, from architect Mark Lechowski, who unfortunately opted, as Davis did, for overpowering monumentality in the wrong place.

Nevertheless, it is an improvement over the first addition of Alta Bates, finished ten years ago, which was done by the same firm before Lechowski became a partner. That one is a very heavy-handed job of massive concrete walls, striated in a corduroy effect made popular by architects such as Paul Rudolph in the 1960s, and punctuated by coarsely framed windows.

In the much bigger second addition, no less than 260 feet square, Lechowski did not settle for small spans, but opened up his building in tremendous clear strokes. This is illustrated by the colonnade that girdles the building at ground level with beautifully defined columns 36 feet apart, finished in silvery gray concrete stucco that is a sensitively related palette of silvers and grays, including the ribbed asbestos panels and silver mirror glass of the long window bands — which are not individual windows at all, but long continuous strips.

Again, all has been simplified to the point of oversimplification. Inside this monumental exterior is a mighty internal structure of 78-foot steel trusses that allow the flows to be rearranged virtually at will as needs change. The trusses also accommodate intermediate service levels — full floors 10 feet high — which easily contain the complex mechanical equipment that will continually be modified and improved.

Some of this big-span structure is apparent within the building, in large public rooms such as the auditorium and cafeteria, and especially in a colonnaded "mall" nearly 300 feet long, where the same robust columns as on the exterior have been brought indoors. The effect is handsome, but this is drama, for the rounded columns are unnecessarily large. They suggest concrete construction, whereas within their ample girths slender uprights in steel are concealed.

In the hands of less skillful architects, this might be simply a case of architectural overkill. But it is all softened by plays of light that enter through great glass openings overhead, framed in pipe trusses that match the scale of the design with great consistency.

This is a prelude to the comfort and grace that, even if one can quarrel with minor aspects of the design, make the whole interior very comfortable. Not only in the cordial lounges and visitors' spaces, but almost everywhere up to the topmost floor, there are the carpeted floors, the decent furniture that was too costly for San Francisco General, the beautifully organized nurses' stations, even the telephone booths expressly designed for patients in wheelchairs. It all adds up to a mood of totally civilized health care.

If this could have been done on the outside, too, where the architects wish the ivy would grow faster to soften the powerful unadorned surfaces, the overscaled hospital might have lived on better terms with its neighborhood.

December 5, 1977

■ THE SOCIAL ART OF ARCHITECTURE FOR THE
POOR AND SICK

Public-interest architecture for the poor and helpless is so rare nowadays that when a pro bono outfit such as Asian Neighborhood Design emerges, creating humane environments on low budgets, it deserves thanks from everyone who cares about the unfortunate.

Asian Neighborhood Design, known as A/N/D to do-gooders in San Francisco, does wonderful things not just for Asians, but for all kinds of people who need help.

Architecture is only one facet of A/N/D's four-part operation, which includes housing management, community counseling and job training for unskilled youths in a furniture shop where recently arrived Asian craftsmen teach.

All that is impressively managed by a staff headed by Maurice Lim Miller, who is of Mexican, Chinese and German descent, but it is the architecture and planning division of Asian Neighborhood Design that is most remarkable.

Financed principally by San Francisco's creative use of federal community block grants, which were cut severely during the Reagan years, the design group offers its services to other nonprofit organizations at fees they can afford, and sometimes for no money at all.

The four young architects on the staff are of Chinese and Japanese ancestry, although A/N/D welcomes collaborators of other ethnic backgrounds. Tom Jones, who was its director of design until he became Mayor Art Agnos' adviser on low-cost housing a few months ago, is conspicuously Anglo-Saxon, and studied at Cornell when its architecture school was one of the most elitist in the Ivy League.

A/N/D was started in the early 1970s as an outgrowth of the civil rights movement by Asian American architecture students at the University of California at Berkeley, and the designers were volunteers. For the past 10 years, they have received modest salaries, but because young architects are notoriously underpaid, they make about as much as they would if they were beginning with big commercial firms.

They are expert in low-cost housing and particularly adept in transforming flea-bitten hotels into decent dwellings in the Tenderloin and other neighborhoods, as well as Chinatown.

The group's best work to date has been the inspired renovation of the old Swiss-American Hotel, above the empty restaurant that used to be New Joe's, at 534 Broadway.

Lately it has branched out into two specialized buildings, each a mix of new and recycled construction: the Coming Home Hospice for dying AIDS patients at 115 Diamond Street in the Castro and the equally remarkable Women's Alcoholism Center at 2261 Bryant Street in the Inner Mission, which includes accommodations for children who usually would be separated from their mothers as they undergo a cure.

It is possible to pass these three unassertive buildings without realizing that they are serious works of architecture, and that is one of their virtues. Vulnerable people need calm and solace and whatever joy inexpensive surroundings can give them under very tight budgets.

The exterior of the Swiss-American Hotel, where Lenny Bruce fell out of a window in 1965, is virtually unchanged except for fresh paint. To discourage graffiti, the soft colors have been applied in imaginative patterns on the side wall along the steep rise of Romolo Alley. So far, the building has not been seriously defaced.

Inside, all is bright. The somber workingmen's hotel and sometime brothel, later a hippie flophouse, is cleaner, more cheerful and surely safer than at any time since it opened around 1910.

The 65 rental rooms have been completely redone and seem perfectly tailored to single elderly people or couples. Some accommodate families with small children and look cramped to visitors, but they are incomparably superior to the hives of single-room-occupancy units that infest the tenements of Chinatown. There also are four two-room units for sick residents who may require an overnight nurse or attendant.

But the vital point is that the rooms that once held such loneliness and despair have been transformed into a community. This is especially apparent in the handsomely equipped communal kitchen and dining areas, very neatly kept, and the new communal bathrooms — thoughtfully designed for the differing needs of women and men — that have replaced the dank old toilets.

Corridors have been rearranged and broadened in some stretches to provide sitting areas. Playful little pediments and moldings are really directional markers that help elderly people not to lose their way.

Skylights bring light to the center of the building. The old staircases have been saved, together with most of the old interior walls, and sensitively repainted in soft blues or rose, again in order that the elderly may know where they are. The wiring is all new, as is the plumbing. Smoke detectors and sprinklers have been installed. Most important, as in all of the group's projects, the building is carefully but unobtrusively managed.

The revitalized hotel is only a few miles across the city from the hospice for AIDS patients, but the distance in human experience is immeasurable. This is America's first hospice for the dying on the British model, and hundreds more are needed across the country.

Nothing in their lives can prepare patients for the sorrow and suffering within this former convent, part of the Most Holy Redeemer Church complex along Diamond Street.

Yet if there is no hope in the hospice, there is almost limitless love expressed for the 15 patients, both by the attending staff and in the care the architects have lavished on the project.

The mutual regard between the patients and staff is tactfully enhanced by the design. Little was done to the building, but the interior was reorganized and refurbished almost inch by inch to provide maximum comfort. The nuns' parlor is a discreet reception room. An outdoor deck now adjoins their dining room. The bedrooms, formerly shared by nuns, are now nearly filled with hospital beds, but there is no extensive medical treatment here, only an attempt to reduce the pain, and the spaces are dimly lit to protect the patients' eyes.

In these quiet spaces, the design group received much help from community volunteers, including some of the best artists and interior designers in town, who not only contributed some excellent paintings and furniture, but stained glass to complement existing glass in the lofty upstairs chapel, which is now a lounge room for this special community and its visitors.

Next door, in what had been a sacristy, a soundproofed room with heavily padded walls allows for the release of grief.

By contrast, the Women's Alcoholism Center is almost a place of joy. In this sunny Mission neighborhood of stalwart old Victorians, A/N/D found a three-story, bow-windowed house with an empty lot next door, which perfectly suited the expanded program of the Women's Alcoholic Center, created 10 years ago by a group of recovered alcoholics and community leaders as a facility for working-class women. The problems of such women, defenseless and frequently battered, are radically different from those of their more affluent sisters. Without household help, and usually with no household at all, they cannot properly care for their children and invariably lose them, often forever, while they try to kick their habit.

The design problem was to transform the old house into a residence for the women and their children and to build a therapy and counseling facility and child-care center on the adjacent empty lot. The architectural problem was gracefully solved with a three-story wooden building that is not literally Victorian in detail, but so traditional in spirit and scale that it resembles old San Francisco row houses.

From the street, the adjacent buildings seem to be separate dwellings, each with a tall staircase. A gate between them leads to the child-care facility and outdoor play area in the rear, serving not only the children living here, but other children whose mothers, having partially recovered, are now outpatients of the center.

They are in much better shape than the women who are in the desperate early stages of a cure. The refurbished interiors of their residence, like the new offices next door, are unexceptional architecturally but are socially and psychologically of considerable interest.

Small groups of children, not necessarily brothers and sisters, share bedrooms separate from their mothers, who sleep two to a room. The women often cannot perform the simplest tasks for themselves or their offspring, but there are kitchens and dining areas where they can help prepare meals and, if they are able, eat with the children, who are looked after by the staff.

All this is far from luxurious, but somehow not Spartan. The architecture, unobtrusive to the casual visitor, is part of the healing process. As the women learn to nurture the children and to respect themselves, the significance of architecture as a social art becomes powerfully clear.

For helping to teach us that half-forgotten lesson in an age of private extravagance and public squalor, when the homeless sleep in doorways and these women might otherwise be on the streets, bravo to Asian Neighborhood Design.

February 6, 1989

■ ITALIAN LOOK FOR DELANCEY STREET

Delancey Street has built up so much goodwill by turning former addicts and convicts into self-respecting citizens that no one except a heartless Modern architect could object to the Italian stage-set design of its nearly completed headquarters on the Embarcadero.

Architecturally, all that this Venetian or Roman street scene needs is a soundtrack of "O Sole Mio."

But this is camouflage. Delancey Street's architecture, beneath its traditional exterior, is a masterpiece of contemporary social design.

For Delancey Street's new home is far and away the greatest halfway house in the country, and probably the world. In plan, organization and mood, the design is tailored to suit perfectly a program that is unsurpassed in making winners out of losers.

Jauntily facing the outer world on the prime triangular site bounded by the Embarcadero, First Street and Brannan Street, the complex of three long buildings also looks inward — again, in a very Italian way — to a protected interior court.

Here, among an array of support facilities, workshops, meeting rooms and recreational spaces, with flats and dormitories upstairs, vulnerable people can work out problems within an extended "family" where almost everyone, from murderers to ex-prostitutes, has done time.

It is a place where Mies van der Rohe and Le Corbusier, or even Frank Lloyd Wright, are not exactly household names. What counts in this unique community are "old-fashioned" values, in architecture and everything else, that all of its members can share.

What's more, they themselves have built their healing environment, performing about 95 percent of the work with little professional help from outside.

In a stunning example of "affirmative action," for many of them had few previous skills except bad ones, they have beautifully finished the stucco facades, replete with loggias and balconies, flower boxes and ornamental ironwork they have made with their own hands.

They have installed the fine copper flashings, gutters and drain pipes. The red-tiled stairs and terraces, like the overhanging tile roofs, are almost all theirs. They have cut and shaped the cedar corbels beneath the eaves.

Inside, the craftsmanship is equally impressive. Union plumbers and electricians provided instruction, but the bathrooms and kitchens, like flooring and fireplaces, were all put in by people who formerly built nothing at all. Stained-glass windows came from Delancey Street's glass shop.

Thanks to its own labor, plus some materials donated or marked down by the construction industry, Delancey Street got about $28 million worth of architecture for half that much in actual cash. It also obtained a good deal on the land. The valuable site just south of the Bay Bridge, owned by the port but leased to the Redevelopment Agency, was slated for low-income housing in the midst of upscale residential developments. When ordinary below-market-rate housing proved unattractive to investors, Delancey Street stepped in, cajoled neighboring developers to accept its presence and negotiated an excellent 66-year lease for one of the best spots on the waterfront, opposite Pier 36. Even so, the project could not have gone ahead if Bank of America, and especially its chairman, A.W. Clausen, had not opened a $10 million line of credit. Delancey Street is repaying the loan regularly through income from its various businesses and from sales of other properties from a ragtag collection of buildings that it now can vacate.

Although Delancey Street's current "family" of 500 men and women won't start moving in from other places in the city until February or March, and the buildings won't be altogether finished before summer, it is already possible to see why this picturesque but very controlled environment should become a model for comparable institutions everywhere.

If such architecture is to succeed, it must be as noninstitutional as possible — the rationale of Delancey Street since it was opened in improvised premises by the late John Maher in 1971.

Since then it has expanded prodigiously and embarked on a number of profitable ventures. Without taking a cent in public money, although the private sector helps a lot, it has evolved into a partly self-sustaining community, with shops of its own that will occupy the arched Roman storefronts at street level.

The residents will live above the stores, recalling European immigrants who settled in the tenements of Delancey Street on the Lower East Side of Manhattan.

According to Mimi Silbert, the extraordinary UC Berkeley Ph.D. who founded Delancey Street with Maher and now heads the whole operation, the idea is that the residents, after a hard journey, are also newcomers to American life, with a full future before them.

And if she has not actually designed the buildings, it is her thinking that has enabled the architects Backen, Arrigoni & Ross, with Howard Backen as partner in charge, to create the remarkable communal image that suddenly rises up on the Embarcadero.

Seen from the north, the great rounded corner of the main building, where Brannan Street intersects the Embarcadero, is a welcoming presence — and will seem much more welcoming when the construction fence is removed and the ground-floor restaurant opens.

Directly above the public restaurant is Delancey Street's own lofty dining hall, reached not from the street but from the interior court. On the level above, the facade opens in a deep-set loggia, with theatrical balustrades sweeping around the curve of the building. It serves a spacious social room for the residents, with one of the finest views in the city of the Bay Bridge, but at the same time the loggia establishes a vigorous three-dimensionality that travels down the strongly modeled facades, extending 260 feet along Brannan and 390 feet along the Embarcadero.

Both of these long perspectives could seem arid, as the flat barebones Modern of the Bayside Village apartments in fact appears on the other side of Brannan Street. But the facades are saved from monotony by robust projections and indentations, slightly varied from one another, that give the effect of row housing.

These are not row houses at all. Behind the facades are ingenious living arrangements that vary from rudimentary shared flats for fresh arrivals to gracious apartments, overlooking the bay, for the most senior residents. It is a little like the old Ivy League system of assigning the worst rooms to freshmen and the best to seniors, as a reward for lasting the course.

The logic of the Delancey Street program is strikingly revealed when one enters the courtyard through the rather grand entrance on the Embarcadero or the corner gardens at the far end of the site. The center of the court is occupied by three key buildings: a central meeting hall for rap sessions and socials, a fitness center and swimming pool, and a cinema, equipped with the latest technology by Lucasfilms.

The perimeter of the court is lined by rows of "practice shops," which provide goods for Delancey Street residents and serve as training facilities. The rears of the practice stores meet the rears of the exterior stores, which serve the public.

This is clever architecture. The question is whether it is to be considered fine architectural art.

Backen, Arrigoni & Ross are among the leading residential designers in the country. They are not only excellent Modernists, but also avowedly "eclectic" and "contextual" architects, and even "historicists" on occasion, not only for Delancey Street but at Jordan Winery, say, where they have unashamedly imitated a French chateau, in reinforced concrete.

Even though they have done tens of thousands of units of commercial housing, none of it, I'd say, comes close to Delancey Street's feeling of community in which people help each other to live with great kindness and candor.

Could the same be achieved, or surpassed, in richly organized Modern architecture — instead of ersatz Italian traditionalism? Neither Backen nor Delancey Street, confronted by overwhelming social realities, was willing to take the chance.

December 28, 1989

VIII. Stadiums and Museums

■ NO WAY TO BUILD A BALLPARK

Summer is upon the pleasant land, and this fun-loving nation once more is being taken — out at the ballpark. The taking is being done by genial club owners, politicians, contractors, financiers, lawyers and sports writers — who in this age of *panem et circenses* have convinced several cities that they dearly need not only major-league baseball, but new stadiums to go with it. Although insufficient money is available nowadays for housing, schools, hospitals and even modest neighborhood playgrounds, there seems to be no shortage of funds for the national pastime, which was described by F. Scott Fitzgerald as "a boy's game with no more possibilities in it than a boy could master, a game bounded by walls which kept out novelty or danger, change or adventure."

More than a boy's pocket money is required, however, to stage big-time baseball. In New York for example, $19 million has been appropriated — and such sums have a way of growing — for the construction of a 55,000-seat arena on public parkland in Flushing Meadows. Los Angeles, another metropolis with no lack of slums, is spending $18 million for the Dodgers' stadium in Chavez Ravine, a site once designated for low-cost public housing. Washington, Houston, and other cities also are erecting expensive homes for their teams; and one can hope that in the planning stage, they have considered the experience of balmy San Francisco, which can serve as a model of kindly hospitality to commercial baseball.

This is the Giants fourth season in San Francisco and their second at Candlestick Park, the controversial stadium beside the bay which — at a cost of more than $15 million — was rushed to completion when the team was induced to abandon New York in 1958. (At the same time, it will be remembered, the Dodgers moved from Brooklyn to Los Angeles.) The first two years in San Francisco the Giants played at old Seals Stadium, near the downtown breweries; and it was there that they nearly won the pennant in 1959. When Candlestick Park opened the following spring, therefore, enthusiastic fans had reason to hope that the 45,000-seat structure would be the scene of the next World Series.

Instead — in a setting worthy of a Greek amphitheater — the Giants

Louise M. Davies Symphony Hall, San Francisco, California, 1982.
By Jane Lidz. Courtesy Skidmore, Owings & Merrill.

enacted a classical drama of the diamond, starting the 1960 season as heroes, and finishing (if the ambiguous term will be pardoned in Brooklyn and Los Angeles) as bums.

The team's ignoble feat aroused not only pity in the bosoms of nearly 1,800,000 paying customers (more than the pennant-winning Yankees drew the same season in New York), but, apparently, terror in the mind of owner Horace Stoneham, who promptly conducted purification rites. A devout new manager, Alvin Dark, was put in charge of what had been a notably lighthearted group of ball players. The insouciant outfielder Willie Kirkland was bartered to Cleveland. So was the prideful pitcher Johnny Antonelli. Harvey Kuenn, a worthy batsman, was acquired in exchange. And now, at midsummer, the Giants, led by the incomparable Willie Mays, who hit four home runs in a single game on April 30, once more hope to conquer.

But if the team's fault lies not in its stars, it may reside in the seemingly blameless stadium. For if Candlestick Park, when first sighted from the Bayshore freeway on the southern limits of the city, appears radiantly innocent in the sunlight, it is far from a simple monument of healthy sport. Like professional baseball itself, however, the great semicircular structure of exposed concrete does make a cheerful show of outward vigor. The top of the grandstand, particularly, is very forceful and clear. Its rounded lid (which is a wind baffle only, rather than a true roof for the upper tier) is mounted on spectacular sculptural elements, shaped like inverted Y's, which bend with the shell and then fork downward into the structure below. For this feature alone architect John Bolles and engineers Chin and Hensolt of San Francisco deserve high commendation. It places Candlestick in a category well above the run of major-league parks, which are probably the worst-designed large stadiums in the world.

Yet on closer view Candlestick rapidly loses glory. The tundra of parking lots, which can accommodate 8,000 cars and 300 buses, contributes to this melancholy effect, for no effort was made to relieve the expanse of blacktop with greenery. At the crest of the steep approach (nicknamed "Cardiac Hill") the uninviting main entrance bears some resemblance to a prison gate; and in the structure which lifts heavily behind it, what had appeared gleaming, strong, and decisive at a distance now seems muddled, unfinished and somehow cheap.

The raw, unpainted concrete, for example, which would have been perfectly acceptable if carefully surfaced, was left slovenly, as if the workmen had hurried from the job. The ramps leading to the upper deck seem brutally flung about at hazard. In fact, on the exterior, only the tall, steel floodlight pylons — the most elegant in the country, perhaps — fulfill Candlestick's first promise.

The story of the financing and building of the stadium, which would have been complex under any circumstances, has been further complicated by lawsuits, some of which remain unsettled. A Grand Jury investigation of Candlestick in 1958 came to the conclusion: "The City did not get a good deal." (Two jurors dissented, however, and commended the city on "a very efficient and excellent job.") The Grand Jury report led to an angry exchange between Mayor George Christopher and the foreman, Henry North, which culminated in a slander suit against the mayor, its withdrawal after a public reconciliation and a mutual pledge to "work toward a greater-than-ever San Francisco."

The Grand Jury's findings related chiefly to land acquisition, financing and costs.

By failing to use its power of eminent domain at the time when the Candlestick Point site was under consideration in 1956, the jury said, the city allowed prices to rise and therefore paid from $650,000 to $1 million over a fair market value for the land. The greater part of the 77 acres was a property of 41 acres owned by Charles L. Harney, some of it under water. Mr. Harney, the contractor for the job, received $2.7 million from the city for the land — approximately $66,000 per acre, though it had been assessed in 1956 for only $26,730 per acre. (Some of this Mr. Harney had purchased in 1953 for about $2,100 per acre.)

As to costs, the Grand Jury pointed out that the voters had authorized $5 million for the land and stadium; but by 1958, estimated costs "may exceed $15 million." To arrange for additional financing, a nonprofit corporation, Stadium, Inc., was formed in 1957, with Mr. Harney and two of his employees as officers and directors.

"It was illogical," said the Grand Jury, "for Stadium, Inc., with its directorate of Harney men, to act for the City and County of San Francisco, and, at the same time, have Harney, the contractor, selling land to the city and constructing a stadium, so on February 28, 1958, it was decided to substitute other officials, and three prominent and influential men [Allan K. Browne, W. P. Fuller Brawner, and Frederic P. Whitman] were asked to serve as directors. . . . The nonprofit corporation is in a very literal sense the alter ego of the city."

Although the Grand Jury said it believed the nonprofit corporation may be a useful financial device, it said that, in this case, if city bonds had been issued instead of those of the corporation, "a very considerable saving of interest would have resulted." The Grand Jury explicitly denied "inferring that we found anything dishonest about this deal," but it stated:

"The end result, therefore, of the establishment of this nonprofit corporation is that the city could avoid securing the voters' approval of an additional expenditure of approximately ten million, could by-pass the Charter provision with regard to bidding, and could and did channel this vast project without competitive bidding, to the contractor of their choice. . .

"It is our conviction that where so much additional money is involved, a few city officials should not accept responsibility for the investment of millions unauthorized by the voters, despite their conviction that major-league baseball would be a fine thing for San Francisco."

Precisely what motives animated the responsible officials during this period — other than frantic haste to bring a major-league ball club to a city which does not possess a decent theater — will probably never be known. But Supervisor James Leo Halley proposed that the grateful municipality name the ballpark Harney Stadium.

This struck a note which vibrated among the citizenry. Many San Franciscans suggested instead that the name Candlestick (taken from the harbor point) be changed to "Candlestink." This is because of the aroma of the nearby tidal flats which is often picked up by the breeze. On many days, of course, the breeze is a wind powerful enough to play havoc with hitting and fielding, and the visitor feels its force soon after he enters the stands.

Yet the visitor forgets the wind momentarily and is oblivious to most of the stadium's tawdry details (such as the poorly joined railing on which I scored my hand upon first entering), as soon as the great sweep of space toward the bay opens before his eyes.

Here the taxpayers get something like their money's worth. Candlestick commands a magnificent view of harbor, sky and distant hills. Across a broad cover of the bay are the giant cranes of the Hunters Point naval station, and, often, standing out to sea is a destroyer or a high-riding tanker. The water is alive with white sails, and on game days some fans arrive by boat, a very San Franciscan touch. The shoreline in the foreground, between the stadium and the water's edge, remains unsightly, to be sure, but it can easily be cleared by some wise municipal government of the future, and then Candlestick Point can become the green, multipurpose recreational grounds it might have been from the start.

So far so good. The remarkable spaciousness of the stadium's interior is enhanced by an extremely open seating plan and generous aisles. The pastel seats, which vary in hue according to price, add charming color (although the concrete remains brutally raw); and the overall lines of the stands, which do not rise too steeply, are handsome. A mezzanine hung from the upper deck emphasizes the tremendous curve of the structure and provides a superb horizontal line which shows how distinguished the architecture might have been.

Yet, as on the exterior, inspection again reveals serious failings. Although engineering today makes unobstructed space possible even in vast buildings, the architect here relied on columns — the bane of spectators unlucky enough to sit behind them — to support the upper deck. These round steel pillars are well set back in the lower stand (granted, they do not interfere to the same degree as the forest of columns in the Giants' old Polo Grounds in New York), but the architect concedes that they could have been omitted at an additional cost of only $250,000. The figure seems high. Probably a different structural concept could have been column-free at little or no extra cost, if only because these columns are of solid steel and quite expensive.

There are also vexing blind spots in the column-free upper stands, however, and they reveal how complex is the job of designing a large baseball stadium. On paper it must have seemed a good idea to bring the stands rather closer than is usual to the playing field. But the result has been that, from broad areas of the upper deck, sharply pulled balls are lost from sight, and low-traveling home runs close to the foul line cannot be seen clearing the fence except on the side of the field. . . . That is, *if* drives which normally would go out of the park even reach the fence in the face of the wind.

Home runs — both by Giants and their opponents last year in Candlestick — were remarkably scarce. The barriers are being brought closer to the plate this year for precisely that reason, and a 45-foot-high backdrop has been installed in center field — at a cost of $45,000 — in order to improve visibility for the hitters. But outfielders will probably continue to leap forward for balls which first seem to be flying far over their heads. For perhaps the most appropriate name yet offered for Candlestick is "Temple of the Winds." The air currents, sweeping off the hills and the harbor, move not only with exceptional velocity, but in an unpredictable variety of directions.

Sometimes one flag in the outfield will be rippling toward the bay, or hanging limp, while another is stiffly directed toward right field. In this corner of the stands the rounded shield of the upper deck apparently acts not as a baffle but as a wind scoop, funnelling great blasts of air around the diamond until they come whirling out over left field again. In their artless, vociferous way the players have complained about these gusts which, they claim, affect even pitched balls.

At night — and of course a good half of the games are now nocturnal

— the wind subsides, but the fog rolls in from the bay. Candlestick is probably the only major-league park where the umpires delayed a game for an hour, although no rain was falling, because a solid bank of fog, worthy of the Labrador shelf, floated into the stadium and stayed there one night last summer. And again like a Labrador fog, this one was cold. Although nearly half of Candlestick's seats are equipped for radiant heating (another unique feature of the stadium), the system thus far has proven remarkably ineffective, and prudent spectators dress for night games as if they were camping out in a Sierra winter.

Such are Candlestick's major failings. Among its minor shortcomings it is enough to mention that the screen behind home plate is crude; the scoreboard resembles, and in fact is, an advertising sign; and the grass is far from being a lush greensward.

How many of these faults could have been avoided? Surely the wind might have been controlled in so large a structure, since from the earliest stages of the project the severity of the wind problem should have been obvious. When work had scarcely begun, a construction superintendent pointed out to a Chronicle reporter that an eight-degree change in alignment might have allowed the upper grandstand to shut off the wind coming into right field. But, he added, "there ain't gonna be nothin' to stop it. And man, does she blow!"

Only now has the city put up $54,925 — another of the high figures which have a way of creeping into the history of Candlestick — for meteorological tests which may not even be final. Possibly the only way to correct the wind condition will be, as has been suggested, to cover the entire structure with a geodesic dome or some other kind of roof. R. Buckminster Fuller, inventor of the geodesic dome, estimates the cost of such a translucent covering at $3.5 million.

As the baseball season waxes, so do the lawsuits, and soon, unless there is an out-of-court settlement, San Franciscans may be treated to a gamy trial. On the basis of a 10-page list of 61 disputed items drawn up by Mr. Bolles, Stadium, Inc. is asking for a $2,522,400 indemnity from Mr. Harney for alleged failure to fulfill his contract. Mr. Harney is charged not only with failure to complete the stadium on time, but also with inadequate filling, grading and paving of the parking area; installation of defective seats, electrical outlets and plumbing fixtures; and failure to provide proper heating and waterproofing systems.

But this is only a cross-complaint against a larger claim which Harney himself filed last August against the city. The affluent contractor charged that an undue number of changes were made in the original design for which he said the city owed him an additional $2,734,480.

The Giants for their part, although the value of the club's stock has soared since it moved to San Francisco, unsuccessfully tried to claim a refund of $117,487 which they said the city overcharged them for taxes in 1960.

But the Giants are now being sued by a San Francisco lawyer, Mel Belli, who asserts that the failure of the heating system represents "a breach of contract" to him as a ticket holder, and has caused "extreme discomfort" and thereby endangered the health and well-being of the plaintiff and his guests."

Such, such, are the joys of the national pastime in the most easygoing of American cities.

August 1961, *Harper's Magazine*

■ A'S COLISEUM AN ARCHITECTURAL MARVEL

So far as modern stadium design is concerned, the A's are already champions. The majestic Oakland Coliseum, scene of today's third game of the American League baseball playoffs, is unsurpassed architecturally — if not in every other way — among major U.S. sports facilities built since World War II.

Calm and powerful, the great circular form lifts in three successive tiers, growing steeper as they ascend, the topmost level flung upward as a spectacular cantilevered rim for the huge sunken bowl. In a counter-movement, the stands sweep horizontally from left field around home plate and onward to right field, leaving the broad arc of centerfield open — above an upswept greensward — to reveal tremendous views of the East Bay hills.

As monumental architecture, almost on the scale of the bridges spanning the bay, it is an irresistible work of structural art.

The only catch is that since 1912 the Boston Red Sox, the A's playoff foes, have had an all-time winner of a stadium in Fenway Park. As a place to enjoy the National Pastime, so close to the field that you can hear the players' voices and see if they have shaved or not, it is hard to beat this historic ballpark.

Filled with legends, packed into an intensely urban cityscape rather than isolated on a tundra of parking lots, Fenway Park and its charming contemporaries in Chicago — Comiskey Park (1911) and Wrigley Field (1914) — are wonderfully eccentric mementos of the days before baseball teams became corporate organizations. It doesn't matter that their architecture was clumsy or naive, in some ways even ugly. They were lovable. Standardized field layouts had not yet replaced wild improvisations such as Fenway's Green Monster fence in left field. Home runs were a lot easier to hit in one direction than another.

Foul balls were hard to catch, because baselines ran so close to the stands in an age of single-use stadiums designed for baseball alone, and the conflicting needs of football did not create large areas of foul territory, which is the chief fault of the multipurpose Oakland Coliseum, which was completed in 1966.

Yet all that can not deprive the Coliseum of its grandeur.

The key to the design is a perfect circle. Or rather, a series of nearly perfect concentric circles, dynamically expanding in three distinct movements, so that the overall diameter of the stadium, from edge to edge, is 770 feet.

The rim is mighty. The precast concrete double cantilevers of the top deck soar nearly 50 feet above the curving main concourse that is still another circle, at the crest of a landscaped earthen ring that adds another round form to the succession of circular shapes.

The Coliseum is thus based on an ideal geometry, which Euclid could have drawn, and Plato might have praised.

To drag ancient Greek philosophy into the design of an American ballpark may seem farfetched, but abstract Platonic purism — applied to machine technology by Modern masters such as Mies van der Rohe — has been one of the chief aesthetic strengths (as well as an oversimplified social weakness) of 20th-century architecture.

It is no accident that the pure form of the Coliseum was conceived by Mies' chief followers, the nationwide firm of Skidmore, Owings & Merrill, now lapsing in Post-Modernist confusion but at the height of its powers when the Coliseum was conceived in 1962. The design team was headed by Myron Goldsmith of Chicago, an architect, engineer and student of both Mies van der Rohe and the Italian engineer Pier Luigi Nervi.

While Nervi did famous Olympic sports palazzos in Rome in the 1950s, Goldsmith conceived his own visionary designs in competitions for other Olympic facilities, including an unbuilt velodrome for bicycle racing. As the Coliseum would be, the velodrome was to have been inexpensively built within landscaped earth forms — shaped with soil dug from the sunken inner bowl — that were conceived as environmental sculpture on the grandest scale.

At Oakland, the vision came true in a multipurpose sports and exhibition complex that cost only $25 million. (Candlestick Park, built a few years earlier, cost $29 million for baseball alone and doubled in price when it was converted to football a decade later.)

But the real payoff was in beauty, evident as soon as the Coliseum complex is glimpsed from the Nimitz freeway. Better still, it should be seen from a plane above Oakland International Airport, where the 770-foot circle of the 53,000-seat stadium can be appreciated beside the equally perfect circle of the basketball arena, with its extraordinary cable-hung roof measuring 420 feet across.

The arena, technically bolder, is in some ways even more splendid than the stadium. Together, they are unmatched in sports architecture. A spectacular interplay of related, curving shapes is set up by the two structures, unlike any other large-scale spatial experience in ancient or modern architecture. The stadium and the covered arena share a brotherly strength, facing each other across a raised plaza.

From the plaza, which covers a lofty underground exhibition space, the stadium is entered at mid-level in the stands, dispensing with the need for cumbersome outer ramps, which mar even Dodger Stadium in Los Angeles.

The surrounding outer promenade is bordered within by a concourse lined with refreshment and souvenir stands, decent rest rooms and other service areas, far better placed than in any other stadium of this size. From here it is also possible to watch play on the field.

Once inside, it's a pleasure not only to watch baseball, but to relax — in a way that has nothing to do with sport alone — within the unhurried splendor of the architecture. This is a stadium without frills, and its precast concrete structure makes up in clarity and frankness what it lacks in luxury.

The handsome piers, taking the main loads at the back of the stands, come fully into view at the ends of the curving structure, in left and right fields, as skewed asymmetric T's which project straight outward, but also slant sharply upward, effortlessly carrying the rows of seats.

There is a sense of harmony and order, of simple heroic dignity, that is everywhere expressed in perfection of proportions and line. The graphics are excellent; the fine white-and-black scoreboard (unfortunately overloaded with vulgar ads) complements the white masts of the lighting towers, which are among the most elegant in baseball.

In contrast to torn and disorderly Candlestick, everything at the Coliseum is decent, clean and civil. Perhaps it is all a bit too laid-back for a major league ballpark. One sportswriter told me that the Coliseum is the most tranquil stadium he knows, and attributes its serenity to the distance of the baselines from the seats, so that the fans are not on top of close plays at first and third.

The architects have made the best of this situation by providing handsome bullpens in spacious foul territory, in contrast to the ugly huts at Candlestick. Both facilities must accommodate baseball as well as football, even though the gridiron can't be reconciled with the diamond unless some compromises are made.

At Candlestick, and many stadiums across the country, for instance Robert Kennedy Stadium in Washington, D.C., this has been done with violence. At the Oakland Coliseum it has been achieved with a perfect architectural form.

The price has been the loss of the thrilling closeness to play, the rousing unpredictability, and old-fashioned American excitement of Fenway Park. But in the intelligence, sensitivity and elegance of the Coliseum — broadly democratic but uncommonly handsome — honor has also been done to the national game.

October 8, 1988

■ A STILL-REMARKABLE GIFT OF ARCHITECTURE
TO OAKLAND

Rarely has a single building launched the career of an architect with such brilliance as the Oakland Museum, Kevin Roche's first design after the tragic death of Eero Saarinen in 1961, when he and John Dinkeloo found themselves at the head of one of the finest architectural offices in the world. Yet few architects had heard of either man. Dinkeloo, who had left Skidmore, Owings & Merrill to become the mainstay of Saarinen's production staff for great projects such as the General Motors Technical Center, was the slightly better known because of his formidable abilities as an administrator with a rare grasp of aesthetics, economics and refined technologies. Roche, on the other hand, although obviously a special person, highly intelligent, deeply cultivated and very winning, could also be reticent, and was something of an enigma except to good friends. He had been educated in his native Ireland, where he experienced the intense literary and creative life of Dublin, but where there was simply not much to build; and after short stays in England and in Mies' Chicago he had worked, happily enough, in Saarinen's shadow since 1950.

That Roche was extraordinarily gifted in his own right, and potentially a more profound architect than Saarinen when he succeeded Saarinen at the age of 39, was thus clear only to a small group of advanced designers, mainly in the Saarinen office itself, where men such as César Pelli were aware of Roche's role in the firm's best work. Probably Roche's most significant contributions were to the eloquent headquarters of John Deere, the first building sheathed in Corten steel, of which he was really codesigner. But the building in the end was Saarinen's, as were CBS, Bell labs and the famous last essays in structural expressionism: the Yale rink, TWA and the much superior Dulles Airport.

Roche was involved in all of these projects, and saw through construction those which were unfinished at Saarinen's death. Yet, except for the most logical functional programs, for instance the careful consideration of passenger movement at Dulles, which resulted from systematic analyses of users' needs that the office dubbed "problem solving" or "responsible architecture," there was nothing in the forced drama — should one now say, melodrama? — of Saarinen's expressionism which anticipated the masterly lesson in rational city building which Roche would give in Oakland, Calif. The contemporary movement, badly torn by the early 1960s between Miesian orthodoxy and confused, self-indulgent heresies, was taken unawares by the humane splendor and social vision of his concept for the Oakland Museum.

Little wonder, for the concept was unique. Unless one hunted back through history to the hanging gardens of Babylon or, better for Roche, to the once verdant terraces of Hatshepsut's temple overlooking the Nile at Deir el Bahari, there was no analogy for his unprecedented garden environment that in fact was a three-level regional museum — another original idea — of science, history and art. Lifting in luxuriant tiers of trees and shrubs and vines, thousands of plants in all, set out in carpeted beds, edging lawns, climbing trellises, tumbling over walls in delicate sprays or profuse masses of green, so that the beautifully proportioned concrete structure would be softened, overgrown and in time largely effaced by foliage and flowers, the museum would not be a conventional building at all, but a new kind of parklike urban fabric — an incomparable setting for art, festivity and noble events — that would be an intimation of the possible grace and dignity of a democratic city of the future, extending freely beside Lake Merritt.

For in theory the continuum of low, horizontal forms and verdurous spaces could go on indefinitely. Just as the museum does, with its theater and classrooms, offices, bookstore, workshops, restaurant and outdoor dining areas, it could accommodate a wide variety of uses, expanding across the urban grid in directionless patterns, much as the museum covers four downtown blocks, courteously meeting the existing cityscape with its richly planted, unassertive borders, half-hidden by thickets of cedar and redwood, eucalyptus and oak. The great promise of the concept — which SOM failed to see when it built a pugnacious community college on the museum's southern side, perhaps to show how tough inner city kids could be — was that the garden architecture could be continued, in different materials if need be, but in an organic idiom similar to the museum's, making overtures to people of all ages and backgrounds, opening into inviting plazas that lead to majestic inner courts, sunken pools, quiet patios and shadowy walks, with parking hidden beneath and unsightly utilities behind banks of shrubbery.

The museum consequently must be seen not as an isolated tour de force, but as a prototype. The whole complex entity was conceived, quite literally, as a biotechnic megastructure that today, nearly 16 years after Roche began the design, is everywhere green and flowering, fragrant and fresh, unpredictably delightful, as the lovely terraces step upward, each providing a roof garden for the level below, ascending from the lawns of the central courtyard, past lines of pear trees and clusters of lemon, tree ferns and fir, roses, jasmine, bright bottlebrush and trumpet vine, to the topmost platforms where, amidst olive trees and pine, azalea and rosemary, creeping strawberry, hawthorne and myrtle, there are exhilarating views of the lake, the downtown towers and the distant hills.

Thus, whatever else this masterpiece may be, and among other things it is an excellent museum, its chief significance is as a model for a potential civic order which, far from being utopian, was achieved on what even in the 1960s was a modest budget: $4.5 million for the building and $1.5 million for landscaping, which used up the bond issue; and $2 million in contributions for furnishings and installations.

Even if the total of $8 million–at that time the price of a suburban high school — were doubled or tripled today, it would still be an astonishing bargain for a poverty-wracked, very ordinary city which, when the bonds were passed (at a time when blacks and other minorities scarcely voted), had almost no inkling of what it wanted or actually needed in a museum. For Oakland may fairly be called the hole in the urban doughnut. Like Brooklyn, Camden or East St. Louis, although infinitely more pleasant than those benighted places, it is a "second city," terribly troubled by the preeminence of San Francisco across the bay, and so deprived of cultural identity that Gertrude Stein, its most famous daughter, could gibe that "there is no there there."

Although conditions would become worse in the next decade, and only now are starting to improve, Oakland in the early 1960s was already afflicted by unemployment, racism, ubiquitous violence, declining neighborhoods, terrible schools and the panicked departure to the suburbs of many whites, retail business and heavy industry.

Not for nothing did Oakland become the home base of the Black Panthers, the scene of spectacular shootouts, draft riots and political trials in the Alameda County Court House just north of the museum site. The jail at the top of this pseudoclassical, Art Deco pile, built by the WPA, gave prisoners a bird's-eye view of the razing of dozens of older buildings by the redevelopment agency, which cleared the land for the museum. These doomed structures — not much different from those left in the vicinity — were mostly the dwellings of whites, some of them elderly, none of them rich, almost all of whom, if they had the money, would have left central Oakland anyway. It is sobering to consider that diehard urban conservationists today (they didn't exist in Oakland then), joined by the now vocal representatives of the poor, would probably fight bitterly to save such housing in a city where more homes are annually declared derelict than are built.

Oakland therefore provided a physical diagram of economic injustice and the irresponsibility of the wealthy: an unlikely situation for serious humanitarian architecture. The most prosperous community leaders, indeed those who pushed hardest for museum bonds and envisaged the building as a sort of club with pictures on the walls, didn't even live in Oakland, but in the privileged enclave of Piedmont. From the hauteur of this genteel purlieus they enjoyed sweeping views of the city, as well as very good schools, their own police force, immaculate streets and lightly taxed, fastidiously maintained residences that were solidly built half a century ago by architects such as Julia Morgan and Willis Polk.

How, then, did the museum refute Lewis Mumford's dictum that every community receives the architecture it deserves? The answer is that behind every great building, particularly a public building in an unjust city, there must be an individual who is a great client. In Oakland it was not someone who figured in the society pages of Senator Knowland's *Tribune*, but a diminutive member of the museum commission, Esther Fuller, who with her husband, Fenner, owned one of the few decent restaurants in town, where artists showed their work. Mrs. Fuller was herself an artist, when she had time, but now all her energies and fiery determination (which she cheerfully attributes to her Armenian ancestry) went into the conception of the museum.

Mrs. Fuller did not yet know much about architecture, but she knew where to find informed judgment she could trust and which would carry weight with other commissioners. On one key point she was already decided: The design could not be entrusted to any of the local firms which had perpetrated Oakland's recent public buildings, some of which stand not far from the museum to justify her opinion. She wanted architects of the first rank; and after a search that took her to almost every distinguished office in the country, she and the museum staff, especially the art curator Paul Mills, drew up a list of 10 firms (later expanded slightly), which was an honor roll of American architecture a decade and a half ago, and still reads rather well. Eero Saarinen from the start was a strong candidate for the job.

Of the noted designers considered, only Mies van der Rohe, who was ill, could not come for an interview. Most of the others rushed to impress the provincial city, some brimming with a priori notions that would have concocted a version of the Taj Mahal (in vogue at the time) as redone by Il Duce. But in the course of the interviews, which were conducted at an admirable level, a vexing difficulty appeared: There was no program.

The bond proposal, hastily sold to the voters, had never been properly formulated. Scrutinized later, it was as ludicrously thin as the meager collections it was supposed to rehouse. By first-rate standards, Oakland strictly speaking had *no* collections, but merely random assortments of Bay Area art, historical curios such as hoop skirts and moth-eaten stuffed animals — with visible patches — that represented natural science. These treasures were on display in three different buildings, administered as separate institutions. History and, less logically, science were installed in old mansions (one of which, the Stanford-Lathrop House beside the lake, at last is being carefully restored). The small collection was better, containing work by Hassel Smith, Richard Diebenkorn and other leading California painters, but it was not really crowded in leftover space in the neoclassical civic auditorium, directly east of the present museum.

Saarinen emerged from the first interviews as the leader; and he and two runners-up were asked to return for a second round. In the interim he was stricken with brain cancer, and died in less than a month: He was 51 years old. It was then, although Oakland might well have played it safe with either of the architects still in the running, that Esther Fuller insisted that Kevin Roche be given the courtesy of a hearing. Perhaps a more pretentious city — San Francisco, for instance, which was then getting insipid architecture for the Brundage collection from an aging Gardner Dailey — would not have taken a chance on an unknown. But Oakland had found its architect.

Roche did not so much announce to the city what he could do, as he asked what Oakland truly needed. What was obviously required, in a city changing so rapidly that in another decade the population would be more than 50 percent nonwhite, was not a museum which only an elitist minority would visit, but a new kind of building — transcending traditional museum functions — which could heal some of Oakland's deep social and physical wounds. A parvenu Oakland could never compete with the richer, but hopelessly conventional art museums across the bay, just as it could never be, and should not try to imitate, an international metropolis such as San Francisco.

But Oakland could honestly be *itself*, like any city worth its urban salt. Seen from this perspective, all of the handicaps — the nonexistence of collections, the barrenness of the inner city, the weakness or venality of official leadership, and most demoralizing, the absence of a genuine higher culture that the fragmented community could share — by paradox could be seen as advantages if they were only recognized frankly. They would then become the basis of architecture.

All this is by way of preamble to the development of the design, a turning point in architecture, even though a confused profession doesn't know it yet. Many experts on museums and other consultants were brought in to assist the design team, which included one of the few landscape architects in the country, Dan Kiley, who was capable of understanding architectonic problems on this order and who had worked with Saarinen on Dulles Airport and other projects where the landscaping mercifully doesn't look overdesigned. A New Englander, Kiley had little firsthand knowledge of West Coast conditions, and so he was joined by Geraldine Knight Scott of Berkeley, a redoubtable lady with sane ideas of design, as well as a thorough knowledge of Bay Area climate and plants. Together their contributions were immeasurable.

But the main effort came from the Saarinen staff itself (the firm's name would not change to Kevin Roche, John Dinkeloo & Associates for a few years), which pitched in to sustain both partners when grief of Eero's loss hung heavily over the office. It was remarkable, during this trying period, to see the skill and resolution of these young architects, creating — among other things — the famous study models which since the 1950s have been unequaled in architectural practice.

One by one the different aspects of the problem led to the general solution. The arid cityscape almost cried for a garden concept; and half a decade before Berkeley students shouted for a "People's Park," Roche spoke calmly of a *building* that would be a "park for the people," where people of all ages and backgrounds — not just counter-culture types (although they were welcome) — would find themselves at home. Such a building, by its very size and purpose, could not escape monumentality, but there now appeared the idea, for the first time so far as I know, of a "nonmonumental" or even "antimonumental" monument whose premise was not to impress or overwhelm. On the contrary, it should belong even to the humblest citizen, who after all owned it, as he would feel he owned a public park. "The building," said Roche, "must be cordial." This cordiality applied, moreover, to the surrounding urban scene, which has its share of obtrusive, bullying buildings. And so the self-effacing museum would respect Lake Merritt, for instance, by stepping back in low terraces, so that no views would be blocked, unlike the towers which usurp views elsewhere on the lake.

And finally (although Roche saw this possibility early), the terraces — indispensable to the garden concept — could in a single stroke be integrated with the idea of a three-level *regional* museum which, of course, originated in the three separate municipal museums that seemed so hopeless.

But now they fitted so naturally in ascending sequence, the roof of each gallery becoming a terrace for the gallery above, that the design became inevitable. For this was a museum which could evolve with Oakland itself, as the essentially new collections grew:

1. On the lowest level, closest to the earth, there would be a gallery devoted to the nature of the region and the varieties of life it supported: in other words, what providence had given to Northern California, from the Pacific to the Sierra. This was proposed a full decade before the United States was swept by the ecology movement.

2. But human beings alter the earth; and on the next level, appropriately, a gallery of history and technology would show how people and institutions, machines and social and political life, have changed the region, from neolithic Indians and Spanish colonists to the Gold Rush and the industrialization of an urban northern California. This has turned out to be the gem of the museum, a miniature Smithsonian, which surely ranks with the transportation and communications museum at Lucerne, Switzerland, as one of the best things of its kind.

3. Yet, there is a higher level of human expression: the creative arts which one day may provide a summa, or ethos, in this part of the world that everyone may share. What is more, as the visitor steps out of this topmost gallery of painting and sculpture, photography and other media, there is a breathtaking view of the supreme regional work of art — the still imperfect, but magnificent metropolis surrounding the bay — and the great flowering museum lifting and falling on every side to show what it all might be.

Once this extraordinary program was established, all the other elements of the design fell easily into place. Spaces for temporary exhibitions were provided at the northern ends of the three superimposed galleries; to the south they were flanked by a great hall for major shows. Curators' offices, with charming private patios, were placed beside the galleries. Overlooking the southern side of the central courtyard was the restaurant and its terraces. Classrooms for school children were tucked into the lowest level, beside the sunken pool with its lilies and water reeds and golden fish, where there would be a warm play of changing light. A theater was put in the southeast corner. The garage was located under the high end of the building to the west.

Gradually, after a point when most firms would have thought the design completed, the museum became architecture. Grand staircases and walks joined the complex together, intersecting in plazas and courts, threading through gardens, passing beneath parts of the building that spanned broad promenades, so that there were always transitions from light to shadow, and then optimistically into light again, as the great space of the main courtyard opened, framed by the architecture into an amphitheater where Mozart or rock could be played. Into this tremendous composition the court house and civic auditorium were brought almost humorously, as foils for the museum's new premise of what a just public building should be. And always there was the city beyond, placed in a new urban focus.

To achieve such richness of effect the architects relied only on the natural wealth of the planting and trees, and on the sparest of palettes in the actual building. Only three materials — reinforced concrete, plate glass and wood — were used throughout the construction. The concrete was sandblasted, inside and out, making it a soft, powdery background for all kinds of art and other exhibits, and a lovely surface for rosemary or ivy spilling down over the walls. The tremendous windows and glass doors, in which Roche's unfailing command of proportion and scale is consistently revealed, were all framed in oak. Only in trellises and arbors, carrying bougainvillea or wisteria, ficus or honeysuckle, where oak would not stand up to the plants or the weather, did he turn to rough-sawn redwood, with a strength and majesty that had not been attained by the local Bay Area school since Maybeck's Christian Science Church.

As construction progressed in the mid-1960s, the whole generous vision seemed to be coming true. Then it was discovered that a roofing subcontractor, who later went bankrupt, had not succeeded in waterproofing the planting beds. The building leaked; and a bitter quarrel followed, in which the architects were certainly not wrong, but were wronged by a city administration that had never grasped what kind of architecture it was receiving. A piranhalike bureaucracy had long been nibbling at the building (and, alas, still does today); and, in the name of safety, city officials demanded handrails in the center of staircases rather than at their side, and all kinds of silly railings and barriers that started and ended nowhere, sometimes in the middle of shrubs, so that gardeners would not fall and hurt themselves in an earthquake.

Finally the differences became irreconcilable, and the longstanding deficiencies of Oakland, always lurking at the perimeter of the project, erupted in ugly ways. The upshot was that the original design group never finished the building; and this had lamentable effects on the interiors. What they might have been, had Roche kept on with them, perhaps together with Charles Eames, can be guessed only from the exquisite proposals for the National Aquarium in Washington, D.C., on which they collaborated in 1966. That design developed in many ways from Oakland; and it was carried very far before it was killed on grounds of economy by a House committee headed by — of all people — Wayne Hays.

But not everything was lost in Oakland. Fortunately, Gordon Ashby, who had worked with Eames, and understood Roche's intentions, was brought in to do the science and history galleries on the first and second levels, and he did an exemplary job. A captious critic might object to his use of walnut for furniture and displays, rather than oak which would have complemented the architecture; and the lighting also seems too restless, dropping below the ceiling coffers to disrupt the architectural volume, and detracting from the intricate play of the structure overhead, where forms step upward and downward in alternating patterns, expressing the movement of stairs and the slanting lawns of the terraces above, and leading to see-throughs from level to level that the staff today keeps mainly closed. Otherwise, especially in the stunning history gallery, Ashby is hard to fault. He has responded to the building with wonderful wit, displaying a hand almost as deft as Eames' own, and a highly civilized intelligence. I only wish that the most recently installed spaces, by Ashby's former assistant Bruce Collins, had been as good. But they are terribly cluttered, and much less selective toward artifacts, so that they seem like parodies of the Eames approach.

In the topmost art gallery, the tallest of the three and potentially more handsome than the others, the museum's own curators, led by Paul Mills, decided to do the interior themselves. Mills had been extremely helpful in the basic planning, but as an amateur designer he committed many errors, erecting false walls that interrupt the flow of space and chop up the room's proportions; and he also studded the floor with cumbersome oak mountings, like little billboards, which display paintings on one side only, and simply block views on the other. All this should be redone, as well as the lighting, which belongs in some department store.

But this was a minor misfortune compared to the calamity perpetrated in the great hall. When Roche left it unfinished, this aristocratic room had the solemn grandeur of an Irish baronial castle. At one end a heroic staircase, cantilevered from the wall, was its single sober adornment, while overhead the girders of the structural ceiling formed massive coffers. For reasons that remain baffling, although ostensibly they were attacking an acoustical problem caused when they installed a hardwood floor, the Oakland firm of Mackinlay/Winnacker/McNeil & Associates tarted up this masculine space as a giant boudoir, with movable chandeliers festooned with hundreds of small bulbs. To compound this mistake, they concealed the structure behind cheap acoustical panels, not only the upper walls — where tapestries might be hung — but the magnificent ceiling, too, so that the great coffers have vanished.

Where architects left off, the city's personnel took over to mar the building in smaller ways: plunking down concrete refuse containers of the wrong size, shape and texture; using ceramic cigarette urns as doorstops for the noble portals; strewing the restaurant terrace with metal furniture that looks acquired at a garage sale; protecting a skylight (through which a teenager had managed to jump) with a ponderous redwood coping that is no more effective than a hidden metal grille would have been, but manages to conflict with both the architecture and Claire Falkenstein's wall sculpture above it. Worst of all, perhaps, was the fencing of the pool with a barrier through which small children, whom it was supposed to save from drowning in two feet of water, manage to slip with ease.

Yet these transgressions fade before the exhilarating splendor of the gardens, lovingly cultivated by a saintly public servant, the chief gardener Bruno Filardo, who with two hardworking assistants is struggling to maintain five acres of planting in the midst of one of the worst droughts in California history. As the garden has matured, it has grown lusher than anyone anticipated; and it is becoming one of the horticultural pilgrimage stops of the world, like Sissinghurst or Villandry. Miraculously the garden has withstood even the loss of a stand of three immense atlas cedars (*Cedrus atlantica*), planted in 1911 when the civic auditorium was built, which Roche made the glory of the central court. These astonishing evergreens, which an architectural renderer would have given anything to draw, perished during the museum's time of troubles in the 1960s, when the new lawn was heavily watered, and these semiarid trees died for lack of drainage. But the fast-growing deciduous alders which have replaced them are now crowning out, and seem acceptable enough.

At any rate the people think so. They come by the thousands (in spite of the city's imposition of an admission fee to the galleries). And to appreciate the museum it is best to come on a Sunday, when whole families arrive from the affluent hills and the plebeian flatlands, intellectuals from Berkeley and hard hats from San Leandro, curious San Franciscans and foreign architects, Chicanos and Chinese, native Americans, hippies, squares, artists, old people and, above all — for this is Oakland's hope — black families and white families side by side, sharing a gift of architecture.

The children are irresistible. They race on the lawn, swing on the trees, hop on the parapets. They use Peter Voulkos' tubular bronze sculpture as a slide. They set George Rickey's giant red scissors in motion and send them flying back and forth above the court. They do not notice, as an architect might, that it is not very sensitively placed, and probably not a fine enough vertical element to contend with the great horizontal lines of the building. Nor do they care that the petrified log on which they climb and play is clumsily installed, and furthermore one of the few science and history exhibits in a garden that is almost exclusively dominated by sculpture. This was not what the architect had in mind.

But neither they nor their parents realize how many possibilities of the architecture have not been fulfilled: that they can enter each gallery only at one end, for instance, and leave the same way, because the security men have locked the garden doors, even though there has been little pilferage (in a museum where almost everything is replaceable anyway), and almost no vandalism since it opened in 1969. Roche hoped, of course, that there would be cross movement in the galleries, with people entering and leaving at will through the garden doors to refresh themselves on the terraces, as one might go outdoors to a garden from a home.

No matter. Someday the museum will be cordially used everywhere. A decade is only a moment in the life of a great institution or in the life of a city that can be great. The collections are growing so quickly that the museum suffers from an acute shortage of storage space and work room for preparing exhibits, something no one could have predicted when the design was conceived for a museum that had no collections at all. The curators grouse about this, just as they complain about many minor technical difficulties; and there is talk about acquiring extra service and storage space in nearby buildings, even though it might make more sense to create storerooms and workshops in the big garage, where stalls are simply rented by the month, and let cars park somewhere else.

But the crowds moving happily through the galleries do not care, are scarcely aware, of such matters. Their verdict is Yes, everything seems to be going well, or well enough, as they applaud musicians and dancers, and eat and drink at the ethnic festivals in the great courtyard: Greeks and Russians, Latinos and Japanese, as well as Indians who set up teepees on the grass. All this is a part of the museum's outreach operation (once bitterly opposed by conservative politicians) that is run by Ben Hazard, a black artist in charge of "special exhibits," many of which take place in other parts of the city, such as the awards ceremonies of the Black Filmmakers Hall of Fame that are held each year in the restored Paramount Theater, a marvelous Art Deco picture palace that was empty for years, and now is the home of the Oakland Symphony.

There is an undeniable sense of an expansion of life, and enlargement of human possibilities. But is this not what modern architecture, from the days of Sullivan and Wright, Gropius and Corbu and Mies, has ultimately been all about? And isn't that what the architectural profession (and even worse, the architectural schools), demoralized by enormous social and physical problems that seem beyond control, has tried to ignore or forget in the 16 years since the museum's design was begun?

Modern architecture has been experiencing a bad failure of nerve, simply because — in an age of Vietnam, Watergate and the decline of cities — architects have been afraid to think of the full potential of the future, just as they have failed, intellectually and spiritually, to renew the movement's founding principles.

But the future is open, and modern architecture may be perennially new. "The architect," said Kevin Roche in one of his rare written statements, "is a servant of people. He leads, if he leads at all, by showing what is possible in creating an environment. . . . There should be no limits. He should move to this end using every energy, asking every question, exploring every possibility." Any architect who can understand this will rejoice that he is not living in another time or place.
June 1977, *AIA Journal*

■ DAVIES HALL — PROSE, RATHER THAN POETRY

"Haut bourgeois" is a tactful way of saying upper-middle class. In French it means not so much the lack of great wealth, for burghers may be richer and more powerful than princes, so much as the absence of true aristocracy. There is in bourgeois art a certain ponderous complacency, a heavily conventional sense of art and manners, and that overfed love of tradesmen's luxury.

And that, architecturally, is what we have in Louise M. Davies Symphony Hall.

Granted, the acoustics—the raison d'etre of the whole $28 million enterprise — promise to be far better than that. Opening night was merely a trial run, like the shakedown of a ship, which produced uneven results. But once the 3000-seat hall is properly tuned, the quality of sound should be superlative. [Note: the acoustics remained poor until a $10 million retrofit in 1992.]

This alone makes the strongly-modeled auditorium, where the "sculptural" embellishments of the walls, ceiling, and balcony fronts are in fact acoustical devices, a much more significant piece of architecture — because its design is truly functional — than the wraparound neo-Baroque exterior, with its three tiers of glittering concourses enclosed by a great curving facade.

The deliberately mannered exterior, composed of precast concrete panels that are chamfered and rounded like artificial stone, is purely pictorial. Skidmore, Owings & Merrill, the architects, have been avowedly inspired by the Beaux-Arts monuments of the Civic Center, now half a century and three-quarters of a century old. Davies Hall does not literally ape the Opera House on the other side of Grove Street, or the still more magnificent City Hall across Van Ness Avenue, but it echoes their monumental scale, ornate mood and civic pride — or pridefulness.

Hence the bulky "rope courses" sweeping around the symphony hall facade, plus innumerable other neoclassical motives justified only by the presence of the historic buildings on the other side of the street.

To SOM's chief designer, Edward Charles Bassett, this is justification enough. Although he is the author of a number of hard-boiled downtown office buildings, which led some people to condemn him as some sort of Miesian technocrat, he has also been a romantic classicist, starting in 1959 with the shapely but partly fictional arches of the John Hancock Building (now Industrial Indemnity) on California Street. From there he went on to a series of historically reminiscent buildings, all steel framed, like Davies Hall, and clad in cast concrete that simulated stone.

To a strict modernist, this may be decadence. But there can be fine decadent art, like Proust's. Seen in that context Davies Hall is a veritable *Remembrance of Things Past*.

Certainly it is a remarkable feat of architectural recollection: a tribute to the Civic Center, of which the late Arthur Brown, Jr., who did the City Hall and the Opera House, might have approved.

In a single stroke, for instance, the great arc of the facade solves the problem of the ragged southwest edge of the Civic Center, which had eluded our city planners for a couple of generations.

Quite apart from some strange formal devices, such as the concrete "teeth" that frame the middle band of windows, or the outsized balconies that have been nicknamed "ears," there are some basic architectural weaknesses.

The first is the failure to provide a real entrance. Instead of a generous staircase at the center of the facade, which needn't have been "grand" in the old pompous sense, but which one would naturally expect at the corner of Grove and Van Ness, there is only a meager entrance down the block — about the size appropriate for an art-movie house. It seems like a side door, if not an afterthought. To either side are staircases — handsomely detailed, but too narrow — that lead to a tiny entrance plaza above, execrably paved in brown and cream tiles, also much too small for so large a building.

That entrance, and a similar staircase and terrace on the Van Ness Avenue side, are the only ways to get into this huge building. There are service doors between the semicircular concrete bastions that roll around the base of the facade (they're not machine gun emplacements, but planters, which soon will be provided with clumps of shrubbery, and enriched with an edge of vines trailed down from below the great windows of the main floor). And there is also Henry Moore's splendid "Reclining Figure," a bit too small, and not quite convincingly placed.

Ostensibly this daunting exterior is to be relieved by the indoor pageantry that will be visible to passersby on the street — before and after performances and during intermissions — through the immense glass surfaces. Because neither the concourses nor interior staircases are quite finished, however, it was impossible — especially in the opening-night crush — to envisage whether this theatrical effect will be truly rich or merely flashy.

My guess is that it will please the audiences. The colors and fabrics, meant to recall the velvets and damasks of the *Belle Epoque* — dove grays, creamy whites, soft beiges and pale roses — should be popular in a period of nostalgia. So should the strips of mirroring inserted between the plaster half-rounds, rather like half-columns, that enliven the 18-foot-high walls.

But it's doubtful that anything can redeem the thin mat of a pink rug — vulgarly adorned with violin "f-hole" motives — that is supposed to suggest serious music but belongs in some hotel lobby.

Thus this lobby architecture strives for the parvenu grandeur of the old Beaux-Arts monuments, without matching their verve and panache. In the great auditorium, one's expectations of Davies Hall come closer to fulfillment. The tremendous space opens at both orchestra and balcony levels with a rich surge of energy; and the colors — cream that now seems a subdued peach, dusty rose that alternates (in the loges and balcony) with wine, the beige acoustical banners (only partly visible) that lighten in tone as they approach the stage — blend into a composition of curved and angular forms that may fairly be called symphonic.

The basic configuration was dictated by the acoustical experts Bolt, Barnaek & Newman, with Ted Schultz in charge of the project. To avoid costly failures such as Avery Fisher Hall at Lincoln Center, he reported directly to the trustees rather than through the architects.

This made possible a genuine collaboration. The chief requirement was to mix sound evenly throughout the hall, returning it to the center at the same time that it is diffused beneath the balcony or dispatched to the topmost row.

It called for a proscenium-less stage, with seating on three sides behind it, as well as the staggered arrangement of the "terrace" seating, in which the rolled fronts of the loges (really, boxes by another name) act as sound diffusers.

For economic reasons, the room, like most big-city concert halls these days, is, of course, too large, but the sight lines are excellent. The architects have saved the space from seeming chopped-up and arbitrary, like Berlin, although they met the complex acoustical program without oversimplifying it.

The angular projections of the walls rise to a ceiling of exceptionally hard concrete that is studded with little truncated tetrahedrons — four-sided pyramids that the architects call "pods" — that neatly contain down-lights and other mechanical equipment, which is messily obvious in halls such as Denver's, but here unobtrusive.

The "continental" seating, uninterrupted by a central aisle (thereby providing many additional seats in the best part of the house) is equally well done. The seats themselves are comfortable, and there is enough space between them and the next row for people to pass easily.

On the other hand, the concrete floor, like in a sports arena, is troubling. It has been justified both on the basis of acoustics (as an undeniably hard surface) and economics (it's surely cheaper than the wood floor originally contemplated). Perhaps if less money had gone into some of the protuberances of the facade, there would have been some available for a lovely hardwood surface.

But that is where the imperial pose of Davies Hall is always breaking down. It is simply not so nouveau riche as the monuments of the robber barons, and one therefore wonders at the attempt to simulate the old effect.

The interior, for all its virtues, is like the facade: a bit too heavy, somehow missing in grace, Mahler rather than Mozart, not poetry but prose.
September 18, 1980

■ SF MOMA: AN EXTRAORDINARY WORK FOR SAN FRANCISCO

Dominated by a huge upslanting skylight that will be larger than the western rose window of Notre Dame of Paris, the new home of the San Francisco Museum of Modern Art will be an extraordinary work of Modernist art in its own right.

This majestic building, privately financed except for the gift of the site by the Redevelopment Agency, will belong to us all.

It will be stronger and more sumptuous even than it appears in models and drawings, and my hunch is that citizens at large, once they get accustomed to architecture of such integrity, are going to love it.

Here, finally, San Francisco has an uncompromising contemporary building, utterly free of passing Post-Modernist chic, that was conceived first and last by the Swiss Italian architect Mario Botta as a civic monument on the order of a cathedral.

Perhaps the severe exterior, stepping back in three brick-clad tiers to either side of the granite-faced central tower, also suggests a castle. Certainly it derives from the fortresslike hermetic houses Botta has built in his native Ticino, on the southern slopes of the Alps, where buildings are meant to last.

This is the price of a Botta building, and it will be redeemed, I think, in the resplendent luminous interior that should be one of the top places in the world to experience art.

It is going to be a terrific museum. With about 200,000 square feet of galleries, offices, a theater, bookstore, restaurant and much-needed storage areas and shops, it will be four times larger and incomparably superior to the museum's cramped old quarters in the Civic Center.

Yet the deepest meanings of the museum are not merely practical. They are spiritual, a metaphor of timeless things.

Hence the ideal geometric forms, the calm grandeur of the horizontal and cylindrical volumes, the facings of richly textured brick or stripes of dark and light stone, above all the sudden upthrust of the central glass opening, like the transept lantern tower of a church, but raked upward to a height of 145 feet — as high as a 14-story building — that will flood the center of the museum with natural light.

Such a building would not be out of place in Siena or Orvieto, but it is going to look marvelous in San Francisco.

Compared with a forced structural stunt like St. Mary's Roman Catholic Cathedral in the Western Addition, whose big windows are detailed like a bank's, the new museum seems positively exalted.

That took some doing. For nearly two years, Botta carefully restudied his original design of 1990, making many subtle changes. Then, in 1991, he suddenly brought the whole concept into focus by a single spectacular stroke, shearing away the dubious crown of ficus trees which were to have encircled the great central skylight.

Whether or not it was so hard a decision as he claimed (a captious critic, me for instance, might suspect that the trees were put there to be sacrificed if other features of the design were threatened), Botta lovingly called these trees "angelic presences."

In fact, he is planting a ring of similar trees around the skylit roof of a small cathedral he is doing in a suburb of Paris.

Yet the skittish ficus trees were a strange fancy of an otherwise reasonable architect.

They probably would have perished in the chill afternoon winds that sweep over Yerba Buena Gardens. At best they would have been difficult to maintain.

Instead of a soft rim of greenery that would have blurred the outline of the tower, the skylight — set at a 45-degree angle — will be bordered by a hard edge of granite, laid in alternating bands of black and silvery gray that is carried over to the round shaft below, imparting tremendous drama to the whole composition.

It should be one of the finest displays of stonework in modern architecture — unless the museum's trustees decide to save some bucks, perhaps $250,000, by substituting precast concrete for the nobler gray granite.

My guess is that they won't. Up to now, their architectural decisions, such as the reduction of office space in the rear of the building, have been based more on an analysis of real needs than on a mean sense of thrift.

The local cultural Establishment can take pride in what it has wrought. This is a case of the upper crust pretty much doing what it wishes, without undue bureaucratic interference or populist compromises with unlettered neighborhood sages.

The museum's own trustees alone have donated some $60 million in construction funds, or nearly three-fourths of an $85 million project that includes a $25 million endowment for operations and maintenance. Only $5 million remains to be raised from corporations and other donors.

Such sums sound large at a time when the homeless haunt the museum's surroundings, but the outlay is not so expensive in the context of an overheated art market that has lately cooled down with the rest of the economy. In the late 1980s, though, a single Van Gogh (and a poor one at that) fetched almost that much.

But this museum will make San Francisco visually richer than any painting could.

By day its massed forms will focus the loose design of Yerba Buena Gardens on a new west-to-east cross axis that will shift the emphasis of this confused and misbegotten redevelopment project away from the north-south view toward Moscone Center. At night, the skylight will shine forth like a great circular beacon in the South-of-Market cityscape, signaling the cultural facilities that are under construction along Third Street.

To get an idea of the museum's heroic scale, the steel-framed stagehouse of the new YBC theater, at 90 feet, is only two-thirds the height of Botta's lantern tower, which in turn will rise nearly half the height of Timothy Pflueger's 26-story Pacific Telephone Building of 1925, directly east on New Montgomery Street.

Botta's building will not defer to this romantic "skyscraper" so much as be a courteous neighbor with its own agenda of urban design. Two highrises are scheduled to go up on either side of the museum when the real estate market recovers from the slump, and Botta has had to anticipate their presence.

This is one way to create a coherent American cityscape.

And once inside the museum, the visitor will enter a special city of the mind — a city of art — that Botta has devised as a progression of light. From the drawings, it is hard to visualize the first effect of this interior, but it should be comparable to the overwhelming impression of Frank Lloyd Wright's Guggenheim Museum in New York, which is entered through a low doorway, and suddenly "explodes" — I guess that's the word — in a swirling luminous space.

Botta's central space will be less bombastic, but it, too, will be a *coup de theatre*. Beyond the low glass doorways, flanked by the bookstore and restaurant, is a veritable indoor piazza, about 100 feet square, paved in light and dark granite, bordered by meeting rooms, forming an interior townscape that by day will be filled with natural light and by night lit by lamps.

Directly ahead is the entrance to the auditorium, framed in a double staircase superb enough for a chateau like Chambord.

They curve round to landings that overlook the main space, on four levels, lifting some 60 feet to the upper galleries (you can take elevators if you don't wish to climb).

At this point, the great lantern tower — 35 feet in diameter — enters the spatial drama, and in a Piranesian play of interpenetrating structure and space, fulfills the promise of its powerful outer form. The skylight, supported by a pair of bowstring steel trusses, plays another geometric drama of its own, since the cylinder sliced away at an angle forms not a pure circle — proper to Renaissance architecture — but a Baroque ellipse.

The concept is truly grand. And what will make the design doubly rewarding is the calm of the exhibition galleries. These unencumbered spaces, lit by skylit vaults which also contain lamps and are fitted with baffles to filter the even flow of light, may be the most serene places to enjoy art since those of the late Louis I. Kahn's Kimbell Museum in Fort Worth, Texas, perhaps the greatest museum architecture of our time.
April 8, 1992

■ BLOWING IT ON WILSHIRE BOULEVARD

Whether the big new wing of the Los Angeles County Museum of Art is regarded as a wild Art Deco put-on or a practical improvement that at last allows LACMA to function as a halfway decent museum — and it's possible to see this mixed-up building both ways — there's no question that the Los Angeles cultural establishment has blown a $35 million chance to transform its worst mistake of the 1960s into an exalted work of architectural art. Why LACMA should get such poor results on Wilshire Boulevard while the Museum of Contemporary Art was doing far better downtown is anyone's guess. MOCA, achieved against considerable odds, may not be a museum of the future, but LACMA, with more money and plenty of room to expand, is turning out to be yesterday's museum of tomorrow today.

Everything about the Robert O. Anderson Building, as the new wing is called after the beneficent former head of ARCO, harkens back half a century and more to a mythic Los Angeles of the palmy days of the movies, all creamy Deco and dreamy streamlined Moderne, when buildings could be tricked out as stage sets. By now, of course, Los Angeles should have outgrown false-front architecture; but here on Wilshire, like a hangover from the 1930s, is a tremendous piece of Hollywoodish scenery, 300 feet across, and stepping up like a bland, asymmetrical ziggurat to its full height of 100 feet.

The materials carry a nostalgic aura. Broad horizontal bands of tawny Minnesota limestone and bluish-green glass blocks, favorites of the Moderne era, are laced through by thin emerald lines of glazed terracotta, another nearly extinct material that has been lately revived by Post-Modern historicists. And cut out of the predominantly yellow wall, as if it were butter, is a mock-imperial portal — as high as a five-story building and 50 feet wide — that could have been cribbed from an extravaganza by Cecil B. de Mille.

This stroke of drama, or farce, through which horsemen might gallop in Roman armor, is obviously meant to upstage the older parts of the museum, which are partly screened from Wilshire, but not totally eclipsed by the new wing. It's a pity that they couldn't be altogether erased (although eventually they will be disguised by new masonry shells) because the whole original scheme by the late William L. Pereira — an architect who himself seemed straight from central casting — is a certifiable dog that was hopelessly out of date when it opened in 1964.

Indeed, the aim of the present architects, Hardy Holzman Pfeiffer Associates of New York and L.A., with Norman Pfeiffer in charge of the design, can't be understood except as a *riposte* to Pereira's triad of weakly pompous pavilions, flecked with marble chips, that were set back deeply from Wilshire in a U-shaped pattern, without the slightest respect for the street, like a suburban mortuary.

Of all the pseudocultural monuments that went up in America during the 1960s, when Mussolini's notions of architecture were resurrected in Lincoln Center and exported westward from New York, LACMA was probably the most bogus. Although the buildings were straightforwardly framed in steel, to lighten their loads on the squishy terrain near the La Brea tar pits, the spindly uprights, coated with concrete, had about as much structural vitality as congealed toothpaste. The banality of the exteriors was topped, if that is the word, by the *nouveau riche* fussiness of the galleries and the intractable three-part layout of the buildings, which hampered all the operations that were administered in a dingy netherworld of basement offices that have now been nicely brightened up.

The final embarrassment occurred after primordial tar seeped into the museum's outer circuit of shallow moats and fountains, which in the 1970s were filled and turned into a crude sculpture garden festooned mainly with posthumously cast Rodin bronzes that have an ersatz look. By the end of the decade — before serious planning got under way, incidentally, for rival MOCA — the powers that be at LACMA knew that drastic overhaul and major expansion were needed if the museum were to accommodate its growing and vastly improved collections. What LACMA could have used at that point was dynamite. But donors of the Ahmanson, Hammer and Bing pavilions were very much on the scene; and out of tact or terror the museum authorities and Pfeiffer hit on a strategy that would convert the U-plan into a square by adding a new wing on Wilshire, leaving the three existing buildings to be put right as time and money permit.

The concept made economic sense, and included the dividend of a spectacular enclosed space, which has ended up as the Times-Mirror Central Court, that has twice the area, at 40,000 square feet, of the great hall of the Metropolitan Museum of Art in New York. Such a court, done properly, would provide the clear focus — a grand place of arrival — that LACMA with its scattering of elements had always lacked. At the same time, if the court were properly entered from Wilshire, the problem of a missing main entrance would be solved in a museum that hitherto confronted the visitor with a bewildering choice of trivial doorways.

Besides, the Anderson Building, with 115,000 square feet of exhibition, storage and administrative space, would be a sizable museum in itself, slightly larger than MOCA, where the Japanese architect Arata Isozaki was faced with the difficulty of placing most of a 90,000-foot museum underground.

Even though Pereira's buildings would remain largely intact, thus ending the chance for an ideally great museum, there was still the promise, or at least the possibility, of outstanding and perhaps extraordinary architecture in the rest of the expansion program. That promise was not kept. Quite apart from the theatrical facade on Wilshire, basically a slickly manipulated blank wall that makes no overtures whatever to people passing on foot (and also partly belies the nature of the spaces inside), the Anderson Building starts to fall apart as a concept as soon as the grandiose portal is entered.

If the effect on Wilshire was Babylonian-Roman, the mood in the towering entry passage, sloping up to the central court, is Pharaonic. The musical accompaniment here should be the triumphal march from

"Aida." Pillars clad in deep green terra-cotta — the same glazed veneer as outside — soar 70 feet to support a translucent plastic canopy that looks very cheap in a major museum. Natural light filters downward, eerily enough, through this honey-colored covering of tilted panels, which are open at the sides — appropriate for Southern California — and are therefore only a shelter against hot sun or rain, rather than a true roof.

But they are so lofty that the scale is overwhelming, or seems to be, until the whole pastiche is revealed as a toy Temple of Karnak. The tall rounded pillars are shams. Pfeiffer, by no means merely a Post-Mod collagist, is enough of a straight Modern architect to expose at top and bottom pins of steel that signify the structural cores; and in any case the plastic canopy far overhead is so lightweight that one side comes down in a what-the-hell gesture on top of the Bing Building that hems the passageway on the right.

Now a discordance sets in between old and new because the Anderson Building on the left is no longer walled in limestone, but with painted metal panels that extend around the sides and back of the new wing. These pale industrial surfaces, "pillowed" so as not to appear overly flat, are not too obtrusive in the entranceway because attention is diverted to a channel of water running downward beside the lifting ramp, next to a low wall — reminiscent of the Vietnam War Memorial in Washington — which in a very Southern Californian way is inscribed with names of contributors to the museum.

The funereal mood subsides when the central atrium is reached. There is a sudden opening of space, an elating play of light beneath the high translucent canopies and friendly bustle in the Times-Mirror Court. Open-air cafes, festively done, are a striking contrast to the squalid old cafeteria; and a certain civilized air prevails.

Yet although the space is big, it is not truly great, and indeed seems smaller because trivial elements, including the remaining hulks of the Ahmanson and Hammer buildings, clamor for attention on all sides. It's too early to pass final judgment on the court in its unfinished state, since the upper levels of the various wings must be linked by a grand staircase, more bridgeways and additional rows of tentlike coverings, popped down on the older buildings as well as supported by magniloquent green columns. They seem too easily flung up.

Perhaps when Pereira's buildings are resurfaced, in stone that hasn't yet been selected, the court will become less restless, and the space can come into its own. But the odds are that a busy, cut-up quality will persist, in latter-day Art Deco details, glitzy lighting and abrupt changes in scale, from the Brobdingnagian colonnades to Lilliputian doorways and balconies. At this state they seem leftover from an imaginary world's fair.

These failings are partly redeemed by the new galleries of the Anderson Building, which provide the museum with sorely needed elbow room. The high-ceilinged spaces, painted a soft silvery gray, are reticent compared to the strident exterior; and the surprisingly fine collections of 20th-century art — more extensive than commonly thought — are for the first time amply displayed in a coherent way.

The art does more for these essentially traditional rooms than the architecture does for the art. In a sense the sequence of spaces, which museum people call an *enfilade*, is simply a carefully done update of Pereira's bourgeois salons, except in the spaces directly behind the Wilshire facade where natural light pours gently through clerestories of glass blocks. In this part of the building the prowlike end of the Wilshire front, which from the outside seems an arbitrary formal device borrowed from I.M. Pei's East Wing of the National Gallery, can be finally understood as a more or less utilitarian stairwell — a dubious use for such an assertive triangular form — where the curators have crowded in odd pieces of sculpture that deserve a more generous setting.

Unfortunately, that's the closest LACMA gets to an inspired ambience for large-scale contemporary art. The Anderson Building has nothing to compare with the thrilling pyramidal spaces of MOCA, particularly the first lordly room where Isozaki has transformed a subterranean gallery into a magical skylight stage for David Smith's sculpture. If MOCA never again comes up to that magnificent opening experience, and in fact winds down to some anticlimactic boxes beneath its administration building, Pfeiffer at LACMA has understated the problem of designing a museum for the virtually limitless array of art — growing, changing, unpredictable as well as familiar — which the people of Los Angeles now have a right to expect.

For that reason it's instructive to walk over to the curious new pavilions for Japanese art, conceived by the late Bruce Goff, Frank Lloyd Wright's maverick follower, which LACMA is building, virtually as an afterthought, next to the Hammer and Bing wings, at the corner of the complex.

Like most works by the uninhibited Oklahoman, who did some of the most madly endearing houses of the century, the pair of small, circular buildings, slung by cables from round towers faced in strange greenish quartzite, looks so disorganized, especially while construction is going on, that the startled beholder may suspect that the model fell off the table, and was haphazardly pushed together again.

Yet these buildings, which should have been given a secluded, landscaped site of their own, present an *idea* — not an anthology of historic quotation — of how architecture may be put at the service of art. In this case the art is a very special collection of Japanese scrolls and other exquisite objects, donated to LACMA (together with half the money for the $12.5 million buildings) by Goff's fellow Oklahoman, Joe Price.

Goff sought an original, nonhistoric equivalent for subtly lit Japanese houses, which are made for such art; and as high-tech substitute for shoji screens, he chanced upon an unassuming commercial product called Kalwall, which happens to be the same synthetic insulation material that Pfeiffer — designing at LACMA a few years later — chose to cover his court.

Goff has used the Kalwall panels as translucent walls, which are just being installed along the curving perimeters of the buildings by Goff's associate Bart Prince, who took a schematic concept and turned it into a final design. Whether it will have Goff's crazy legerdemain is another question. My hunch is that the exterior, at least, will always look extremely odd.

But the principle of meeting art with searching architecture remains intact. Fearless buildings need not be oddities; and there are museums all over the world to prove it. Instead of the bombast on Wilshire Boulevard, LACMA might have tried to achieve the nobility of the late Louis I. Kahn's Kimbell Museum at Fort Worth, or the quiet splendor and intelligence of Renzo Piano's Menil Collection in Houston, to name a living architect. But that would have required a patron so brilliant, so uncompromising as Dominique de Menil, and we have yet to see her like at LACMA.

November 29, 1987

■ WHAT TO DO WITH THE PRESIDIO

Now that the Army must surrender the Presidio to the National Park Service, it is high time to make sure that this unique opportunity is not frittered away.

The stakes are enormous. The magnificent old base deserves an equally magnificent new use, not merely as a great historic park but as a cultural institution — perhaps a new kind of "World University" — that could be the key to San Francisco's whole future as a center of Pacific civilization.

If Nirvana, the final beatitude, had floated down on San Francisco from on high, it might bear some resemblance to the 1,440-acre forested preserve, which has the most spectacular natural open space in any large city in the world. That the Presidio is also an architectural treasure, with the finest ensemble of U.S. Army buildings this side of West Point, only enhances its cultural value. Dating back to the 1850s, but largely from the late 19th and early 20th centuries, 400 buildings (out of a total of 900 on the base) contribute either historically or aesthetically, usually both, to the Presidio's status as a national landmark. Under no circumstances should this heritage be trashed. Even if its uses were as fine as Fort Mason's, which we don't need two of, the Presidio must be much more than a recreation facility.

But therein lies the danger that this literally priceless resource will be chopped up and degraded by a strange melange of opportunistic politicians, middlebrow bureaucrats, populist nuts, arts and crafts innocents and Fisherman's Wharf concessionaires. A stampede of would-be squatters is already under way.

Paradoxically, there is also a certain danger from environmental purists who think that the western edge of San Francisco, once barren dunes that have been almost entirely planted by man, is the wild Mendocino coast.

None of these piecemeal approaches will work. The Presidio must be seen whole, as an incomparable urban resource. All of its secondary uses must accord, or at least not conflict, with its highest possible use as a cultural and educational resource.

There is no question that it can be transformed into a university — not a conventional University of California campus, but an unprecedented, profoundly democratic international institution that all nations could share.

The stage is ready for this great intellectual drama.

Two campuslike spaces especially recall university environments: the immense parade ground of the Main Post, degraded to a blacktop parking lot but easy to restore as a greensward, and the long grass centerpiece of Fort Winfield Scott, used by the soldiers for sport and seldom visited by tourists, although it is almost directly on axis with the Golden Gate Bridge and commands one of the most thrilling views of the great reddish web of steel.

Each of these "campuses," put to peaceful purpose, could in time become as famous as the central lawn of Jefferson's University of Virginia. Their strong surrounding architecture could easily accommodate many uses: the Main Post as the university proper. Fort Scott perhaps as a low-cost conference center — much needed in San Francisco — on the order of Asilomar, but in a setting of rare grandeur.

Even then, plenty of buildings and spaces would be left for a wonderful variety of uses, from nature study to child care. The officers' and noncommissioned officers' clubs, with few alterations, can be opened to the public. So can the golf course and clubhouse, whose civilian membership is now snootily limited. The beautiful stables, disused for decades, could again be filled with horses, and bridle paths opened. The chapels already are virtually public places of worship. At Crissy Field, the nearly completed commissary, part of a $30 million Army construction program that never should have been undertaken in the 1980s, can become a visitors' reception center.

The military police station, guardhouses and fire station would be turned over to the Golden Gate National Recreation Area, just as warehouses, repair shops, garages and other utilitarian structures will be occupied by park crews. And a good chunk of the Presidio's ample housing should go to national park rangers, who make as little as $16,000 per year and are priced out of the local residential market.

Opportunities for museums abound. I'm not thinking of mass-cult shrines, such as a College Football Hall of Fame, which state Senator Quentin Kopp wants to move from the Ohio boondocks and dump on the Presidio, but of cultural institutions of very high order, which would be worthy neighbors of a university.

A "Smithsonian of the West," for instance, superseding the fascinating little Army museum installed in a 19th-century infirmary building, could be distributed in period structures as authentic as the airplane hangars near Crissy Field that date from pioneer days of Army aviation.

The Palace of Fine Arts, with its incomparable Exploratorium, presently cut off from the Presidio by major traffic arteries, should be brought into the whole cultural complex and perhaps allowed to expand within the Presidio's walls.

Added to this is a huge stock of housing — ranging from monumental barracks to family dwellings for officers and enlisted personnel, including fine houses for the brass — that are arranged in formal groups or meander along tree-shaded roads.

At the moment, it all seems up for grabs while our liberal congresswomen, Mesdames Boxer and Pelosi, foes of the battleship Missouri, fight to prolong the Army's departure, in a bitter irony, for the sake of a Pentagon payroll.

But sooner or later, the soldiers must go, and then the Presidio, by law, thanks to the vision of our late Representative Phillip Burton, will become part of the "crown jewel" of the Golden Gate National Recreation Area.

Topped by windswept ridges of pine, cypress and eucalyptus, opening to tremendous views of the sea, the bridge and the bay (that could still be improved by selective clearing and replanting), the Presidio has turned out none the less handsomely for never having had a master plan.

Only after World War II, when some truly terrible buildings went up, replacing nice old ones, was the site desecrated by monstrosities such as Letterman Medical Center, a third "campus" that is seismically unsafe for hospital use and mars the whole view westward to the Presidio.

Letterman may be a candidate for demolition when the Golden Gate National Recreation Area takes over, but almost everything else seems worth saving, except the hideous Wherry housing, overlooking the ocean beaches, which was built in the 1960s and should be returned to nature forthwith.

How such decisions will be made is still a very open question.

Some proposals, such as the rock-and-pop amphitheater that Bill Graham thinks would be dandy beside the Golden Gate, are bound to be outrageously inappropriate. Others may make sense, such as a museum commemorating the role of minorities in the armed forces as well as the history of American Indians, whose extermination was conducted partly by Presidio-based troops.

After sorting out popular notions of what the Presidio should be and conducting specialized studies for the site (for example, of 100-year-old trees that are cracking and dying and perhaps should be replaced in slightly different patterns), it will take a couple of years to complete a general plan and still longer for it to be approved.

Because the Presidio is in fact urban, locked into the very fabric of the city, it is seen by many worthies as a heaven-sent chance to relieve the housing crisis in general, and in particular to shelter the homeless, AIDS patients and crack addicts. Fast-buck artists would like to install motels and hotels (there goes Letterman Hospital and rehabbed barracks), fast-food joints and souvenir shops.

Fortunately, the Presidio cannot be sold off by panicked federal officials — right up to the environmentally incompetent Interior Secretary Manuel Lujan — who are scared stiff of assuming heavy new responsibilities when, after years of Reaganish parsimony, there is hardly enough money to run the Golden Gate National Recreation Area as it is. Parts of the Presidio may be legally leased, however, presumably on the Yosemite model, and Park Service officers, prodded by the press, have spoken of potential "revenue centers" that sound ominously like tourist traps.

May heaven forfend such an omen. For one thing, if a World University is created, there's no reason for hand-wringing over money, even if the Presidio, according to slightly overwrought present estimates, will actually cost $17 million annually to operate and maintain as a park once the Army departs.

That will probably occur in a phased withdrawal, lasting well into the 1990s, which gives time to the nation — for this is too important for local sages alone to decide — to consider the Presidio with the intelligence and respect it deserves.

May 15, 1989

IX. Books and Exhibitions

■ ARCHITECTURAL THEATER OF THE ABSURD:
THE WORK OF FRANK GEHRY

Ten years ago Frank Gehry might have been dismissed as another beachfront nut from Venice, Calif. The fractured forms, wildly conflicting materials and inchoate spaces of his impromptu buildings seemed hardly distinguishable from the enlarged shacks lining the hippie streets of the topsy-turvy community.

Today Gehry is the hottest "architect-artist" in America, and by all odds the foremost practitioner of "deconstructivism," a term borrowed from literary criticism, which in architecture comes close to nihilism.

For "deconstructivist architecture" — or "no rules" architecture, as Gehry calls it — is a contradiction of terms. Architecture by its very nature is primarily a rational building art. It has plenty of room for individual genius, even mad extravagance, but it does have rules, or at least used to have rules of scale, proportions and "correct" building practice, like correct syntax in language and harmonics in music.

All that has dissolved in the crucible of Gehry's work. Whether or not he even understands classical principles, and there is evidence that he doesn't in his barbarous recollections of ancient Rome at the Loyola Law School of 1981–84 in Los Angeles, this 59-year-old iconoclast knows that historic culture has ceased to prevail in mass-cult society, especially amidst the technocratic chaos of Southern California.

Just as Los Angeles has unraveled the historic web of urban civilization, Gehry has ripped apart the fabric of historic architecture, including the Modern architecture of the 20th century that is now part of history. With a kind of blunt anger, he has pieced the fragments together, in no perceptible order or hierarchy of forms and materials, often left unfinished, to create an artist's architecture of disconcerting energy, gratuitous crudeness and seemingly aimless intentions that are more like accidents than deliberate design, like a crash on the freeway.

The closest musical equivalent to this "collision architecture" is punk rock. Dramatically — and Gehry can be a magical stage and exhibit designer — it could be theater of the absurd.

If this suggests a gigantic put-on, a false approach to the permanent art of architecture even in ephemeral Los Angeles, Gehry's method has produced buildings which in many ways are unlike any ever built before.

Interior of the First Church of Christ, Scientist, Berkeley, California, 1991.
By Richard Barnes. Courtesy Richard Barnes.

Seen separately, as *faits divers* in the cityscape, the buildings may appear to merge with vernacular environments, like his "life guard's" shack shooting out of the Norton House (1983–84) to scan the beach at Venice. Or they can cause an innate lack of meaning to erupt into a higher random confusion, as in the Wosk Residence (1982–84) — one of his many studio houses for artists — that Gehry plunked atop a nondescript Beverly Hills apartment house as an outlandish collection of unrelated, multisurfaced forms.

But these disparate designs fall apart only when experienced as three-dimensional *buildings.* Viewed indoors as *art,* in the spectacular retrospective exhibition at the Los Angeles Museum of Contemporary Art (MOCA), his ideas gather unexpected coherence. For this we can partly thank Mildred Friedman, the design curator of the Walter Art Center in Minneapolis, who originated this traveling show, and specially commissioned the handsome models and systematic drawings.

But the show is really Gehry's. And it strikingly reveals the degree to which he has been inspired by artists such as Claes Oldenburg, from whom he borrowed the giant pop binoculars for the portal of an office building project. Contemporary art helps him, Gehry has said, to rid himself of the "burden of culture . . . I want to be open-ended. There are no rules, no right or wrong. I'm confused as to what's ugly and what's pretty."

The exhibition, despite fine moments of focus, shows remorselessly how much confusion remains. One impression received from the most striking exhibits is that Gehry is a sculptor *manqué* and that his message is partly messianic. At the entrance to the show, for instance, in the white pyramidal space of MOCA's noblest gallery (designed by the Japanese architect Arata Isozaki), the theme is introduced by a giant fish — Gehry's most deeply personal symbol — that is actually a small wooden structure, covered with lead fish scales. The creature is arrested in full movement, as if it were arcing through water. The idea is to achieve the immediacy of a fresh brush stroke.

In other words, the fish — like the coiled snake that also figures in his buildings, lamps and drawings — is a paradigm of dynamic architecture, but it is fraught with other meanings, some of which have not escaped the burden of culture. Several writers in the splendid exhibition catalog allude to nuances of the symbol.

A huge fish, perhaps 30 feet high, is incorporated with a restaurant in Japan, not too different from Southern California establishments built in the shape of a derby, an orange or a duck. In an unbuildable design for Manhattan, a colossal fish soars 1,500 feet to anchor one end of a dream bridge threaded through the World Trade Center and the Chrysler Building to a huge pylon by the sculptor Richard Serra.

Whether this is simply fun or the biblical leviathan (which also appeared ominously on the beach at the end of Fellini's *La Dolce Vita*), it invites a psychobiography of the artist, who was born Ephraim Goldberg in Toronto and not only changed his own name on his way to the top, but persuaded his parents to change theirs, too, after the family moved to Los Angeles.

Gehry is distressed by this now, even though Gehry seems as good a pseudonym as Le Corbusier, if less resonant with implied poetic associations. Yet it is haunting to learn that he was called "fish" by anti-Semitic schoolmates, as if he had a bad smell; and his subsequent development and success in a sense has made it sweet. As recently as 1984, however, when he was already on the rise, he ruefully remarked, "Being accepted isn't everything."

As one passes through exhibit after exhibit of "no rules architecture," the forced and disorderly designs can be partly understood as the valor of an artist to be accepted on his own terms.

Very little information is provided about the beginnings of his practice after he left the big commercial firm of Victor Gruen to set up his own office in 1962. By the next decade he was doing a few relatively "straight" and rather large buildings, notably the heavy-handed steel trusswork of the Concord Pavilion (1975–77), and the Santa Monica Place shopping center (1973–80) whose only exceptional feature is a great outside sign screen in cyclone fencing, a cheap common material that he elevated to veillike immateriality, and has become a trademark of his work.

Then he suddenly hit his stride in a series of eccentric houses for special clients, starting with himself, which carried idiosyncrasy further than "follies" in Victorian England. Topping the list is his own famous home of 1977–78 that has scandalized a quiet Santa Monica neighborhood. Here he has enveloped an ordinary older house — mostly stripped to raw interior studs and lathing, then partly recovered with unpainted plywood panels and furnished with his signature cardboard furniture — with a lopsided enclosure of cyclone fencing, screen "walls" of corrugated metal and tilted cubistic "windows" that are small, airy structures in themselves.

Compared to sumptuous modern houses, this dwelling is almost squalid, but that is not the point of deconstructivist architecture. It is to abolish preconceived notions of what a house can be, not quite on the level of Neitzche's philosophy, which sought to overturn all previous canons of thought, but with the real Superman kick in the pants of fat-bottomed clods whose cars, pickup trucks, RV's and boats parked in the driveways, Gehry notes, disfigure the neighborhood more than his architecture.

That makes the design an art of *criticism*, but it does not make it profound architecture. There is a sense of mounting anger, and terrible impatience, in the unpainted Sheetrock surfaces and other slapdash details of the Indiana Avenue houses in Venice (1982).

Then the mood lightens, and a certain refinement and humor appear, with a note of almost unbearable poignancy in the unbuilt design for a camp for terminally ill children in the Santa Monica mountains, done with Oldenburg and his wife Coosje van Brugge, which called for playful buildings like wave forms and billowing sails, a giant milk can for a kitchen, and a Gehry fish canopy as an open-air shelter from the sun.

Faced by the challenge of a competition to build a media center facing the Maison Carrée in Nîmes, however, Gehry could respond only with an arrogant incivility that verged on insult to one of the loveliest temples of ancient Gaul. An impartial observer was forced to ask if he could be equal to such a problem of civic design in a contemporary American setting, and he responded with surprising suavity under a very tight budget, with the California Aerospace Museum (1982–84) close to USC.

Here the building's external form seems arbitrary and from certain angles clumsy (although like most of Gehry's work it photographs well), but the bulging shape — so weak compared to the exquisite Lockheed Starfighter attached to the wall — was in fact generated by an interior program that has since been scrapped, so that the inside of the building reveals little of Gehry's intentions.

One wonders if his anger will subside, and how truly radical his architecture can be now that he has been entrusted with a 1,000-foot office building in Manhattan, and has been named one of the four final contenders for the new Disney Symphony Hall in Los Angeles. Planned to be the finest music facility in the world, with a lavish budget permitting superb materials, it cannot escape some of the grandeur inherent in great historic monuments.

If Gehry as an Angeleno is picked for the job over very accomplished architects from elsewhere in the world, as I have a hunch he will be, "no rules" architecture will be facing a moment of truth.

March 27, 1988

■ WRIGHT'S MONUMENTAL CONTRIBUTIONS:
FRANK LLOYD WRIGHT: IN THE REALM OF IDEAS

Frank Lloyd Wright was the greatest artist America ever had. Apart from
Walt Whitman, Mark Twain and perhaps one or two other writers, no
one else equals his stature in our national culture, except Thomas
Jefferson, the last Renaissance man, who, among his many attainments,
was an excellent architect.

But Wright, too, was more than a supremely American architect. He
not only subsumed the roles of painter and sculptor in his many-faceted
art, but he also wrote wonderfully. He was particularly eloquent in
books such as *In the Cause of Architecture* — his own personal cause of
"organic" architecture, which could mean rather different things at
different stages of his career.

By definition, however, his architecture always reached out to every
aspect of "organic" life, based on self-reliant "sovereignty of the individual" and reverence for nature — ideas that derived from Emerson,
Thoreau and Whitman, but went back ultimately to Goethe and
Rousseau. These political, social and economic theories, always united
with his aesthetics, qualified Wright as a home-grown philosopher who
was naturally "an architect of democracy."

Wright the revolutionary designer was of course inseparable from
Wright the libertarian thinker, which is the basic concept of the extraordinary "Realm of Ideas" show at the Marin County Civic Center. No one
will come away from the exhibition without fresh insights into the disconcerting richness of his inventions — the open plan of the affordable,
servantless house, the carport, steel office furniture and other break-
throughs too numerous to list — which were all part of a unified vision
of the world.

A single traveling exhibition — the show moves next to San Diego —
cannot sum up all of this prodigious output or the ramifications of his
personality. This show was largely put together by adoring disciples at
Taliesin ("shining brow" in his ancestral Welsh) at Spring Green, Wis.,
or Taliesin West near Phoenix. It shows the sides of Wright they best
wish to remember at these retreats: communes that are also schools and
architectural offices, where the Master on his stallion was the model for
Ayn Rand's superarchitect in *The Fountainhead.*

The visitor gets little inkling of Wright's patriarchal imperiousness,
still less of the absurd posturing of his last wife, Oglivanna, a harpy born
in Montenegro who hashed Wright's ideas with the mysticism of the
guru Georgei Gurdjieff, and meddled increasingly with design — and

especially daily life at Taliesin — as Wright grew very old. After Wright's death, she was even more domineering as keeper of the flame.

Consequently it is necessary to read between the lines — or read some of the more critical books for sale at the end of show — to get a fuller picture of the master's accomplishments and shortcomings. But compared to other Taliesin productions, this presentation is surprisingly well balanced and lucidly arranged according to major themes Wright elaborated all his life. This is particularly because Gerald Nordland, former director of the San Francisco Museum of Modern Art, was brought in — together with other able consultants — to organize the material, and also because the Taliesin crew has proudly included fevered proposals of the Master's dotage, such as a "mile-high" skyscraper project for Chicago, in which atomic-powered vehicles instead of elevators would run up the flanks of the colossal triangular tower.

Fortunately, the show is otherwise composed of works, many of them endearingly modest, that have changed the history of architecture and express an amazing interplay of art and intellect. To say that Wright's designs and philosophy were fused in a single, magnificent life's work may sound like a truism, applicable to all great architects, but many famous architect/idealogues — Le Corbusier, for instance — have not practiced precisely what they preached.

Wright on the other hand strove mightily, up to his death in 1959 at the age of 91, to live by precept and example according to his defiant family credo: "Truth Against the World."

Today, America — if not the whole world — has turned to his "truth" with a popular devotion, even adulation, that he never enjoyed during his long career. It is still another stunning comeback for his reputation, which has fired up a cottage industry in bogus Wrightian artifacts and ersatz Wrightian buildings, plus a sensational rise in prices of genuine Wrightiana that would have astounded him in his lifetime, when he was often broke but never poor.

But never before was there such an outpouring of public interest in his ideas, rather than his buildings alone. It is a phenomenon that needs explaining.

Architecture, like modern civilization as a whole, has been going through a bad time in the three decades since Wright died. Not only have people begun to see through the reactionary sentimentality of Post-Modernism, the architectural counterpart of Reaganism in politics, but a large part of the public is also fed up with the puristic abstractions of the International Style, which (although the exhibition does not make this clear) partly originated as a stripped-down version of Wright's richly generous early Modern architecture, going back to the 1890s, which caused a sensation in Europe when published in the epochal Wasmuth edition of 1910.

His open-plan structures, especially the Prairie Houses pinwheeling around central hearths, and still more his geometric decorations, predated Cubism and anticipated the nonfigurative abstractions of Mondrian — for instance in the skylights of Unity Temple in 1906 — a good 15 years before Mondrian's austere, rectilinear compositions. In architecture, Le Corbusier, Mies van der Rohe and other Europeans then carried minimalism about as far as it could go until Wright boldly reacquired the lead, enriching their strict formulas with romantic American brilliance in indigenous masterpieces such as the textured, concrete-block Millard House ("La Miniatura") in Pasadena (1922) and above all Fallingwater — his greatest single house — done in 1936.

Locked into a wooded Pennsylvania hillside, but flying free in cantilevered, concrete terraces above a pouring waterfall, Fallingwater epitomized our national ideal of order and liberty, individualism and responsibility. Although built for a wealthy man, the department store owner E.J. Kaufmann of Pittsburgh, its aesthetic and social principles could be extended endlessly.

Indeed, they illustrate the four major themes of the exhibition.

First of all, by "destroying the box," one of Wright's primary aims in architecture, the dynamic, open structure created limitless "freedom of space." Secondly, the house was wedded to land and water, respecting "the nature of the site," and by inference the entire natural world. Third, "materials and methods" — daring projections of reinforced concrete juxtaposed with stone masonry, steel, wood and glass — were resolutely forthright.

Every part of the house was built "in the nature of materials." Each material retained its individual and almost sacred essence: wood as wood, stone as stone, steel as steel, glass as glass, and above all reinforced concrete as an incomparable Modern material that could be used powerfully or playfully.

They added up to a parable of American freedom, for Wright saw these three principles as indispensable to our national ethos, plus a fourth ingredient that he frankly called "building for democracy."

That meant putting the whole organic vision together in an all-encompassing environmental order — expressed in "Broadacre City," an endless metropolis in which every American could have an acre of land for a "Usonian" family home — where public and private interests would be integrated (perhaps after the abrogation of the Constitution of the United States) on the basis of individual creativity.

To this son of the rural Midwest, a Protestant of Protestants for whom European history (but not the Japanese traditions he loved) was mainly a record of injustice, cruelty and poverty imposed by authoritarian governments, truly Modern architecture — his own architecture — was the best hope of democracy.

The past could be literally exploded, as for instance in the spiraling space of the Guggenheim Museum, his most spectacular breakout from "the box," which is a thrilling building but surely one of the most coercive museums of our age, crushing the art on display, and compelling the individual to follow the path Wright has ordained.

By paradox, it is also a way toward true freedom and human dignity. As the crowds move slowly through the (pseudo-Wrightian) Marin County exhibit hall, passing hundreds of designs, realized and unrealized, like the proposed "Butterfly Bridge" for San Francisco Bay and the immense cable-hung fiberglass canopy Wright wished to cover the Marin County fairground, people suddenly became aware of how much he has given us.

And outside, across the lagoon, are the blue-roofed main buildings of the Civic Center, by the master himself, sweeping from hill to hill on broad arches, as the most exhilarating part of the show.

The best view of the county buildings, indeed, is from the terrace of a Usonian (Wrightian for "American") Automatic House, designed in 1955 but never before built, and now ingeniously simulated in Styrofoam rather than concrete block, which has been put up next to the exhibit as a full-scale demonstration of a reasonably priced home for middle-income Americans who could do much of the construction themselves.

Wright was 88 when he conceived this charming and efficient little house (which seems much larger than its actual dimensions), but rarely — at a time when millions of Americans are homeless or badly housed — has a model seemed so young and optimistic, showing once more that there is nothing that we cannot accomplish, nothing we could not hope for, as a lesson to the world.

February 25, 1990

■ THE MYSTERY OF JULIA MORGAN

The most extraordinary woman in the history of architecture, Julia Morgan (1872–1957), hated being known as a "woman architect." The tiny California spinster considered her personal life — guarded to the point of secrecy — and her sex irrelevant to a career that was almost as prolific as that of her contemporary, Frank Lloyd Wright.

When she closed her downtown San Francisco office (and destroyed her files) in 1951, at the age of 79, Morgan had designed 700 buildings. By far the most famous was William Randolph Hearst's fantastic palace at San Simeon, which from 1920 until construction was shut down in 1942 was an architectural career in itself.

Or it would have been, for an ordinary architect. But Morgan also produced an array of churches, YWCAs, women's clubs, educational and commercial buildings and offices, and, not least, several hundred houses, from cottages to mansions. According to her clients' tastes and budgets, and her own powerful impulses, the designs could be done in either the grand historical manner that she was the first woman to learn at the Ecole des Beaux-Arts in Paris, or the redwood regional style that linked her to such early Bay Area Modernists as her friend and mentor, Bernard Maybeck.

Of these modest, rational buildings in wood and stone, so chaste compared to the flamboyance of her work for Hearst, none had more warmth, strength and sure feeling for the land than Asilomar (1913–28), the YWCA conference center beside the sea at Pacific Grove, now a state park.

One would think that a shelf of books had already been written to celebrate such accomplishments. But Julia Morgan until now has been oddly neglected by historians, who are daunted perhaps by a paucity of documents and the wall of privacy that kept even the architect's family and friends at a certain distance. So Sara Holmes Boutelle's long-awaited biography, *Julia Morgan, Architect*, is the first full-length study of this great Californian.

We're lucky to have it. Boutelle has pieced together as much as probably will ever be known of Julia Morgan the woman; and she has earnestly summarized her architectural career. The book is packed with information, some of it new, and the rest hardly known, except to scholars. Facts were culled down from scattered articles on Morgan, allusions to her in general works on the period, and writings on Hearst and San Simeon in particular.

Yet it is still not altogether the book that Julia Morgan deserves, even though it has been beautifully produced by the Abbeville Press and illustrated by Richard Barnes' postcard-effect color photographs, together with reproductions or rare drawings and black-and-white photos of buildings when they were under construction or new.

For several reasons, the brilliant pictorial promises of the book never quite come true in the writing. Boutelle, a great lady in her own right, has been fascinated by Morgan since coming to California in the 1970s from New York, where she taught for years at the Brearley School.

She has been close enough to the Victorian tradition to ask many of the right questions. She wonders, for instance, how so "modest" an architect could have created such "hedonistic" works of art as the magnificent swimming pools for coeds at Berkeley and members of the YWCA, as well as for San Simeon.

Yet if Morgan's life was her work, as she gave every indication it was, her enigmatic personality has direct bearing on her architecture. Critical biography should link the two, but Boutelle runs into difficulty because, in her writing at least, she does not seem to perceive or *feel* buildings very deeply. She has a fair grasp of architectural history, but nothing like the penetrating insight into structure and space, ornament, scale and proportion that is wanted in criticism of the highest order.

Beyond a few allusions to monuments and styles that profoundly affected Morgan's eclectic approach — for instance, the influence of Bramante's sober Roman courtyard of Santa Maria della Pace on the glass-roofed court of the Oakland YWCA — she largely misses the aesthetic chemistry that turned Morgan's Beaux-Arts designs at their finest into architecture of disconcerting richness and originality.

That was especially true at San Simeon, where history is ransacked left and right in a unique amalgam of time present and time past, but Boutelle's appreciation of its wild juxtapositions — the passionate mixing of architectural metaphors — at almost every point is less evocative and searching than architect Thomas Aidala's 1981 book on the Hearst Castle.

More serious, perhaps, in a critical biography, is the lack of a clear view of Morgan's practice at any given moment — and there was usually a good variety of work in the office — because Boutelle has divided the record according to building types. She first deals with campus, church and commercial structures; women's buildings next; then large and small houses; and finally all her varied designs for the Hearsts at other lavish establishments as well as San Simeon, spanning almost half a century.

The upshot is that the reader goes 40 years, from start to end in each category, with no sense of overall continuity. Yet different kinds of buildings rubbed off on one another. Instead of considering the Williams House (1928) at 2821 Claremont Boulevard in Berkeley with dissimilar earlier or later houses, just because they are all houses, it would have been more instructive to relate its Venetian Gothic loggia, tiled borders and other decorative effects that enrich this basically dull house to nonresidential buildings of the period — say, the Gothic encrustations of the luminous mortuary of the Chapel of the Chimes (1926–30) in Oakland.

Neither of those can be rightly understood except as distant cousins of San Simeon, even though the castle was never meant for everyday housekeeping and practical business.

To her credit, Boutelle senses that it was all one thing, and that the castle in the end was the key to the Morgan mystery. The swimming pools, in puritan terms, were sorcery. So were the guest suites, so sensitively designed for lovers, with carefully designed views over the countryside from the enormous beds.

Although Morgan was loyally devoted to Hearst's remarkable mother, and seems to have been on correct terms with his wife, Millicent, she nonetheless dined at the center of the long table, going over drawings amid the revelry with her princely patron and the bewitching Marion Davies.

Boutelle is at her best in describing Morgan's life at the castle, where she had her own room high in a tower, and where she spent almost every weekend for 20 years. Of the thousands of photographs taken there that can be found, she appears only briefly with Hearst in a movie, but her presence was everywhere, not just in the tailored suits whose pockets made a purse unnecessary, but in her spirit, which everywhere animates the architecture and landscaping.

Boutelle gives an indelible picture of Morgan on the job. As architect-engineer-construction manager, she was general overseer of the work, purchasing agent for an immense inventory of *objects d'art* and artifacts, and straw boss of the labor force. Apart from the household staff, there were often as many as 90 construction workers, rarely fewer than 30. Morgan saw to it that they were paid, housed, fed and generously treated on the remote hilltop barony, halfway between San Francisco and Los Angeles.

It was a supreme work of surrealist art. Half palace, half cathedral, the castle emanated from the deepest realms of their beings. It was crammed, like a Joycean stream of consciousness, with bric-a-brac rifled from the ancient monuments of Europe. Wild animals roared in concrete pits and harmless beasts, such as zebras and antelopes, roamed the golden hills.

Above the most sumptuous swimming pool on earth, consecrated to Neptune, the sea god looked down from the pediment of a composite Greco-Roman temple — partly genuine, partly fake — on a mythic province of Eros. Here, and in the still more erotic indoor "Roman" pool, all Byzantine purple and gold, Miss Morgan — it was always "Miss Morgan" and "Mr. Hearst" — turned dreams into buildings for her imperial client-patron-collaborator. Neither could have done it alone.

July 10, 1988

■ THE WEST'S FIRST MODERN ARCHITECTURE

Bernard Ralph Maybeck, the Bay Region's most famous and beloved architect, is best known for the burnt-orange dome of the Palace of Fine Arts. But his real masterpiece — the incomparable First Church of Christ, Scientist, in Berkeley — shows how richly inventive, profoundly humane and strangely elusive this extraordinary designer was in the great days when Modern architecture at last reached the Pacific Coast.

He died in 1957 at the age of 95, sainted in Berkeley and venerated by the whole "humanist" side of the Modern movement.

Lewis Mumford, for instance, the chief enemy of the "restrictive and arid formulas" of the International Style, considered Maybeck's richly informal work — especially his redwood houses, with their pitched roofs and projecting trellises delightfully overlooking the bay — "the West Coast counterpart of Frank Lloyd Wright's prairie architecture" of the early 20th century.

But it really wasn't. The rest of the world would scarcely have been affected if Maybeck had never built in California, even though it would be much poorer without his finest buildings, whereas Wright — in every way the more powerful designer and profound theorist — changed the history of architecture.

Yet Maybeck's Christian Science church of 1910, on Dwight Way between Telegraph and College avenues, showed for the first time in this part of the world that the new architecture of the technological age — far from being merely utilitarian — could use functionalist aesthetics and industrial materials such as reinforced concrete, and even steel factory windows and asbestos siding, to express deep spiritual meanings for modern society.

In a sense, those meanings have nothing strictly to do with the unprecedented sect of Christian Science, conceived in an age of scientific "progress" by Mary Baker Eddy, at a time when Darwin and Marx were forever altering our sense of human experience and cosmic truth.

Nevertheless, the unique structure in the then-unspoiled south campus neighborhood (where it now faces the ravaged environmental battlefield of "People's Park") could only be a Christian Science church, specifically intended for a radically new sect that was striving to meet the future while retaining the most precious associations with the past.

"Christian Scientists are wonderful clients," Maybeck told me late in his life. "They have the fervor of early Christians, and they always pay their bills."

Thus the modern church astonishingly flowers in Gothic tracery windows, not in stone but concrete, and concrete Romanesque piers, complete with cast-concrete biblical capitals that originated 800 or 900 years ago in Burgundy or Provence, beneath an assemblage of broadly sheltering, low-pitched roofs, stacked and canted at different angles, almost Chinese.

How all this is held together is as mysterious as the reddish golden light that plays over the heroic redwood beams beneath the eaves, or over redwood columns stoutly mounted on concrete brackets, and redwood trellises that carry rich sprays of wisteria. Together with innumerable other plants and vines and a splendid redwood placed daringly close to the building, these marry the church with nature, as in Maybeck's houses, where indoors and outdoors seem to merge.

All is stronger, even mightier, somehow more resolutely felt, than in the houses, which occasionally verge on cuteness in Hansel-and-Gretel or Swiss chalet idioms. Always, however, they are redeemed from quaintness by Maybeck's joy and wit, even though his spaces can seem cramped, cut up and jumbled.

In this respect he stands a good distance from Wright at this prime period in their development. Wright's magnificent open plans, interpenetrating spaces, unfailing command of scale and proportions and — not least — his revolutionary protocubist form and decoration before Picasso and Braque invented Cubism, all strongly affected the great Europeans of the next generation. They retransmitted those ideas, still more radically purified, to the United States from the 1920s onward.

Wright was willing — as Maybeck never was — to break completely with historical pictorialism for the sake of an entirely new civilization.

He would have died at the stake rather than resort to Beaux-Arts classicism, as Maybeck proudly did in formulating the rules for the Hearst competition for the UC Berkeley campus, or in his own Palace of Fine Arts, or the theatrical Packard showroom — now British Motors — at 901 Van Ness Avenue.

Thus, to see how fine a regional architect Maybeck was, but to place his uneven work in accurate perspective, his achievements should be assessed against the broad architectural and cultural background of his time. This is something that devout Berkeleyans such as Professor Kenneth H. Cardwell of UC seems unable to do in his *Bernard Maybeck: Artisan, Architect, Artist* (Peregrine Smith). There is a terrible provincialism about this long-awaited book.

At once lazy and complacent, ploddingly written but doggedly packed with trivia, omitting discussion of several buildings as notable as the 1921 studio-house Maybeck did for Cedric Wright in Berkeley itself, Cardwell's uncritical biography exhibits less architectural discernment — in spite of plenty of welcome photographs and drawings — than Esther McCoy's Maybeck chapter in her *Five California Architects* published some years back.

Maybeck's buildings speak eloquently for themselves. Thanks to the very complete *Guide to Architecture in San Francisco and Northern California* (another nicely produced book by Peregrine Smith), it is now easy to see all of Maybeck's buildings — in the case of houses, sometimes only from the outside — and to appreciate the seemingly inexhaustible variety and exuberance in his work.

Besides the Christian Science church, the best seem to be the spirited Marin Outdoor Art Club in Mill Valley and his dining hall at the since greatly expanded Faculty Club on the Berkeley campus. Both use structure in remarkably uninhibited ways; both are wonderfully open to nature; both have the informality of happy homes.

Yet the brooding dome and monumental splendor of the Palace of Fine Arts — once the plaster showpiece of the Panama-Pacific International Exposition of 1915, and now permanently rebuilt in concrete — reveal what Maybeck really dreamed of as great architecture: the grandeur of the past, as he learned it at the Ecole des Beaux-Arts in Paris, but suffused with his personal romanticism.

We should be glad that it has been saved, or at least reproduced (although it was foolish to spend $6 million to preserve the neoclassical carbarn behind it, which could have bought us an Oakland Museum). For the rotunda is — with the City Hall dome — our greatest example of Baroque scale, Michelangelesque in its boldness and richness, and to some extent, making history modern, as Michelangelo did in his own time.

"It is all right to copy Michelangelo," said Maybeck, tapping his chest, "if you copy him from here — from the heart. Beware of those who copy him only in their heads."

That's what he was all about. However boldly he tried to walk out into the sunlight of the present day, he never succeeded at — as

Santayana said of the New Englanders he knew — emerging from the massive shadow of the temple. But there, in the mysterious shadows, he showed us flickering gold, and a tragic sense of eternal things, as in the interior of the Christian Science church, crossed by its gilded trusses of wood, springing from their stalwart piers of concrete, mixing light and shadow, structure and space, and lifting up our hearts with the mysterious presence — beyond the hammered half-medieval glass in the steel window frames — of sunshine and unceasing life and growth beyond.

January 30, 1978

Index

All buildings and structures are in San Francisco unless otherwise noted.

Page numbers in italics refer to images.

Aalto, Alvar, 90
Adams, Mark, 158
Aidala, Thomas, 64, 262
Alaska Commercial Bank, 82
Alcoa Building (renamed 1 Maritime Plaza), 57, 80
Alexander, Christopher, 119
Allen-Drever-Lechowski, 202
Alta Bates Hospital (Berkeley), 202–6
American President Lines Building (renamed International Building), 21
Anderson Building (Los Angeles), 242–47
Anshen & Allen, 21, 35
Art Deco, 104–7, 194–95, 242
Ashby, Gordon, 232
Asian Neighborhood Design (A/N/D), 206–9

Backen, Arrigoni & Ross, 211–13
Bakar, Gerson, 87–90
Bakewell, John, Jr., 158
Bank of California, 80
Bank of Tokyo, 78–82
Barker, Michael, 100–103
Bassett, Edward Charles, 78, 80–82, 236
Bay Area Rapid Transit (BART), 24, 115–20
Baylis, Douglas, 50
Becket, Welton, 21, 79, 114–15, 169
Belluschi, Pietro, 56, 154–56
Benham-Blair & Affiliates, 85
Berkeley, 8, 40–43, 120, 136, 146–49
Bethlehem Steel Building, 21
Birrell, Don R., 173–74
Bliss & Faville, 80
Bolles, John, 171, 216, 220
Bolt, Barnaek & Newman, 238
Born, Ernest, 118
Botta, Mario, 239–41
Boutelle, Sara Holmes, 261–64
Box, Cloyce K., 55
Braccia, DeBrer & Heglund, 121
Bradbury Building (Los Angeles), 28–29
Brandin, Alf, 37–38
bridges, 9, 109–12, 124–28, 161
Brown, Arthur, Jr., 50, 144, 158–59
Bunker Hill (Los Angeles), 29

Burchard, John E., 119
Burgee, John, 105
California Aerospace Museum (Los Angeles), 256
California First Bank. See Bank of Tokyo
Candlestick Park, 215–21
Cardwell, Kenneth H., 266
Cargo West, 86, 88–89
Chen, Carl, 151–53
Chen, Clement, 165
Church, Thomas, 50
City Hall, 49–51
City of Paris, 164, 167–68
Civic Center Plaza, 49–52
Collins, Bruce, 232
Coming Home Hospice, 207–8
container cranes (Oakland), 129–31
Court of Honor, 50
Crissy Field, 249
Crocker Bank, 80
Crown Zellerbach Building (renamed 1 Bush Street), 76, 80

Dailey, Gardner A., 147, 149
Davies Symphony Hall, 214, 235–39
Davis, Brody & Associates, 142
Davis, Clark, 203–5
Day, Clinton, 167
Day, William E., 113
DeBrer, Jacques, 121–23
deconstructivist architecture, 253
Delancey Street, 210–13
DeMars, Vernon, 147–48
Design Research, 59
Dinkeloo, John, 224
DMJM, 196–98
Doane, Larry, 199
Dreyfuss & Blackford, 173–74
Dubin, Fred, 85
Duvivier, John, 96

Eames, Charles, 232
Eastridge shopping center (San Jose), 169–72
Ebony Museum (Oakland), 134–35
Eichler, Edward, 25
Eichler, Joseph, 34
Ellis, Charles Alton, 128
Embarcadero Center, 9, 44, 52–59

Emmons, Don, 119
Environmental Planning and Design
    Associates, 123
Equitable Building, 76
Esherick, Joseph, 148

Fairmont Hotel, 20
Fallingwater (Bear Run, Pennsylvania), 259
Federal Building, 20
Fenway Park (Boston), 221–22, 224
ferry terminal, 123–24
Fields, Howard, 198
Filardo, Bruno, 233
First Church of Christ, Scientist (Berkeley),
    252, 264–67
100 First Plaza, 99–103
Fleck, Roger, 174–75
Foothill Junior College (Los Altos Hills),
    137–39
Ford Foundation (New York), 88
Fourcroy, Louis, 36
Fuller, Esther, 227–28

Gaidano, Mario, 20
Garden Court, 198–201
Gehry, Frank, 253–56
Geiger, David, 140, 142
Gensler, Arthur, 88
Geyserville, 66–67, 69–71
Gilbert, William, 62
Giurgola, Romaldo, 64–66
Goff, Bruce, 246–47
Golden Gate Bridge, 124–28
Golden Gate Park, 10
Golden Gateway, 18, 20, 52
Goldsmith, Myron, 9, 222
Gordon, Sheldon, 181–83
Graham, John, 80, 170
Gruen, Victor, 41
Guadalupe River (San Jose), 30–33
Gutmann, Willi, 59

Haas, Richard, 185
Hall of Justice, 150–53
Halprin, Lawrence, 10, 59–62, 77
Hancock Building (renamed Industrial
    Indemnity Building), 72, 73–78, 80
Hardy Holzman Pfeiffer Associates, 243
Harney, Charles L., 217, 220
Hawley-Peterson, 96
Hearst, William Randolph, 261–64
Heller, Jeffrey, 100–101

Hellmuth, Obata & Kassabaum, 45–46, 88
Herman, M. Justin, 18, 53–55
Hertzka & Knowles, 203
Hilltop shopping center (Richmond),
    169–70, 172
Hilton Hotel, 20–21, 167
Hirsch-Bedner, 198
Hollis, Douglas, 150–53, 186
Hood, Bobbie Sue, 85
Hoover, Albert A., 140
Howard, John Galen, 147
Hughes, Stanford, 199
Hunt, Jarvis, 133–34
Hyatt Regency Hotel, 189–93

IBM programming laboratory
    (Santa Teresa), 96–99
Industrial Indemnity. See Hancock Building
International Style, 47, 258
Irvine Ranch (Irvine), 26
Isozaki, Arata, 244

Jackson Square, 19
John Hancock Building.
    See Hancock Building
Johnson, Fain & Pereira, 185
Johnson, Philip, 105, 164
Jones & Emmons, 35

Kaiser Engineers, 121
Kaufman, Ron, 89
Kays, William M., 145–46
Keating, Richard, 100–101, 103
Keithley, Jerome, 35–36
Kennon, Paul, 140
Kiley, Dan, 229
Knorr-Elliott, 38
Kump, Ernest J., 137–39

Lake Maracaibo bridge (Venezuela), 111–12
Landor, Walter, 123
Landsburgh, G. Albert, 158
Larkspur ferry terminal (Larkspur), 120–24
Leavey Activities Center (Santa Clara), 139–42
Lechowski, Mark, 205
Lee, David, 94
Lee, John Michael, 154
Letterman Medical Center, 250
Levi Strauss, 86–90
Lin, T.Y., 8–9, 46, 119
Los Angeles, 22–30
Los Angeles County Museum of Art
    (LACMA), 242–47

Loubet & Glyn, 113
Lumsden, Anthony, 196, 198

Mackinlay-Winnacker-McNeil, 148, 233
Macris, Dean, 100
Mahar & Martens, 120
Maher, John, 211
Maillart, Robert, 46
Marine Exchange, 79
Marquis, Robert, 85
Marriott Hotel, 188, 193–98
Masten & Hurd, 137
Matsumoto, George, 149
Maule, Tallie, 118
Maybeck, Bernard Ralph, 159, 261, 264–67
Mays, Roland B., 123
McCue Boone Tomsick (MBT), 97–98
McSweeney, Angus, 154
Miller, J.R., 168
Miller, John K., 66–71
Mills, Paul, 232
Modern architecture, 70, 73, 104, 212–13,
    222, 239, 258–60, 264–67
Moiseiff, Leon Solomon, 128
Montgomery Block, 19
505 Montgomery Street, 104–7
Moody, Bruce, 175
Moore, Henry, 237
Morandi, Riccardo, 112
Morgan, Julia, 79, 149, 260–64
Morris Store, 21, 161–64
Morrow, Irving F., 127
Moscone Center, 45–48
Mumford, Lewis, 264
Museum of Modern Art, 239–42
Mutual Benefit Life Building, 79

Naggar, Avner, 170–72
Neiman-Marcus, 164–68
Nervi, Pier Luigi, 154–56
Nevelson, Louise, 59
Newhall Ranch (Valencia), 26
Nichols, Debra, 106
Nichols, Leslie, 36
Nordstrom, 179–83
Nut Tree (Vacaville), 172–75

Oakland, Port of, 108, 129–31
Oakland Coliseum (Oakland), 221–24
Oakland Museum (Oakland), 135, 224–35
O'Brien, Steve, 106
Olmsted, Frederick Law, 144

Olsen, Donald, 148
Osmundson & Staley, 155

Pacific Telephone Building, 103–4
Page, Edward B., 114
Page & Turnbull, 200
Paine, Clifford E., 128
Palace of Fine Arts, 249, 264–66
Palo Alto, 34–40
Parsons, Brinkerhoff, Tudor, Bechtel, 116
Pei, I.M., 203–4
Pereira, William L., 79, 243–46
Perry, Charles, 172, 190
Petaluma, 66–69
Peterson, Charles A., 96
Pfeiffer, Norman, 243–46
Pflueger, Timothy, 103–4
Pier 39, 175–79
Polk, Willis, 80
Portman, John, 55–59, 189–93
Portsmouth Plaza, 19
Post-Modernism, 183, 258
Presidio, 247–51

Qume Building (San Jose), 93–96

Raab, Norman C., 110–12
railroad stations, 132–34
Reay, Donald, 147
Richmond-San Rafael Bridge, 110
Rincon Center, 160, 183–87
Robinson, Mills & Williams, 158
Roche, Kevin, 88, 224–25, 228–35
Rockefeller, David, 54–55
Rockefeller Center (New York), 54
Roland/Miller Associates, 66–71
Royston, Hanamoto & Mayes, 21, 36
Ryan, Paul A., 154

Saarinen, Eero, 224–25, 228
Sacramento, 82–86
St. Mary's Cathedral, 11, 153–56
St. Mary's Square, 19
San Francisco: airport, 112–15; changing
    cityscape, 16, 17–21. See also individual
    buildings and structures.
San Francisco Centre, 179–83
San Francisco General Hospital, 202–4, 206
San Jose, 30–33, 63–66
San Marino, 28
San Mateo-Hayward Bridge, 9, 109–12
San Simeon/Hearst Castle (Cambria), 261–64
Santa Clara, University of, 139–42

Santa Teresa, 96–99
Sazevich, Igor, 183
Schultz, Ted, 238
Scott, Geraldine Knight, 229
Scuri, Vicki, 151–52
Shepley, Rutan & Coolidge, 37, 144
Sheraton Palace Hotel, 198–201
shopping centers, 169–72
Shroeder, Robert E., 94
Silbert, Mimi, 211
Silverdome (Michigan), 142
Simmons, Warren, 175–79
Skidmore, Owings & Merrill: Alcoa Building,
    57; Bank of Tokyo, 79–82; BART
    stations, 117; Civic Center Plaza, 50;
    Davies Symphony Hall, 236; Davis Hall,
    149; 100 First Plaza, 100–101; Hancock
    Building, 73–78; 505 Montgomery
    Street, 104–7; Oakland Coliseum, 222;
    Sheraton Palace Hotel, 199–200;
    Stanford University, 38, 145
Smith, Harwood K., 32
Snaittacher, Sylvain, 158
Snyder, Curtis, 96
Southern Pacific depot (Oakland), 132–34
Southland shopping center (Hayward),
    170–71
Spaulding, Phillip F., 123
Standard Oil of California Building, 203
Stanford University (Palo Alto), 34–40,
    143–46
Stedman, Morgan, 38
Stone, Edward D., 36
Stone, Marraccini & Patterson, 130, 202–3
Stonestown shopping center, 169, 172
Strauss, Joseph B., 127–28
Sun Valley shopping center (Concord), 169,
    171
450 Sutter Street, 104
Sweetser, Arthur, 138
Swiss-American Hotel, 207–8

Tabler, William, 20
Tacoma Narrows Bridge (Washington), 126
Taubman, A. Alfred, 170–71
Taylor, Frank M., 32, 64
Technology Center of Silicon Valley
    (San Jose), 31, 64
Temple Emanu-El, 156–59
Terman Engineering Center, Stanford
    University (Palo Alto), 143, 145–46
Tishman Building, 166–67
Transamerica Pyramid, 79
Trowbridge & Livingston, 199
Turnbull, William, 59

Union Bank, 79
Union Square, 19
University of California, Berkeley, 136,
    146–49
University of Santa Clara, 139–42
Usonian Automatic House (unbuilt), 260
Utzon, Jorn, 65
Utzon, Lin, 65

Vaillancourt, Armand, 60–62
Valencia, 26
Van der Ryn, Sim, 83–86
van der Zee, John, 128
Verrazano Bridge (New York), 125

Walker, John C., 175
Walker, Peter, 138
Warnecke, John Carl, 38, 145, 147, 164–67
Weese, Harry, 117–18, 143, 145–46
Wells Fargo Building, 80
Whisler/Patri, 181
Williams, Gregory, 150
Williams House (Berkeley), 262–63
Women's Alcoholism Center, 207–9
Wright, Frank Lloyd, 21, 161–64, 257–60,
    264–65
Wurster, Bernardi & Emmons, 50, 147
Wurster, William Wilson, 148

Yerba Buena Gardens, 45

Zeidler, Eberhard, 196–98